The Carnivores
of Agate Fossil Beds
National Monument

*Miocene Dens and Waterhole in the
Valley of a Dryland Paleoriver*

Robert M. Hunt, Jr.
Robert Skolnick
Joshua Kaufman

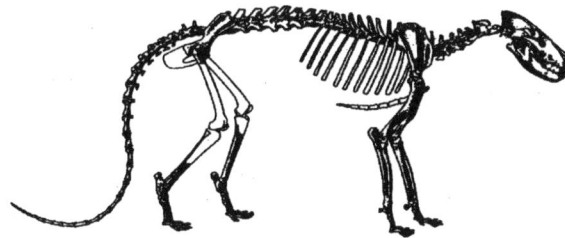

Zea Books
Lincoln, Nebraska
2018

ISBN 978-1-60962-143-8

doi 10.32873/unl.dc.zea.1070

Composed in Chaparral types.
Zea Books are published by the
University of Nebraska–Lincoln Libraries

Electronic (pdf) edition available online at
https://digitalcommons.unl.edu/zeabook/

Print edition available from
http://www.lulu.com/spotlight/unllib

UNL does not discriminate based upon any protected status.
Please go to http://www.unl.edu/equity/
notice-nondiscrimination

UNIVERSITY OF NEBRASKA
STATE MUSEUM

Nebraska
UNIVERSITY OF
Lincoln

Visitor Center diorama of the Miocene waterhole, Agate Fossil Beds National Monument

Contents

Map H 113
Map I 114
Institutional abbreviations 114
Introduction to the Tables 115

Table 1.   Fossils Collected in Carnegie Quarry 3 by
          Olaf A. Peterson and a Carnegie Museum
          Party (1904–1905) 116

Table 2.   Fossil Material Excavated in Carnegie Quarry 3,
          Beardog Hill, Agate Fossil Beds National
          Monument, Nebraska (1981–1990) 117

Table 3.   Postcranial Bones of Carnivores, Quarry 3 123

Table 4.   Postcrania and Teeth of Ungulates, Quarry 3 127

Table 5.   Dental Measurements (length × width in mm)
          of Lower Teeth of *Daphoenodon superbus* 129

Table 6.   Dental Measurements (length × width in mm)
          of Upper Teeth of *Daphoenodon superbus* 129

Table 7.   Dental Measurements (length × width in mm)
          of Upper Teeth of *Delotrochanter oryktes*,
          Megalictis simplicidens, *Promartes olcotti*,
          Phlaocyon annectens, and *Cormocyon* sp. 130

Table 8.   Dental Measurements (length × width in mm)
          of Lower Teeth of *Megalictis simplicidens*,
          Promartes olcotti, *Phlaocyon annectens*, and
          Cormocyon sp. 130

Table 9.   Measurements of Canines (length × width in mm)
          of *Daphoenodon superbus*, *Megalictis simplicidens*,
          and a Small Carnivore 131

Table 10. Cranial and Mandibular Measurements of
          Carnivorans from the Dens 131

Appendix A: Carnegie Hill Quarries—A Brief History of Excavations
             of the Bonebed 133
Appendix B: Reopening of the Carnegie Hill Quarries by the
             University of Nebraska in 1986 137
Appendix C: Sediments at Quarry 3 138
Appendix D: Analysis of Bone at Quarry 3 140

Acknowledgments 142

References 143

Illustrations

Preface

At the beginning of the twentieth century, in the remote upper reaches of the Niobrara River valley, paleontologists discovered an unbelievable trove of fossil bones eroding from two adjacent hillsides. Under these two "fossil hills" were buried entire skeletons of extinct animals that previously had been known only by fragmentary remains. Over the next two decades, leading museums of the day expended great effort exposing and then extracting whole portions of this bonebed for public exhibition and for research purposes.

Many years later, scientists from the University of Nebraska–Lincoln reopened the old quarries to search for clues, long overlooked, that might explain why rhinoceroses, chalicotheres, and entelodonts had perished together millions of years ago at this particular place. In the process, they uncovered carnivore dens unrecognized by the first excavators.

North America in the Early Miocene. Copyright 2013 Colorado Plateau Geosystems. Used by permission. The location of the Agate paleoriver and waterhole in northwest Nebraska 22 to 23 million years ago is shown by the arrow east of the Rocky Mountains. Although the Great Plains and the mountains to the west are positioned much as seen today, the westward expansion of the continent will not take place until the Basin and Range country begins to develop later in the Miocene.

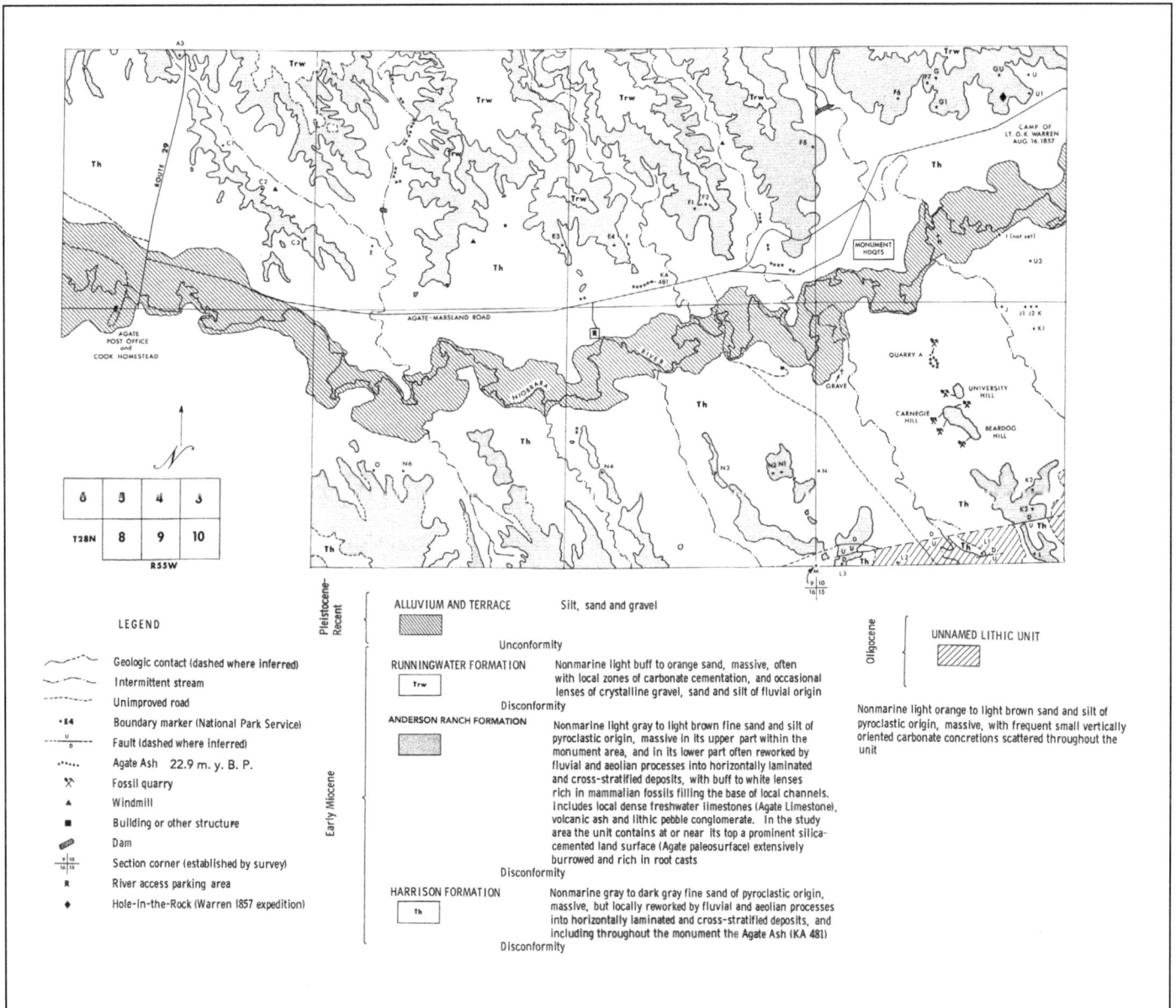

Geologic Map of the Agate Fossil Beds National Monument   R. M. Hunt, Jr.

LEGEND

Geologic contact (dashed where inferred)
Intermittent stream
Unimproved road
•E4 Boundary marker (National Park Service)
Fault (dashed where inferred)
Agate Ash 22.9 m. y. B. P.
Fossil quarry
Windmill
Building or other structure
Dam
Section corner (established by survey)
R River access parking area
Hole-in-the-Rock (Warren 1857 expedition)

Pleistocene-Recent

ALLUVIUM AND TERRACE   Silt, sand and gravel

Unconformity

Early Miocene

RUNNINGWATER FORMATION   Nonmarine light buff to orange sand, massive, often with local zones of carbonate cementation, and occasional lenses of crystalline gravel, sand and silt of fluvial origin
Trw

Disconformity

ANDERSON RANCH FORMATION   Nonmarine light gray to light brown fine sand and silt of pyroclastic origin, massive in its upper part within the monument area, and in its lower part often reworked by fluvial and aeolian processes into horizontally laminated and cross-stratified deposits, with buff to white lenses rich in mammalian fossils filling the base of local channels. Includes local dense freshwater limestones (Agate Limestone), volcanic ash and lithic pebble conglomerate. In the study area the unit contains at or near its top a prominent silica-cemented land surface (Agate paleosurface) extensively burrowed and rich in root casts

Disconformity

HARRISON FORMATION   Nonmarine gray to dark gray fine sand of pyroclastic origin, massive, but locally reworked by fluvial and aeolian processes into horizontally laminated and cross-stratified deposits, and including throughout the monument the Agate Ash (KA 481)
Th

Disconformity

Oligocene

UNNAMED LITHIC UNIT

Nonmarine light orange to light brown sand and silt of pyroclastic origin, massive, with frequent small vertically oriented carbonate concretions scattered throughout the unit

Today, the displays at Agate Fossil Beds National Monument lead visitors through the forensic evidence that discloses a sequence of events culminating in the demise of many hundreds of animals. The exhibits at the visitor center also include murals by artist Mark Marcuson and a diorama that uses full skeletal mounts, all illustrating the fascinating story of the Agate bonebed.

In addition, the park is situated in a 3,000-acre preserve of shortgrass prairie and tells the story of rancher James Cook, who first noticed the bones in the 1880s, and his friendship with the scientists who came to excavate at Agate. Visitors can follow several trails to view the historic fossil sites, where wayside exhibits explain the paleontological investigations, and reconstruct the landscape of a dryland paleoriver valley and its animals, 22 million to 23 million years ago.

The Agate bonebed was excavated from 1905 to 1908 by Olaf Peterson at the flat-topped Carnegie Hill and by Erwin Barbour on conical University Hill in the valley of the Niobrara River in northwest Nebraska.

Introduction

In 1981 University of Nebraska paleontologists came upon an unexpected concentration of carnivore dens at Agate Fossil Beds National Monument in northwest Nebraska. The discovery of bones of Miocene beardogs, mustelids, and canids in their burrows was unparalleled and marked an exceptional event in the fossil record. Survey and excavation (1981–1990) established that six species of carnivores had, over time, occupied the dens with traces of their prey: juvenile and adult oreodonts, camels, and a neonatal rhinoceros. At least nine individuals of the wolf-like beardog *Daphoenodon superbus*, the most common carnivore, were identified from remains of young, mature, and aged individuals that included in one den an adult female and her juvenile male offspring. The carnivores found together in the dens represent a moment in time—the oldest carnivore den community yet discovered with remains of predators, their prey, and their ecology in evidence. Dated at 22 to 23 Ma (million years), the den complex provided scientists with the oldest documented evidence of carnivore denning behavior.

The site was first discovered more than a century ago by the paleontologist Olaf Peterson of the Carnegie Museum (Pittsburgh) and initially excavated by him and his co-workers in 1905. Although they found almost nothing but bones of carnivores, he was apparently unaware that he had stumbled upon their dens. Peterson (1910) named his small excavation "Carnegie Quarry 3," which was located ~200 m southeast of the immense rhinoceros bonebed found by him on nearby Carnegie Hill where he had placed his principal excavation, Carnegie Quarry 1. There groups of small rhinoceroses had died during drought at a waterhole in the broad valley of a dryland stream. It was at the margin of this waterhole that the carnivores had excavated their burrows. Erosion by the modern Niobrara River over thousands of years gradually exposed the buried dens and waterhole within the ancient river valley.

Olaf Peterson, 1865–1933

Erwin Barbour, 1856–1947

Peterson recognized that the bones found at Carnegie Hill represented a wealth of evidence that would bring to light previously unknown species of extinct mammals living during an unfamiliar interval of geologic time, the early Miocene (16–23 Ma). His discovery of the potential significance of the site motivated the Carnegie Museum to carry out major excavations in 1905, 1906, and 1908 on Carnegie Hill under his supervision, and during those same years, the University of Nebraska opened an excavation on neighboring University Hill directed by

paleontologist Erwin Barbour. The foresight of the two men proved essential in systematically excavating the bonebed and in mapping the distribution of the bones. Removing the bones from the rock required considerable time and patience but their dedicated effort alerted the scientific community to the bonebed's importance and singular geological setting. From 1905 through the 1930s, the quarries on Carnegie and University Hills supplied hundreds of bones to universities and museums in North America and Europe.

The Southwest Excavation on Carnegie Hill (Peterson's Quarry 1): The bonebed level extends along the base of the cliff and con-tinues into the hill. The horizontal layers of sediment from the base to the midpoint of the hill are the thin-bedded sands of the Miocene Agate paleoriver. A section of the bonebed is shown below.

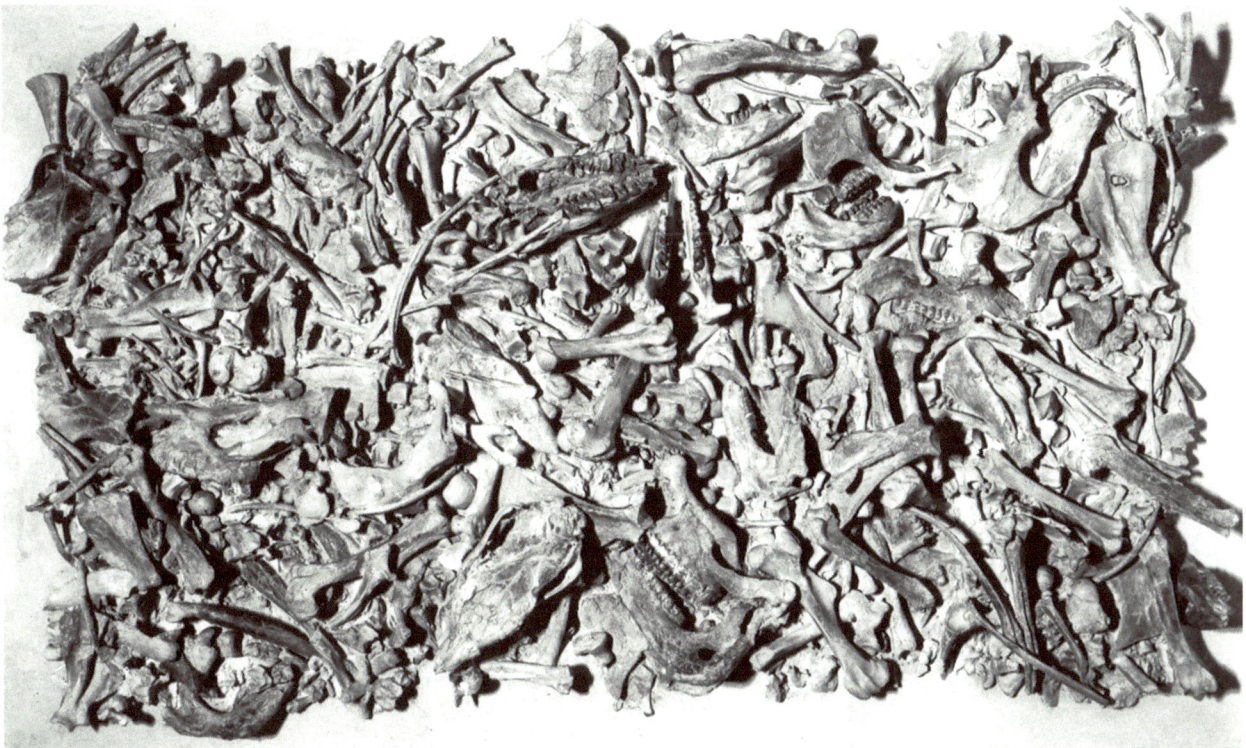

CARNEGIE QUARRY A
Carnegie Museum of Natural History | Olaf Peterson
Discovery Site, 1904

NORTH RIDGE

AGATE ASH
22.9 million years

North Outcrop
South Outcrop

MAP OF THE AGATE SPRING QUARRIES, SECTION 10, T. 28 N, R. 55 W SIOUX COUNTY, NEBRASKA

Surveyed by
R. M. Hunt, Jr. and M. E. Rebone
July, 1983

N

Historic Park Trail
to Visitor Center

UNIVERSITY HILL

UNIVERSITY QUARRY
University of Nebraska State Museum
Erwin Barbour | 1905–1908

PRINCIPAL REFERENCE DATUM
University of Nebraska State Museum
1985–1986

NORTH EXCAVATION
American Museum of Natural History
Bill Thomson
1917–1919   1907

NORTHWEST EXCAVATION
Carnegie Quarry 2 | Bill Utterback
1906–1908

WEST EXCAVATION
Excavator Not Known

Agate Limestone

CARNEGIE HILL

inner
outer

SOUTHWEST EXCAVATION
Outer Part: Carnegie Quarry 1 | Olaf Peterson | 1905–1908
Inner Part: American Museum | Bill Thomson | 1911–1923

SOUTH EXCAVATION
American Museum | 1923

BEARDOG HILL

CARNEGIE QUARRY 3
Olaf Peterson | 1904–1905
University of Nebraska State Museum | 1981–1990

LEGEND

——	Quarry Limits
- - - -	Outcrop Boundaries of Agate Ash and Agate Limestone
-·-·-	Hill Perimeters
— —	National Park Service Trail

0   100 feet

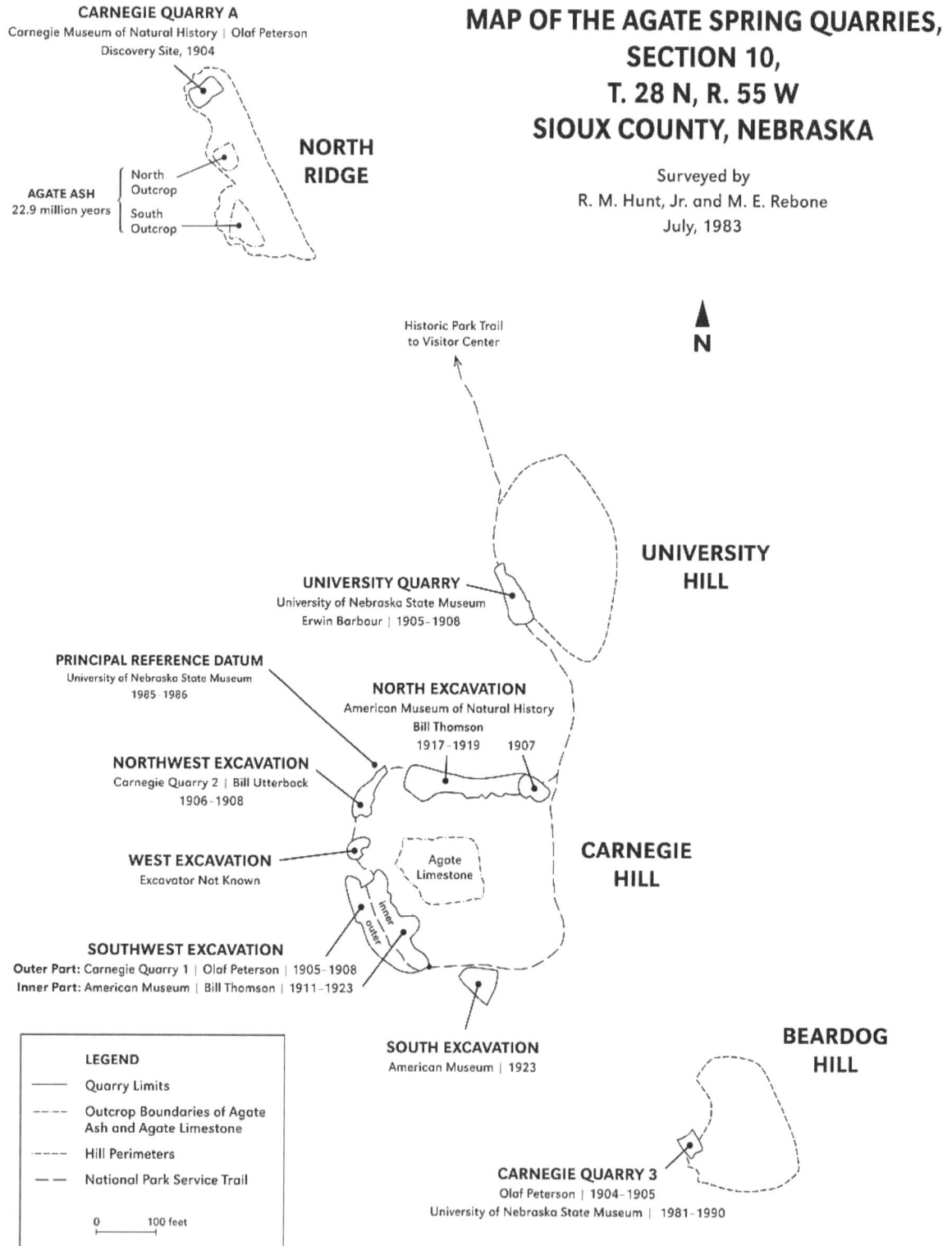

Map of the Agate Spring Quarries: Peterson's discovery site of 1904 at Carnegie Quarry A lies just below the Agate Ash (~22.9 Ma) on North Ridge—the quarries on Carnegie and University Hills occur above this ash bed and so the bonebed is younger. The most productive Carnegie Hill quarry was the Southwest Excavation worked by the Carnegie Museum and American Museum (New York); the waterhole once continued between University and Carnegie Hills and extended as far as Beardog Hill. The gray shading indicates the location of the quarry excavations from 1904 to the present.

The Waterhole

When Olaf Peterson and Erwin Barbour began excavations at Carnegie and University Hills in 1905, they discovered that the bonebed had once continued between the two hills, occupying an area of nearly 6 acres (~24,000 m²). In 1986 University of Nebraska excavations at Carnegie Hill established that the bones had accumulated in a shallow stream channel within a broad Miocene river valley. Sediment filling the channel and analysis of the distribution of the skeletons suggested the site had been a waterhole that had attracted large numbers of a small species of rhinoceros (*Menoceras arikarense*), together with a group of 17 to 20 claw-footed chalicotheres (*Moropus elatus*) and several large scavenging entelodonts (*Dinohyus hollandi*) at a time of prolonged drought.

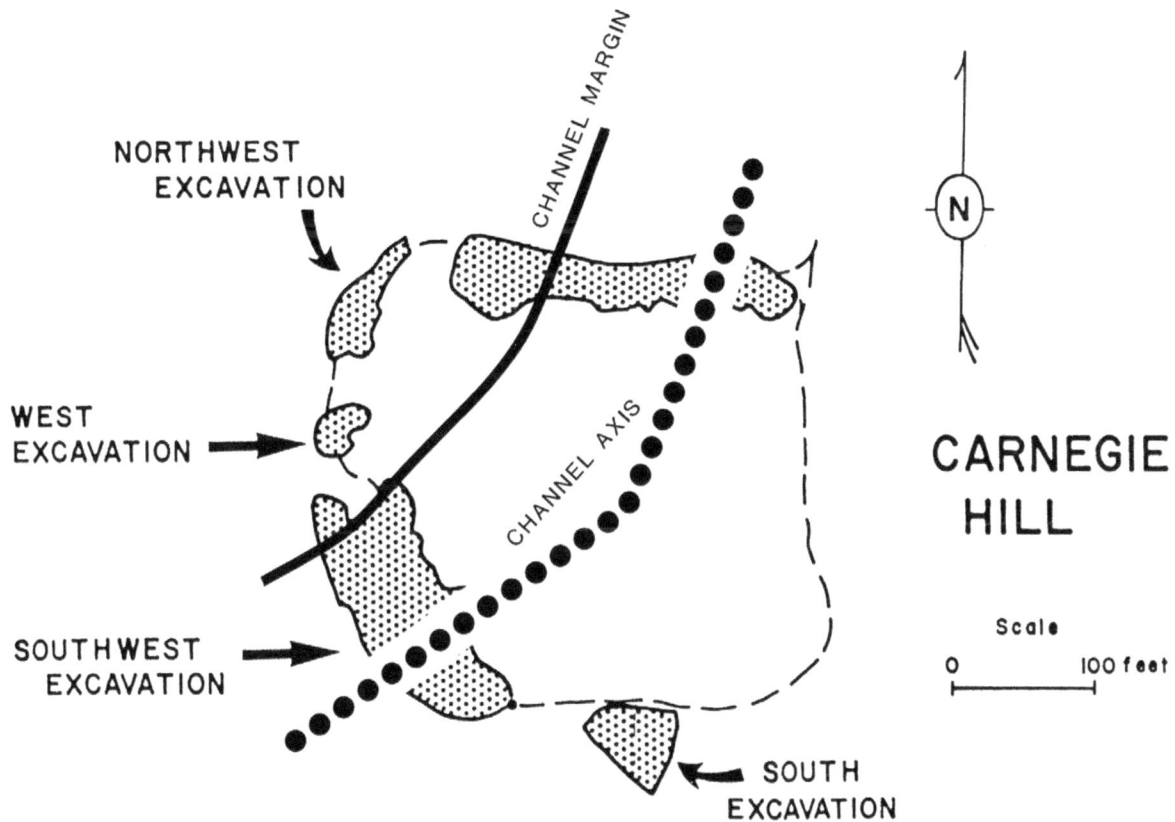

The waterhole at Carnegie Hill developed in an abandoned stream channel deepest in the Southwest Excavation where most of the bones of mammals were concentrated.

AGATE BONEBED - SOUTHWEST SIDE OF CARNEGIE HILL

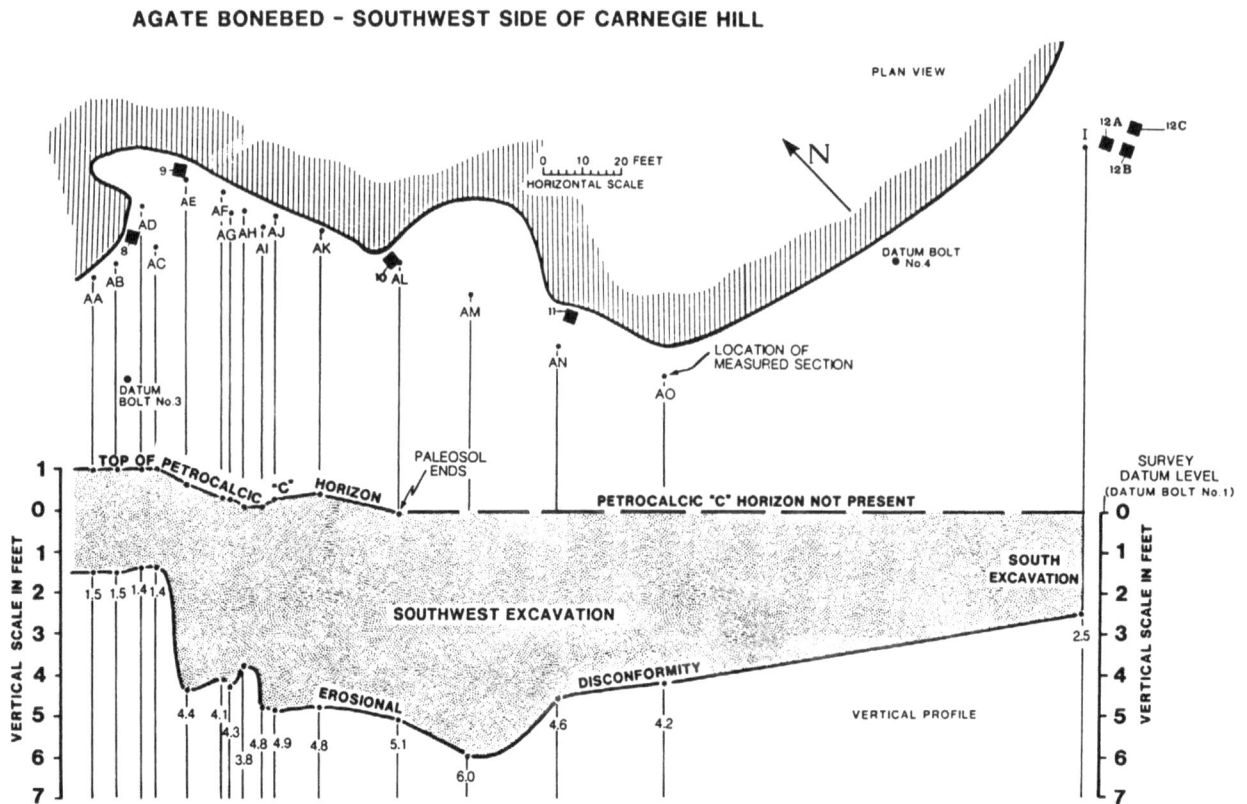

The waterhole was shallow (~1.5 ft) at the channel margin and held fewer bones, but the deepest part (~4–6 ft) contained many rhinos and 17–20 chalicotheres—adult females, large males, and juveniles. Black squares indicate location of UNSM excavated test pits.

Their skeletons were eventually covered by fine sand, volcanic ash, and calcareous mud that slowly accumulated in the warm ponded water. Eventually, plants colonized the sediment that had filled the waterhole, creating a soil recognized today on Carnegie Hill by a *paleosol* (a fossil soil). The paleosol was traced to Beardog Hill where a corresponding fossil soil was present above the dens. The carnivores burrowed through this soil at the southern margin of the waterhole, excavating their dens in the same mud, ash, and sand that had buried the bonebed at Carnegie Hill. Later, thin-bedded sands deposited by the Miocene paleoriver completed the burial of the waterhole and the dens.

During our exploration of the quarries on Carnegie and University Hills and review of Agate fossils in collections of other institutions, we discovered that carnivores were particularly rare in the waterhole bonebed. Nearly all bones of carnivores that we located belonged to the amphicyonid *Daphoenodon superbus,* a wolf-sized species of beardog; its remains scattered through the bonebed amounted to only a few foot bones and teeth apart from a jaw fragment with a tooth of a very young pup.

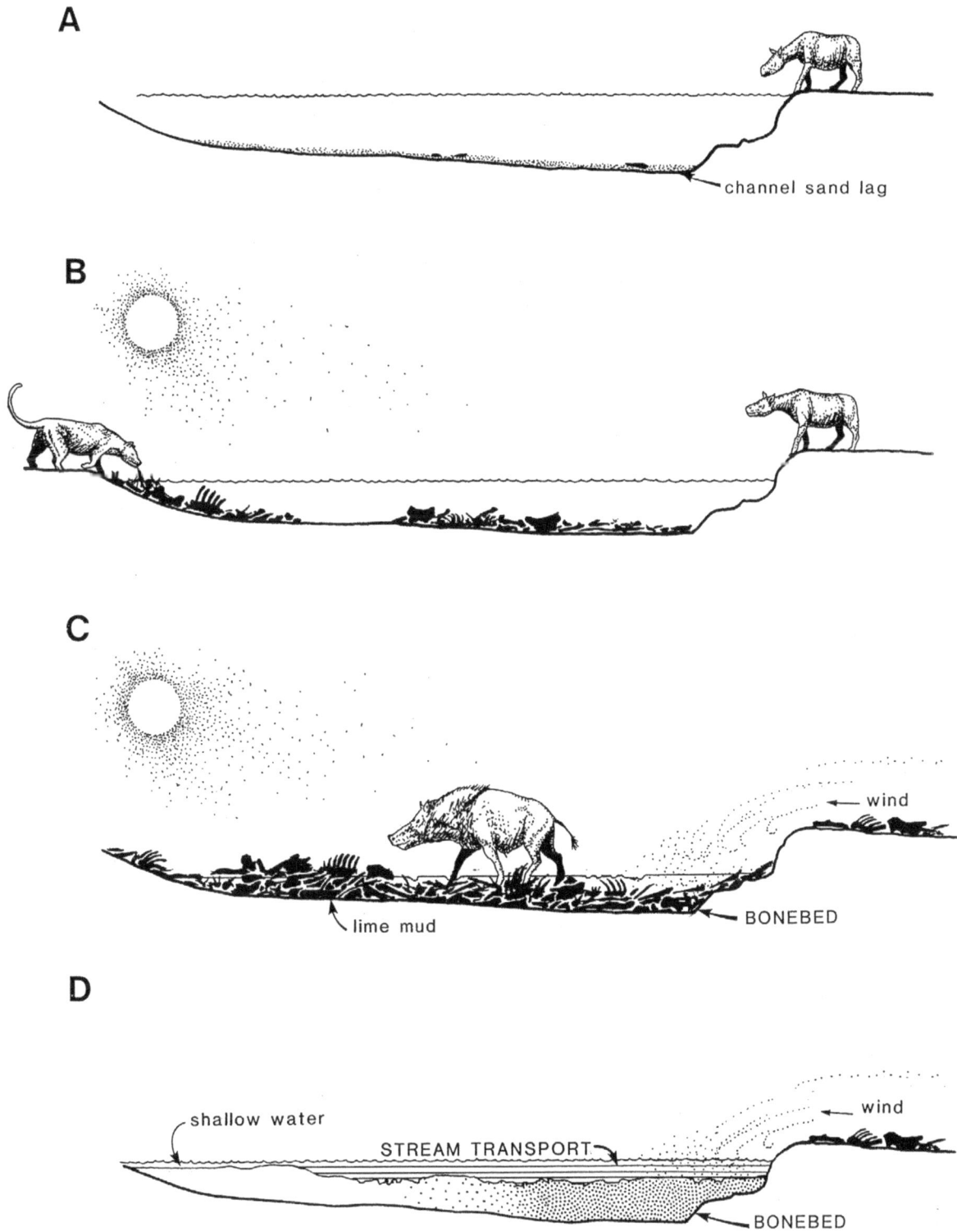

Chronology of the waterhole: (**A**) At times of seasonal rainfall, mammals drink wherever water collects in these depressions; (**B**) When the rains fail, rivers begin to dry—carnivores prey on mammals drawn to the remaining waterholes; (**C**) During severe drought, the Agate waterhole accumulated carcasses as it dried—the mud, fine sand, and ash preserved tracks of scavenging Dinohyus; (**D**) Over time, renewed streamflow and wind buried the bones of rhinos, a herd of chalicotheres, and the tracks of the scavengers (two nearly complete skeletons of Dinohyus were found in the waterhole).

During the severe drought, starving rhinoceros and chalicothere no longer able to find food take final refuge in the warm water of the shallow pool. Nearby the large scavenging entelodont Dinohyus waits patiently in the dried river bed.

The Mark Marcuson Restoration of the Waterhole

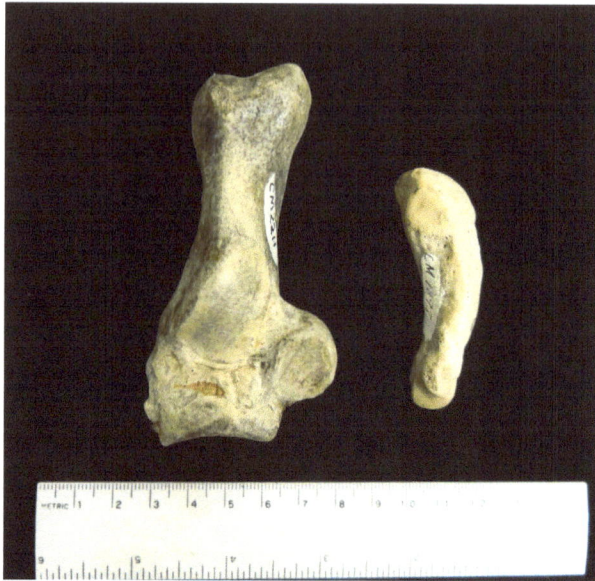

These two foot bones (calcaneum, metacarpal) found in 1904 and 1908 were the first evidence of the entrance of the lion-like beardog Ysengrinia into North America in the early Miocene. Since then no other evidence of this large carnivore has been found in the quarries of the national monument or in the dens.

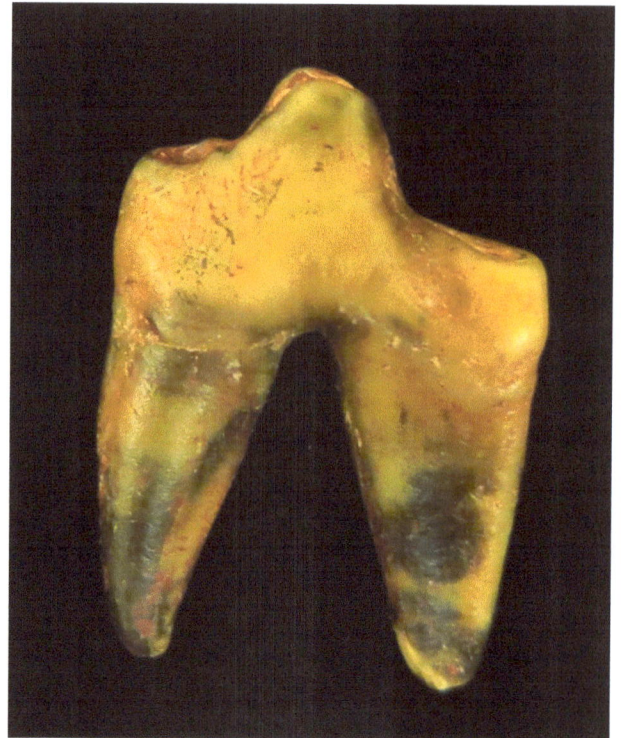

Molar tooth of the immigrant Eurasian beardog Cynelos found by Olaf Peterson in 1908 on Carnegie Hill (Quarry 1).

The few remaining carnivore fossils from the waterhole (other than *Daphoenodon*) turned out to be of unexpected importance. Found in the archives of the Carnegie Museum, a field label written in Peterson's own hand mentioned a foot bone (5th metacarpal) from the forepaw of a huge carnivore that Peterson (1910) thought belonged to a large unidentified canid. He had discovered it in 1904 among "surface fragments" from the as-yet unexcavated University Hill bonebed before it was opened in 1905 by Erwin Barbour. This unusual bone did not come from a canid but from a carnivore not recognized then in North America, a large lion-like beardog, *Ysengrinia*. Later in 1908 Peterson found a hind foot bone (a calcaneum) from this beardog when exploring a nearby pond deposit of the same age as the bonebed on Carnegie Hill. An active predator in the region at that time, *Ysengrinia* proved to be an immigrant from Eurasia, but it did not occur in the dens on Beardog Hill, probably because of its large size.

A few years later, in 1908, Barbour's field men found in University Quarry a bone (3rd metatarsal) from the hind foot of a very small Eurasian carnivore, *Cephalogale*, also unknown in North America. And in the same year, Peterson discovered in the Carnegie Hill bonebed a single tooth (a molar) of the small beardog *Cynelos*, then recognized only in Europe. Remarkably, these three foot bones and the tooth together document the earliest appearance in the New World of *Ysengrinia, Cephalogale, and Cynelos* at ~22 to 23 Ma, based in part on the dated volcanic ash (the "Agate Ash") beneath the waterhole bonebed. These three carnivores found at the waterhole appear in the New World at a time of immigration of Eurasian mammals via the Bering route into North America in the early Miocene. They were found in the bonebed with the rhinoceros *Menoceras arikarense* and chalicothere *Moropus elatus*, two species also recognized as coeval Eurasian migrants that entered North America at the same time as the carnivores.

The entelodont Dinohyus scavenged carcasses at the waterhole shown by its tracks discovered in bonebed mud at Carnegie Hill and by marks made by its teeth on limb bones of chalicotheres. © 2010 University of Nebraska State Museum/ Mark Marcuson

Hundreds of young, mature, and aged individuals of the small rhinoceros Menoceras were found in the waterhole bonebed on Carnegie Hill.

Carnegie Quarry 3
(Beardog Hill)

In September 1981 the University of Nebraska State Museum initiated the first paleontological excavation in the principal quarries at Agate Fossil Beds National Monument since the monument had been authorized by Act of Congress on June 5, 1965. We hoped to find an abandoned early excavation, Carnegie Quarry 3—its location was in doubt relative to Quarries 1 and 2, the major excavations on Carnegie Hill where Peterson and his men focused their work from 1905 to 1908. Quarry 3 had been discovered by Peterson in August 1904 yet, lacking time and resources, he postponed serious excavation until his return in 1905. After that time, except for a visit in 1908, we could find no evidence of later excavation at or near the site. He left no field notes or map, and despite an extensive search of the Carnegie Museum archives, only a few of Peterson's handwritten field labels that accompanied his fossils from the quarry provided any details of his excavation. However, there was a compelling reason for finding and investigating Quarry 3. To Peterson's surprise the bones he found were almost exclusively those of extinct carnivores, unexpected and unexplained in view of the scarce carnivore remains in the principal rhinoceros quarries on Carnegie and University Hills.

After completing a geologic map of Agate Fossil Beds National Monument as background for eventually reopening the Agate quarries, and after reviewing the Miocene fossils from Agate kept at the various institutions that had excavated there in the past, the university received permission from the National Park Service in the summer of 1981 to attempt to locate and reopen Quarry 3 as the first step in this effort. Fortunately we noticed that Peterson had left a single critical clue: in his publication (Peterson, 1910) describing the carnivores he had found at Quarry 3, he included a blurred photograph showing that the quarry occurred somewhere

Beardog Hill: Peterson in 1910 published a distant view of the hill in a photograph but did not indicate the specific location of his excavation (Carnegie Quarry 3).

Initial trenching on the west face of Beardog Hill in 1981. (Carnegie Hill is to the north.)

on a small hill directly south of Carnegie Hill. "Bear-dog Hill" eventually became the name of this non-descript knoll where Peterson had placed Carnegie Quarry 3.

Exploration of the hill utilized hand-dug test excavations placed around the perimeter, and sediments in two test trenches revealed that the water-hole seen on Carnegie Hill had once extended as far

Sediments in the trenches showed that the white calcareous mud and ash (*) seen at Carnegie Hill was also found at Beardog Hill and marked the southern margin of the waterhole.

*Discovery of Carnegie Quarry 3: The site of Peterson's excavation (**a**), where a worker cleans the white bedrock, is situated ~168 m (~550 ft) southeast of Carnegie Hill; our test trench (**b**) at the left margin of the photograph located the southern edge of the waterhole (view looking west from the summit of Beardog Hill).*

as Beardog Hill. The profile of the west side of the hill matched the image in Peterson's photograph and looked promising as the place where excavation by the Carnegie men might have occurred. Encouraged by this, we began with removal of loose rock and topsoil that exposed the bedrock surface over ~10 m² on the hill's sloping western face.

On the third day of the excavation, two large mammal burrows appeared on the face of a low cliff, one leading downward to a broad shallow depression in the bedrock. We realized from its size and dimensions that this depression could have been the pit left by Peterson and his men in 1905 after they removed a large block of sediment with fossils from the quarry—only one block of that size had been taken out and shipped by the Carnegie men in 1905 from Quarry 3. Peterson sent this plaster-encased sand-

stone block to the Carnegie Museum in "Box 17," a designation used for wooden crates containing fossils shipped by him to the museum in Pittsburgh. The box number allowed us to trace the block from the quarry to its final destination. Peterson's numbering of boxes at the quarries and the discovery of his critical surviving field labels in the Carnegie Museum archives made possible identification of the carnivore fossils found in or closely associated with the Box 17 sediment block. Seven of the carnivores and a few ungulate bones collected by Peterson at Quarry 3 were positioned in the quarry based on this evidence and are listed in Table 1. Peterson in the laboratory at the museum discovered that the block contained two nearly complete skeletons of the beardog *Daphoenodon* (CM1589, CM1589A), still the best-preserved skeletons known from the quarry.

Discovery of burrows at Carnegie Quarry 3: The entrance tunnel leading to the chamber of Den 1 appears on the low cliff that marks the southern terminus of the quarry. This well-defined burrow is excavated into white calcareous mud and ash and overlain by the gray sand that includes a fossil grassland soil extending to the top of the cliff.

The large depression where Peterson had removed the Box 17 block with the two beardogs we designated as Den 1. The floor and wall of Den 1 survive today at Beardog Hill together with its tunnel-like entrance burrow—the most remarkable of the Quarry 3 dens.

Burrows at the quarry had never been mentioned by Peterson. We recognized then that the burrows possibly belonged to a den complex—here was the explanation for the unexplained abundance of Peterson's carnivores. But we had found no bone in Den 1 and did not want to disturb the consolidated sediment filling the entrance to the den. Then, during surface exploration on the sixth day, a tooth and skull fragments of a large temnocyonine beardog (*Delotrochanter*) were found only a meter to the north of Den 1; this eventually was identified as the

location of Den 2 and showed that some carnivores even then probably remained in these dens. But could we be certain this was Quarry 3?

Prior to our 1981 excavation at Beardog Hill, through the cooperation of the Carnegie Museum, we brought together the remains of the carnivores found by Peterson at Quarry 3 to familiarize ourselves with his material. Several of the carnivores had been described and illustrated by Peterson (1907, 1910): the beardog *Daphoenodon*, a large mustelid "*Paroligobunis*," and a very small canid "*Nothocyon*," but there were also hundreds of unidentified bone fragments from Quarry 3 kept in trays at the museum. In April 1982 a graduate student, Carl Swisher, while examining these fragments collected by Peterson in 1905, took several from a tray and found one that perfectly fit a

Carnegie Quarry 3 in 1977 before it was realized that this was the site of Peterson's excavation in 1905. The cliff on the right contained the two burrows leading to Den 1.

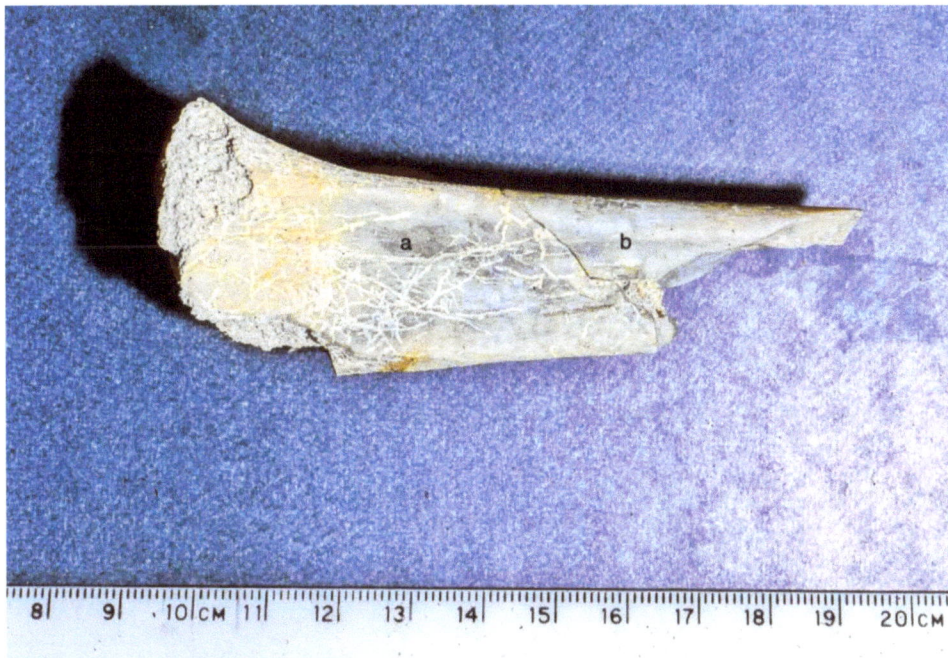

*Limb bone of Daphoenodon that established the site of Carnegie Quarry 3: The large piece (**a**) was found in 1981 by UNSM and the piece on the right (**b**) in 1905 by Peterson.*

broken limb bone (tibia) of *Daphoenodon* that we had discovered near Den 1 in 1981. The exact match of our limb bone, recovered 76 years after Peterson collected his bone fragment in 1905, confirmed that we had been excavating at the location on the hill's west side where Peterson had placed Carnegie Quarry 3.

At Quarry 3 the burrows are mostly evidenced by remnants of the floors preserved as shallow linear flat-bottomed depressions, or "runways," up to 3 m in length and from 10 cm to 1 m in width, filled with laminated fine gray sand. Some floors can be followed into a cylindrical tunnel where stacked layers of the gray sand preserve a nearly complete cross-section of the burrow.

Once soil, sand drift, and rock debris were removed, the face of Beardog Hill on which the burrows stand out forms a gradually sloping surface descending to the west. Most burrows on this surface have had the upper part of the burrow tunnel removed over time by erosion of the hill. Only at the south end of the quarry does the low cliff preserve the exceptional burrow seen entering Den 1 from the Miocene grassland through which the carnivores and other animals excavated their dens. This grassland surface extends to the east into the hill where it is overlain by stream sediments of the Agate paleoriver. At Carnegie Hill these paleoriver sands also directly overlie the waterhole bonebed. The dens could continue into Beardog Hill beneath this grassland surface.

Paleontologist Josh Kaufman points to Burrow A, the first found by us in the quarry. The blue marker in front of him indicates the large depression where we believe Peterson removed Block 17 in 1905. The small yellow marker (a tape measure) identifies the contact between the white sandy mud of the waterhole and the underlying gray sand of the Harrison Formation.

*The extension of the quarry in July 1982, following discovery of the first burrows during the previous year. A strip of unexcavated gray sand (**a**) identifies the as-yet unexplored burrow of Den 2 that produced the beardog Delotrochanter oryktes. A screen used to sieve topsoil and surficial sediment is in the upper left, and a meter grid used to plot the location of specimens is in the lower right.*

The den site was recognized as the oldest paleontological record of denning behavior in large mammalian carnivores, confirmed by the remains of the several species preserved within the burrows (Hunt, Xue, and Kaufman, 1983). The site was worked by the University of Nebraska State Museum (UNSM), first from 1981 to 1985 and then from 1989 to 1990.

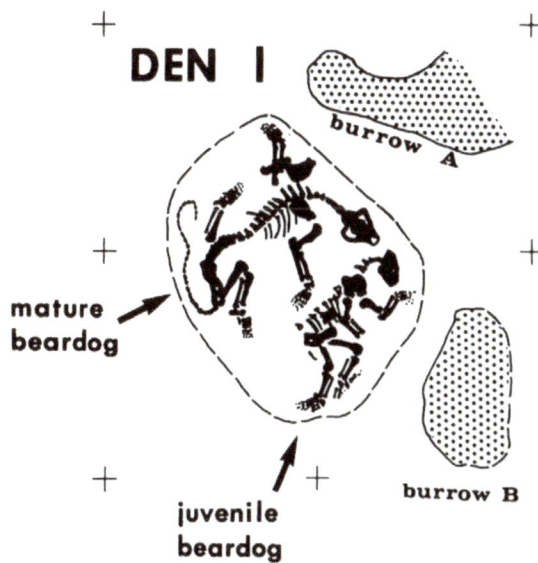

Adult female and young male Daphoenodon placed here in the shallow depression (dashed line) created by Peterson's removal of "Block 17" that contained the two skeletons. Burrow B is an entrance tunnel into the den.

Final Extent of Quarry 3: The limit of the den complex was reached by 1989 on the western slope of Beardog Hill—no evidence of additional dens or burrows was found beyond the northern edge of the excavation. Carnegie Hill can be seen in the distance to the north, capped by the Agate Limestone.

Excavation and Survey Methods

Erosion of the western slope of Beardog Hill had exposed, then removed, much of the den complex. Plant roots seeking nutrients had invaded near-surface skeletons in the burrows. Because so little was known and the site exceptional, a conservative exploration program was adopted to prevent further damage to the remaining burrows and skeletal material. A metric grid network was established—during excavation, reference flags were placed to mark the four corners of each meter. A portable meter grid frame subdivided into 10 × 10 cm sections was used to map objects within each meter. Within Quarry 3, we decided to forego test trenches so that burrows that had survived Peterson's earlier excavation would not be damaged, and instead first removed loose rock and topsoil to bedrock in conformity with the metric grid. Soil was screened (mesh aperture 11.5 × 11.5 mm or 0.5 × 0.5 inch) for bones and fragments from all gridded meters. A finer mesh was used in several test locations for small vertebrate teeth and bones without significant result. Staff of the national monument protected the site so that the dens remained undisturbed over the long intervals when we could not be present.

Map A illustrates the distribution of the burrows over the quarry surface and includes both UNSM and where possible Peterson's Carnegie fossils. They were exposed to view as soil and surficial slope wash were progressively removed meter by meter from the south to north end of the den complex. Over much of the quarry, but particularly in the southern half, the contrast between burrow fill of laminated gray sand and the better consolidated white calcareous ashy mudstone aided in identification of the burrows. The difference in color between gray burrow fill and the white mudstone was critical in mapping the burrow perimeters. When recognized, the identified perimeter of a burrow was plotted on the

A portable meter grid was used to plot the position of all bones and burrow perimeters.

Within the quarry, the corners of each meter were marked with flags during excavation.

meter grid. We regard the burrows so defined as the remnants of random breaching of the Miocene den system through a slow continual erosion of the hill.

Elevations in the quarry were determined with alidade and plane table. A steel datum bolt was initially anchored in bedrock in meter H1 at grid-point C9, and elevations within the quarry were determined from this reference level. In 2007 the National Park Service set an aluminum datum bolt in concrete (4,546 feet above sea level) at the base of the low cliff at the south end of the quarry (at the southeast corner of meter B7) to serve as a permanent point of reference for future study and excavation (North American Datum 1927 CONUS: 42°24'54.5"N, 103°43'33.0"W).

All individual bones and partial skeletons discovered during the course of the excavation were recorded each day on field labels and entered in field notes whether found within or outside a burrow. Our map of Quarry 3 shows that most bones came from either the southern (rows A–K) or northern (rows L–T) quarry where the burrows were concentrated.

Note that the numbering of rows is offset between rows K and L.

The better-preserved bones and teeth, and the partial skeletons provided the most reliable identifications of mammals in the quarry. In addition, the bones and bone fragments sieved from each meter of surficial sediment also included identifiable skeletal elements. Because nearly all identifiable mammal bone screened at the quarry belonged to the same species of carnivores and small ungulates associated with burrows, most screened bone probably came from breached or entirely destroyed dens. A list of the bones and fragments discovered by UNSM paleontologists at Quarry 3 is presented in Table 2.

When each fossil bone or identifiable bone fragment was found, it was assigned a UNSM field number (groups of associated unidentifiable fragments often received a single lot number—in a few cases several identified bones and associated fragments were included together). About 185 specimen lots were catalogued during the excavation of Quarry 3 from 1981 to 1985 and an additional ~230 were

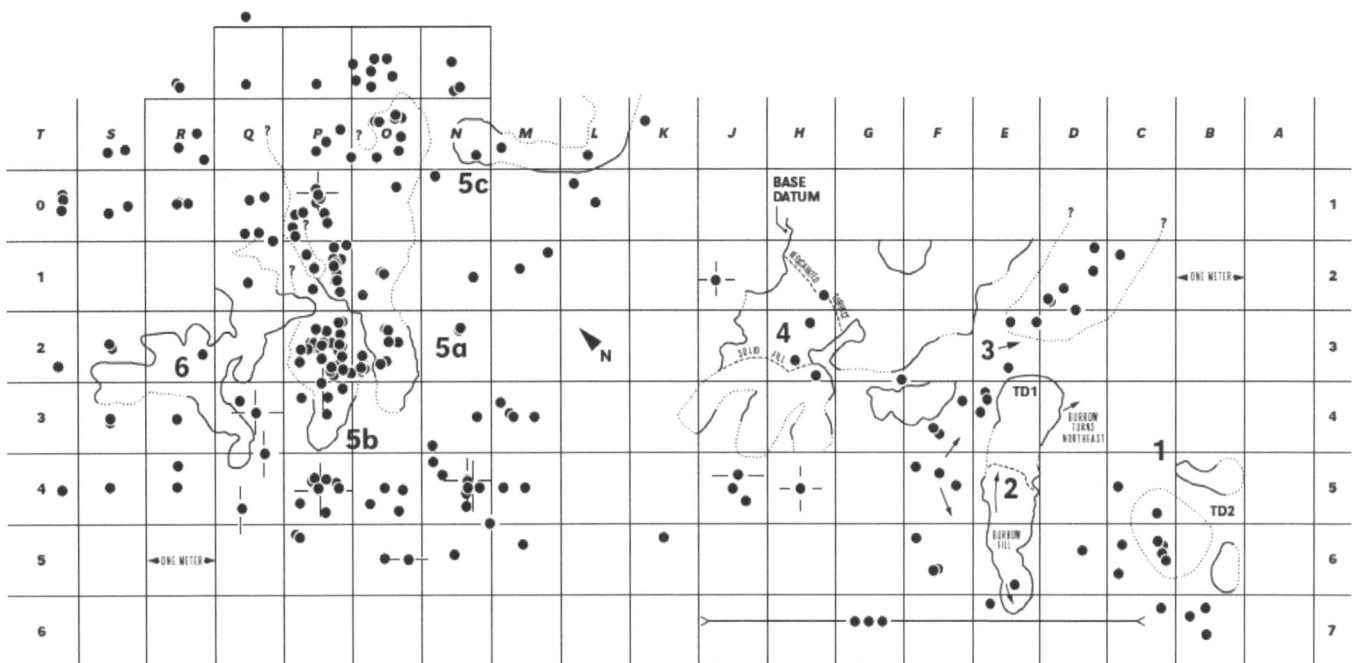

Map A. *Distribution of bones and partial skeletons at Quarry 3 from UNSM and Carnegie excavations.*

added from 1989 to 1990 (Table 2). Fragile bones were hardened with the preservative resin Glyptal in acetone, allowed to air-dry, and numbered and wrapped for transport to the laboratory. If a bone could be identified as to taxon and/or element in the field, that identification was also entered at the time of collection.

During field work, the burrows required protection from inclement weather and were covered with sheet plastic when not actually under excavation. The fill of some burrows was removed over selected areas to measure burrow dimensions and to examine the topography of the burrow floors.

The Den 2 burrow as first exposed before excavation while still filled by gray sand that contrasts with the white consolidated mudstone walls. The burrow slopes upward from its terminal chamber to its unexcavated upper end (marked by the bucket at top left), where the skull of the beardog Delotrochanter oryktes was discovered in 1981.

The Den Community

After completing excavation of Quarry 3 in 1990, we brought together and reviewed what we had learned of the den community and its occupants. Here, highlights of the work set the stage for more detailed analysis later in the chapters "The Burrows of Quarry 3," "The Carnivore Species," and "The Prey Species."

Quarry 3 of the Carnegie Museum as extended by the University of Nebraska from 1981 through 1990 now covers ~160 m^2 on the western side of Beardog Hill. Mapping shows that the fossils were confined to the areas where the burrows were concentrated: (a) in or near burrows that we have called Dens 1, 2, 3, and 4 on the south and (b) in or near those designated Dens 5A, 5B, 5C, and 6 on the north. The general absence of fossils in the intervening area (rows L and K) and their clustered distribution around either the north or south dens told us that the fossils had not traveled very far from their host burrows.

As our work progressed and we began to see that fossils still could be found in Quarry 3 following Peterson's earlier excavation, the probable survival of a relict Miocene den community gradually began to take form and with it the kinds and numbers of animals present, whether skeletons were still intact or now only fragments, the condition of the bones, their distribution in the quarry and eventually, the opportunity to reconstruct the manner of death and burial.

The species at Quarry 3 were identified from a few partial skeletons, from teeth mostly in jaws, and from scattered isolated bones, primarily diagnostic limb and foot elements found throughout the quarry. Beardogs predominated in the quarry and were found with bones of small ungulates, plausibly their prey. Unexpected rare occurrences of lizard, snake, and bird were accompanied by a few bones of unidentified small mammals. Lenses of ponded sediment at the margin of the waterhole were the likely source of bones of frogs, turtle, and a fish.

Carnivores—The carnivores found in the dens included two species of amphicyonid beardogs: *Daphoenodon superbus*, discovered by Peterson in 1905, and *Delotrochanter oryktes*, a hyena-like beardog found in the burrow designated Den 2 during the opening of the quarry in 1981. Both are wolf-sized predators and the largest carnivores of the den community. Peterson in 1905 recognized a jaw and partial skeleton of *Megalictis* ("*Paroligobunis*") *simplicidens*, a large wolverine-like mustelid. A skull and other bones representing at least two additional individuals of this carnivore were discovered in the quarry in 1985, together with remains of three adults and a juvenile of the smaller marten-like mustelid *Promartes olcotti*. In addition, two kinds of very small foxlike canids, *Phlaocyon* ("*Nothocyon*") *annectens*, discovered by Peterson, and a species of *Cormocyon* excavated in 1990, compare respectively in size to the African fennec fox (*Fennecus zerda*) and North American swift fox (*Vulpes velox*), which are among the smallest living canids. Peterson (1907) found *Phlaocyon* with the beardog *Daphoenodon* in or near Den 1; the slightly larger *Cormocyon* (*copeihaydeni*; Wang et al., 1999) found in 1990 was unexpected and had not been encountered by Peterson. Damaged partial feet of this canid found in Den 5B seem to be leftovers from scavenging of its carcass.

Ungulates—Although very few bones of ungulates were found at Quarry 3 by Peterson, his fossils belonged to the same ungulate species discovered by us during our excavation. Most ungulate bone came from in and near burrows in the north half of the quarry. Particularly common was the small oreodont *Merychyus*; we soon saw that many of its bones had been scavenged. Found together with *Merychyus* in Den 5B were bones of the little gazelle-camel *Stenomylus* and among unidentified ungulate bones col-

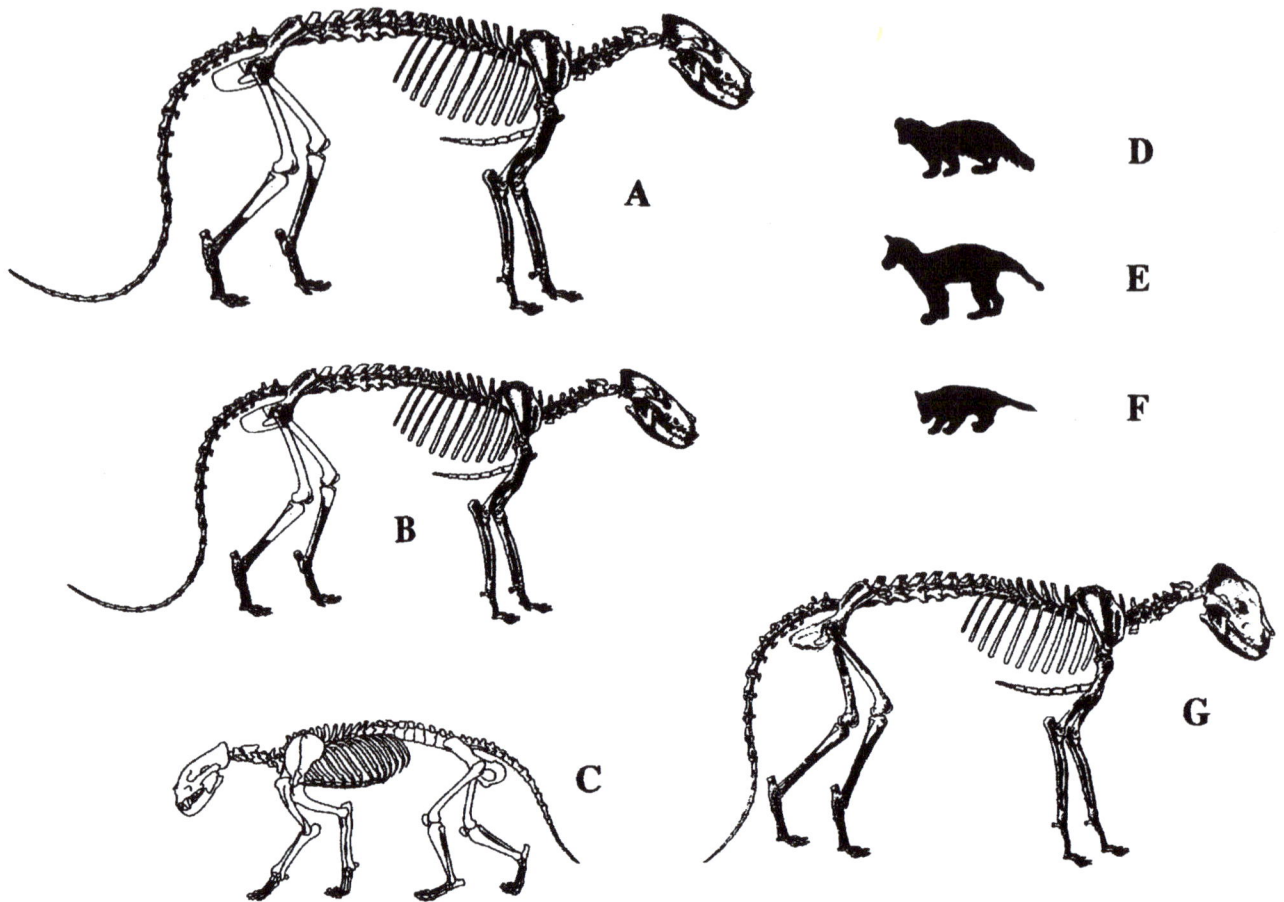

The carnivores of Quarry 3: (**A**) *Daphoenodon superbus (male),* (**B**) *Daphoenodon superbus (female),* (**C**) *Megalictis simplicidens,* (**D**) *Promartes olcotti,* (**E**) *Cormocyon sp.,* (**F**) *Phlaocyon annectens, and* (**G**) *Delotrochanter oryktes.*

lected by Peterson were a number of foot bones of a slightly larger camel *Oxydactylus*. The rarest ungulate was a neonatal rhinoceros *Menoceras*, identified by a few foot bones, perhaps from part of a carcass carried to a den. Other indications of possible prey were unanticipated bones of two "deerlike" cervoids: a tiny moschid and a larger juvenile dromomerycine.

The presence of small ungulates throughout the quarry and their near absence in the bonebed on Carnegie Hill can be explained if the ungulate bone at the dens is seen to be remains of prey carried to the burrows by the carnivores. The lack of ungulate skulls and the axial skeleton, with numerous incomplete and fragmented limb bones when compared to

the many relatively indestructible bones of the fore and hind feet, tells of thorough scavenging of the small ungulates.

Distribution—When all bones from the UNSM excavation are plotted on the quarry map (**Map B**), bones of predators (in red) and ungulate prey (in green) are represented in about equal proportion in the north quarry where isolated bones were the rule. Because the same ungulate species occur throughout Quarry 3, we think it likely that this same proportion once could have existed in the south quarry where during our excavation ungulate bone was scarcer. Possibly its absence is because of failure to screen

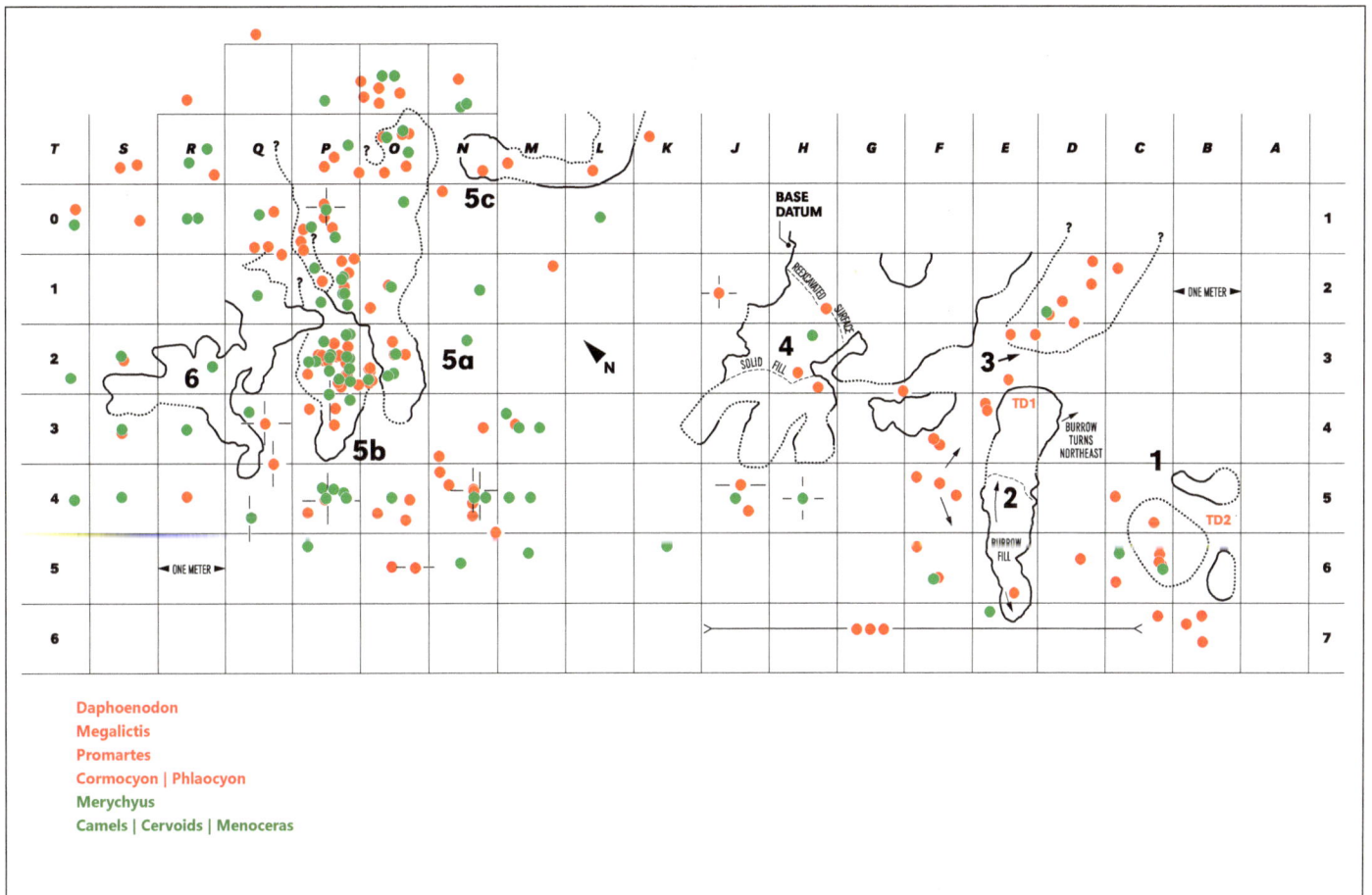

Map B. *Bones from the UNSM excavation plotted on the quarry map, predators in red and ungulate prey in green.*

for small bones by the Carnegie men or to only the single season spent at the quarry in 1905.

The detailed distribution of the species of carnivores and ungulates in the quarry are shown on a series of maps in the chapters "The Carnivore Species" and "The Prey Species."

Completeness—The best-preserved skeletons from Quarry 3 belonged to *Daphoenodon superbus* (Peterson, 1910) and included the two partial skeletons (CM1589, CM1589A) shipped by Peterson to the Carnegie Museum in Box 17 as well as a complete hind foot (CM1589C) of a third individual found nearby. In 1981 University of Nebraska paleontologists discovered the skull and articulated foot bones of *Delotrochanter oryktes* in Den 2 and later the lower

jaws with partial skeleton of an aged male *Daphoenodon superbus* in Den 3. In 1985 we found the skull and a jaw representing two individuals of the mustelid *Megalictis simplicidens* coming from the Den 5 complex in the northern section of the quarry, far from where Peterson found his partial skeleton of this animal to the south in the vicinity of Den 1. Skeletal remains of the small canid *Cormocyon* from Den 5B seem to be bones of a single adult embodied by its scavenged fore and hind feet near a few teeth of a very young pup. A second adult was evidenced by a molar found in Den 5C. However, because of their completeness, Peterson's skeletons of the adult female *Daphoenodon* (CM1589) and her young male offspring (CM1589A) were critical in showing that nearly intact carcasses had been preserved in some burrows, then scavenged, and eventually buried by sediment deposited over time in these dens.

Other than these partial skeletons, identifiable bones in the quarry were primarily individual skeletal elements either excavated from burrow fills or found in consolidated to semiconsolidated sand nearby. Isolated bones sieved from surficial sediment during the extension of the quarry often could be assigned to skeletal element and taxon by comparison with reference skeletons. We also discovered that some bones could be reconstructed from fragments collected by Peterson in 1905 during the Carnegie excavation. From a tray of fragments grouped by him under CM1589B, it was possible to identify two adults of *Daphoenodon* for which sufficient parts of the skeleton survived to allow an estimate of gender and body size. The bones fell into two size groups representing a very large male and a smaller individual (a probable female), both with well-worn teeth. Several bone fragments found by us in the south quarry later proved to be missing pieces belonging to two of the beardog bones under CM1589B found by Peterson.

Condition—The condition of much bone in the quarry appears to be related to decay and scavenging of carcasses within or near the dens. Many bones are broken, whether through scavenging at the dens or through later exposure and weathering at the quarry. Overall, breakage left sharp edges on fragments and otherwise more complete bones. Sometimes broken fragments found in close proximity within a burrow can be joined to form a perfect fit, indicating breakage occurred at or very near that location in the burrow with little or no displacement after burial.

Many small angular bone fragments were present in the burrows and had worked into slope wash on the quarry surface. Table 2 documents more than 1,100 unidentifiable bone fragments of this type recorded in the quarry during the UNSM excavation. Nonetheless, in addition to teeth, we found that many badly broken limb bones, the numerous bones

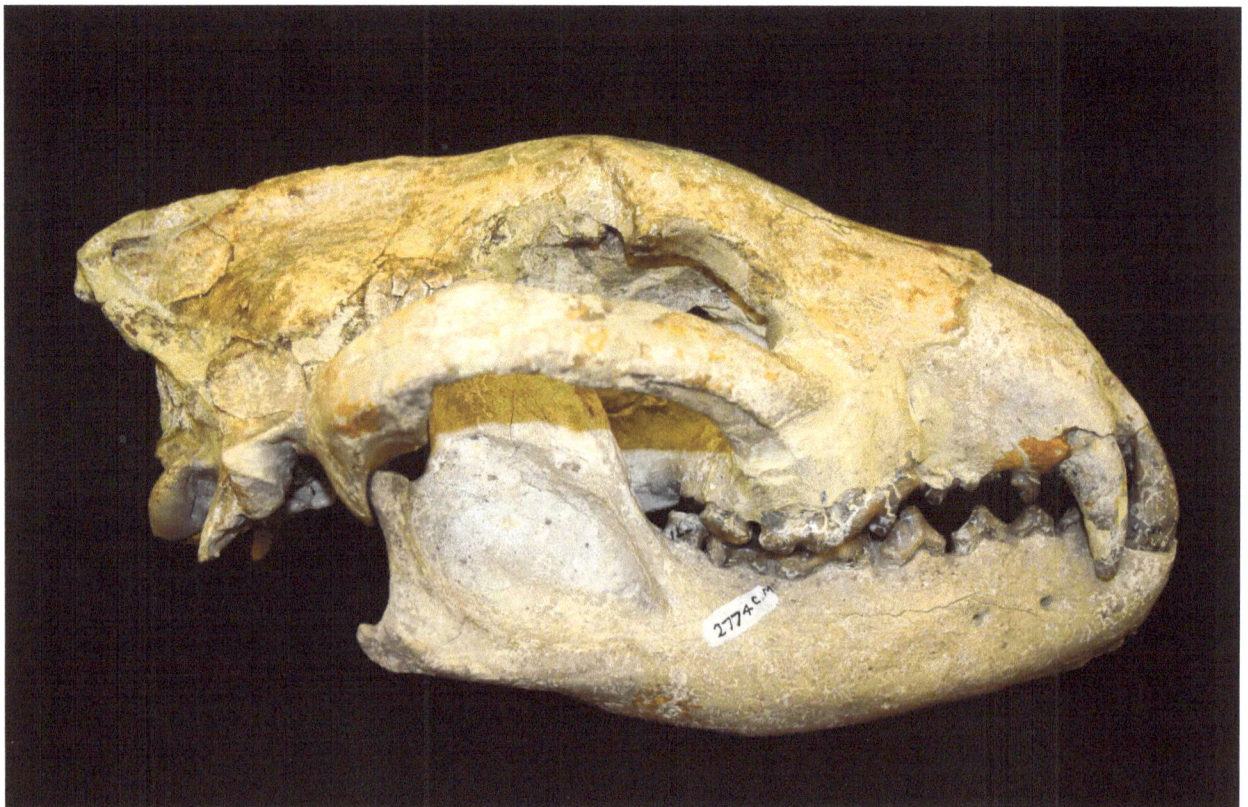

The skull and jaw of the amphicyonid beardog Daphoenodon superbus (CM2774) found by the paleontologist Olaf Peterson at Carnegie Quarry 3.

of fore and hind feet, and some bones of the axial skeleton could be identified to element and taxon.

Weathering of bone at the quarry followed if bone had worked to the surface and was then exposed to the elements and to plant roots (during our excavations, the growth of plants in the quarry required constant attention). Bone fragments from burrows can show leaching and dissolution of the bone apatite from chemical weathering by plant acids and from mechanical weathering by tap roots entering the burrows. Some bone has been corroded and dissolved by digestive acids. However, much bone from the laminated sand *within* burrows shows little evidence of preburial exposure and often preserves pristine anatomical detail. Abrasion of bones in dens is nonexistent—the smoothing and polishing caused by the abrading action of sand in flowing water or by continual exposure to wind-transported grains is absent.

Minimum Number of Individuals (MNI)—The number of individuals of a particular species confirmed in the quarry is estimated by the minimum number of individuals (MNI). It is based on the bones identified to skeletal element and taxon discovered during our excavation combined with the specimens found by Peterson at Quarry 3. For each species, the MNI counts as a new individual any bone or tooth that duplicates that particular skeletal element if already known to have come from the quarry. Logically, if both a right and left limb bone, such as a femur, of a species survived, then the MNI will register one individual if both bones are shown to be the same size. If the left femur is markedly different in size from the right, then they cannot have come from a single individual, and the MNI will be two. If two left femora of a species are present, the MNI of course will be two regardless of size.

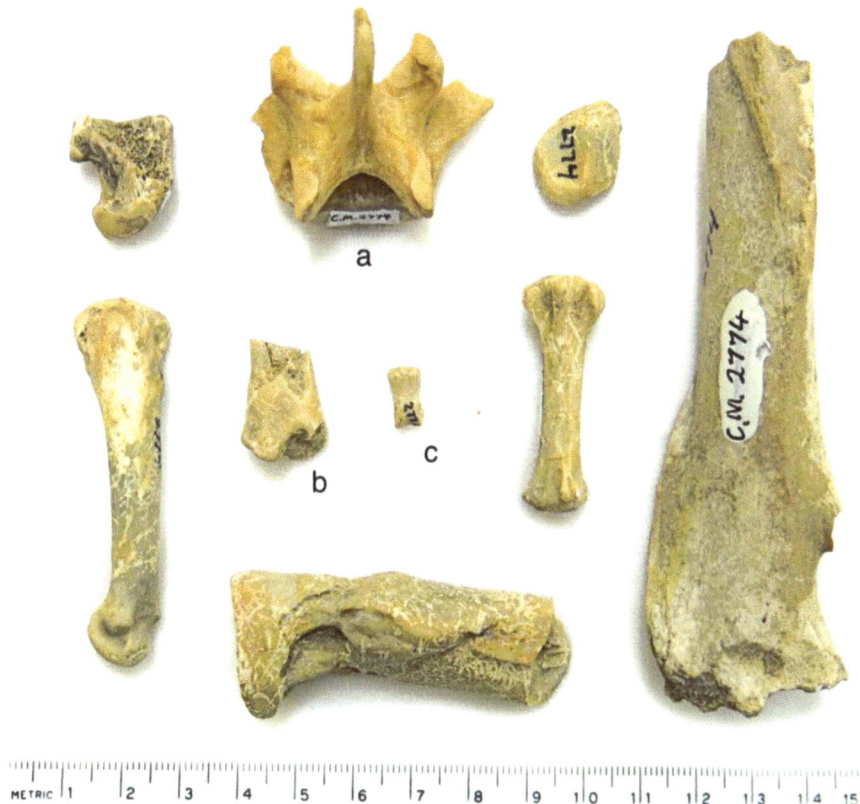

*Bones of prey found with the beardog skull (CM2774): (**a**) gazelle-camel vertebra, (**b**) oreodont tibia, and (**c**) phalanx of moschid "deer"—the remaining bones belong to the beardog.*

Burrow B (Den 1): The best-preserved entrance burrow and den at Carnegie Quarry 3 (letters are described in the text).

The Dens of Quarry 3

Excavation in the quarry beginning at the southeastern end in 1981 progressed steadily toward the northwest until row T was reached in 1985. The quarry at that time was 20 m in length by 8 m in width with the long axis of the excavation aligned N45W. After preliminary cleaning, the quarry surface could be seen to slope gradually to the southwest along the western side of Beardog Hill. Over ~160 m^2 of the western slope, the burrows as exposed varied in extent and dimensions as a result of Holocene erosion. Often only the burrow floor remained, a runway excavated into white calcareous ashy mudstone carpeted with a few centimeters of thinly laminated, semiconsolidated gray sand. Some burrow floors when traced east into the less dissected portion of the hill lead directly to nearly cylindrical burrows preserved in cross-section that represent either the den chambers themselves or large interior tunnels; here laminated sediment packing these burrows reaches a thickness of up to ~50 cm.

Dens 1, 2, and 4 are well defined in the southeastern end of the quarry, and we think Den 1 produced Peterson's partial skeletons of *Daphoenodon* and the mustelid *Megalictis* and jaws of the little canid *Phlaocyon*. Den 2 contained the beardog *Delotrochanter* and a few bones of *Daphoenodon*, but few fossils came from Den 4. The extent and dimensions of Den 3 are uncertain; just its floor could be identified in proximity to a partial skeleton of *Daphoenodon*. At the northwestern part of the quarry, only the terminal sections of the burrows assigned to Den 5 are defined, yet there the bones of small mustelid (*Promartes*) and canid (*Cormocyon*) carnivores were found with beardogs. The northwestern burrows have been breached and in places destroyed by slope erosion, scattering many bones downslope. There we did not find the partially articulated beardog skeletons discovered by Peterson in the southern half of the quarry. However, discovery of a remarkable concentration of bone fragments from a small canid found scavenged in Den 5B demonstrated that burrow fill in some dens remained undisturbed. This brought to mind the report of an African brown hyena (*Hyaena brunnea*) taking remains of a small canid (a jackal, *Canis mesomelas*) to a den as food for cubs (Owens and Owens, 1979).

1981–1982 Excavations

Den 1 (Burrow B)

The early Miocene fossil soil capping the low cliff (in meters A5–A6) at the southern limit of the quarry represents the grassland surface at the time the den complex was in active use. The vertical face of the cliff preserves an undisturbed burrow (meter B6) descending 1.2 m from the entrance at ground level to the floor of the den. The entrance tunnel 30 cm in width passes through the soil zone, widening to 43 cm as the passage opens into the den. The width of this tunnel at the floor of the den increases to ~66 cm. The dimensions of the den chamber measure ~1.1 m in length along its wall and ~38 to 52 cm in height. The greatest diameter can be no more than ~1.5 m because of the proximity of the nearby Den 2 runway.

From this den we believe came the two partial *Daphoenodon* skeletons (CM1589, CM1589A) excavated by Peterson in 1905. Here where the entrance tunnel enters the den chamber, the undisturbed sediment in the tunnel reveals several episodes of filling and re-excavation in the life of the burrow. A loose laminated gray sand (**a**) was first deposited low in the den, initially unexcavated, and then removed in part by digging—the den could have been open and in use at this time. However, partial closure of the den takes place next by deposition of a lighter-toned gray sand (**b**) with fragments of white mudstone, this sand then cut by a re-excavation surface. On this surface is deposited a rather uniform fine gray sand (**c**). This event is then followed by introduction of a breccia of sand and pieces of white mudstone from wall rock (**d**) that begins to fill the den entrance. These

four intervals suggest an interrupted infilling of the den entrance with fine sand mixed with wall rubble, and not a sudden mass influx of sediment. Deposition ceased at this point for a time and was followed by direct deposit of an overlying fine light brown sand (**e**) that completed the filling of the entrance to the den. This brown sand extends upward into the entrance tunnel where it meets a rooted zone (**f**) that marks the base of the overlying fossil soil.

Den 1 (Burrow A)

A second inclined burrow (in meter B5) a meter to the east of burrow B is directed toward and appears to slope into this same den. It contains a finely laminated fill of loose sand, silt, clay, and granular rubble that demonstrates an episodic low-energy influx of water and sediment into the burrow. The burrow narrows from a height of ~45 cm to 30 cm and then to 23 cm where it turns toward the den chamber. Its floor is ~76 cm in length as exposed, rising 15 cm along the runway trending upward to the ground surface. The burrow has been excavated into the white consolidated mudstone: the burrow floor (**a**) is smooth and white, and at its low point (**b**) has begun to turn toward the den chamber. The first sediment (**c**) deposited on the burrow floor—4 cm of finely laminated gray sand overlain by a few millimeters of silt and clay—was introduced by a current of water. A wedge (**d**) of disturbed light gray fine-grained sediment follows. After this, a flow of water carried in a rubble of small pebbles (**e**) and finely laminated gray sand (**f**) and then two layers of silt as flow energy ebbed. This event repeated with a slightly coarser pebble-rubble (**g**) at the base of the second finely laminated sand wedge (**h**). These graded pebbly sediments in burrow A without evidence of re-excavation indicate an episodic yet continual infilling of the tunnel passage, which took place after drought, flood, or other catastrophe had killed the occupants of Den 1. Their carcasses could have been available to scavengers for some time before burial of the skeletons.

Collectively the Den 1 burrows represent the best examples of the partially to nearly completely filled access tunnels in the Beardog Hill den community.

Burrow A (Den 1): Thinly laminated sand, silt, and pebbles filled the burrow (letters are described in the text).

Den 2

Upon cleaning of meter E4 it was the appearance of a broken molar tooth that identified the presence of an unexpected species of beardog in a breached burrow, eventually recognized as a tunnel of Den 2. Unnoticed until after the Den 1 burrows were discovered, Den 2 was the first in which we found intact carnivoran material and a species unknown to Peterson at Quarry 3. Excavation of meter E4 revealed the complete toothrow of the skull: its teeth, adapted for crushing hard food items, identified it as an unrecognized temnocyonine beardog (*Delotrochanter oryktes*).

Its skull and several visible articulated foot bones were removed in a large sandstone block and transported to the preparation laboratory at the university. After removal of our block, we noted the striking similarity of its dimensions to the pit we suspected had been left by Peterson at the nearby Den 1.

The following week during a detailed inspection of the site, we were able to identify a section of the burrow's wall and roof within the excavation that had just produced the skull.

Discovery of a partial molar (M1) of the beardog Delotrochanter found by Joshua Kaufman at Den 2—the first evidence of a previously unrecognized carnivore within the quarry.

The temnocyonine beardog Delotrochanter oryktes (UNSM 47800) from Den 2.

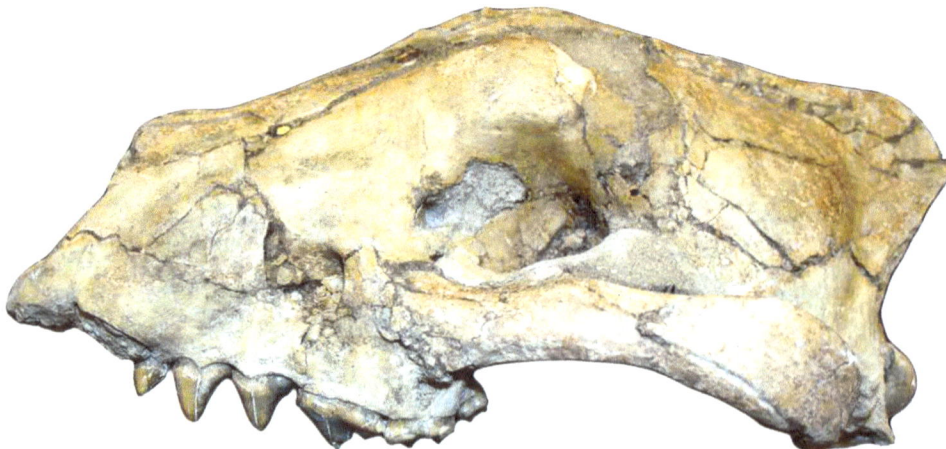

*A portion of the wall and roof of Den 2: The burrow has been excavated in the white ashy mudstone and later filled with dark gray sand. A large pebble of light gray sand (**a**) floating in the tunnel may represent evidence of an earlier re-excavation of the burrow.*

The skull with teeth and foot bones of the beardog Delotrochanter coming into view in the laboratory during the exploration of the burrow fill of Den 2.

A few days after reopening the quarry in 1982, downslope from where the skull had been found in meter E4, a burrow runway appeared, one of the best defined at Quarry 3. When first seen, the runway was floored by semiconsolidated fine gray sand typical of these burrows. A section of the floor when cleaned showed that the runway had gradually filled with thinly laminated pebbly fine sand, from only a few centimeters in meter E5, continuing downslope along the runway to a greater thickness of laminated sand at the terminus of the burrow. We soon realized that the runway led upslope into meter E4, directly to where the skull had been found in its Den 2 burrow; there the cross-section of the den tunnel was packed with laminated sand where the block with its skull had been removed. The block of sediment when examined in the laboratory showed that the skull occurred in the upper part of the burrow fill. At the opposite end of the burrow, two perfect bones of the hind foot of *Daphoenodon* were the only other skeletal parts found in Den 2.

The Den 2 runway before excavation of the burrow fill of laminated gray sand enclosed by white calcareous mudstone. The two anatomically intact and undamaged foot bones of Daphoenodon were found buried in the runway to the left of the bucket.

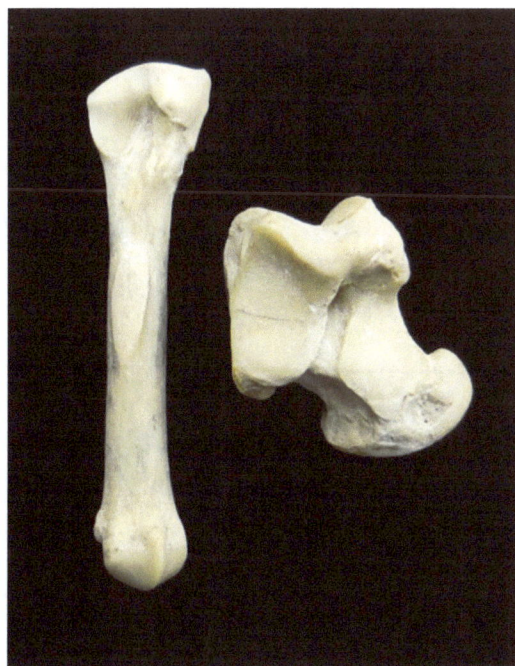

Partial excavation of Den 2: The terminal chamber packed with laminated gray sand can be seen next to the bucket. This sand was removed from the burrow at its midpoint (by the blue Estwing hammer) to expose the floor of the runway. Note the meter grid frame used throughout Quarry 3 and yellow flags marking the corners of each square meter in the metric grid.

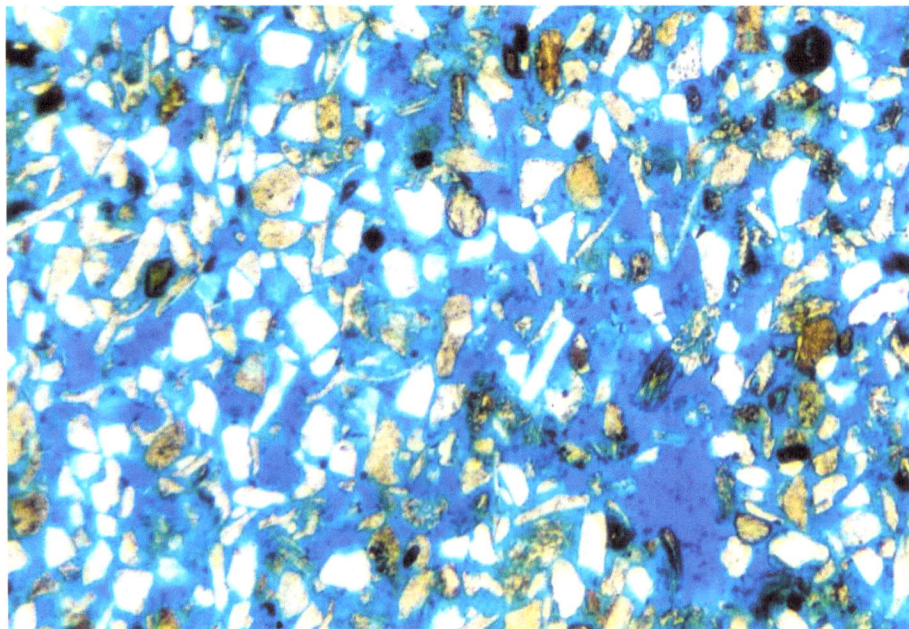

Sediment in Den 2 consisted of semiconsolidated fine sand and volcanic ash; such well-sorted angular crystals and glass shards are typical of the burrow fill in the dens.

Excavation of Den 2 showing the terminal chamber filled with laminated gray sand.

Circular thin layers of sand indicate a gradual filling of the terminal chamber of Den 2.

Den 3

At the opening of the quarry in July 1982, excavation revealed the lower jaws of a large *Daphoenodon* with worn teeth in meter E3. The articulated jaws and parts of the skeleton were found only a short distance from the temnocyonine beardog skull in meter E4 of Den 2. They were embedded in a burrow fill of thinly laminated pebbly light gray sand incised with relief of 2.5 cm into a compact dark gray to brown sand, probably the burrow floor. Here 10 cm of pebbly sand had already been deposited in the burrow before the "arrival" of the beardog, and the face of the exposure showed that several intervals of cutting and resedimentation had occurred. Excavation failed to define a den perimeter—an estimate of width was taken from the visible burrow fill measuring 25 cm. The site was reburied as survey was extended into the northern section of the quarry.

When the quarry was reopened in 1985, bones began to appear on the third day in the area we had designated as Den 3: the skeleton of this aged beardog eventually included its lower jaws, most of the lumbar vertebrae, a scapula, and scavenged humerus near an articulated radius-ulna with the forefoot. Nearby were a few metapodials and a second ulna separated by ~20 cm from the beardog's other radius that preserved the radial exostosis found only in males of this species. The forelimb, still mostly ligament-bound at burial, had survived scavenging.

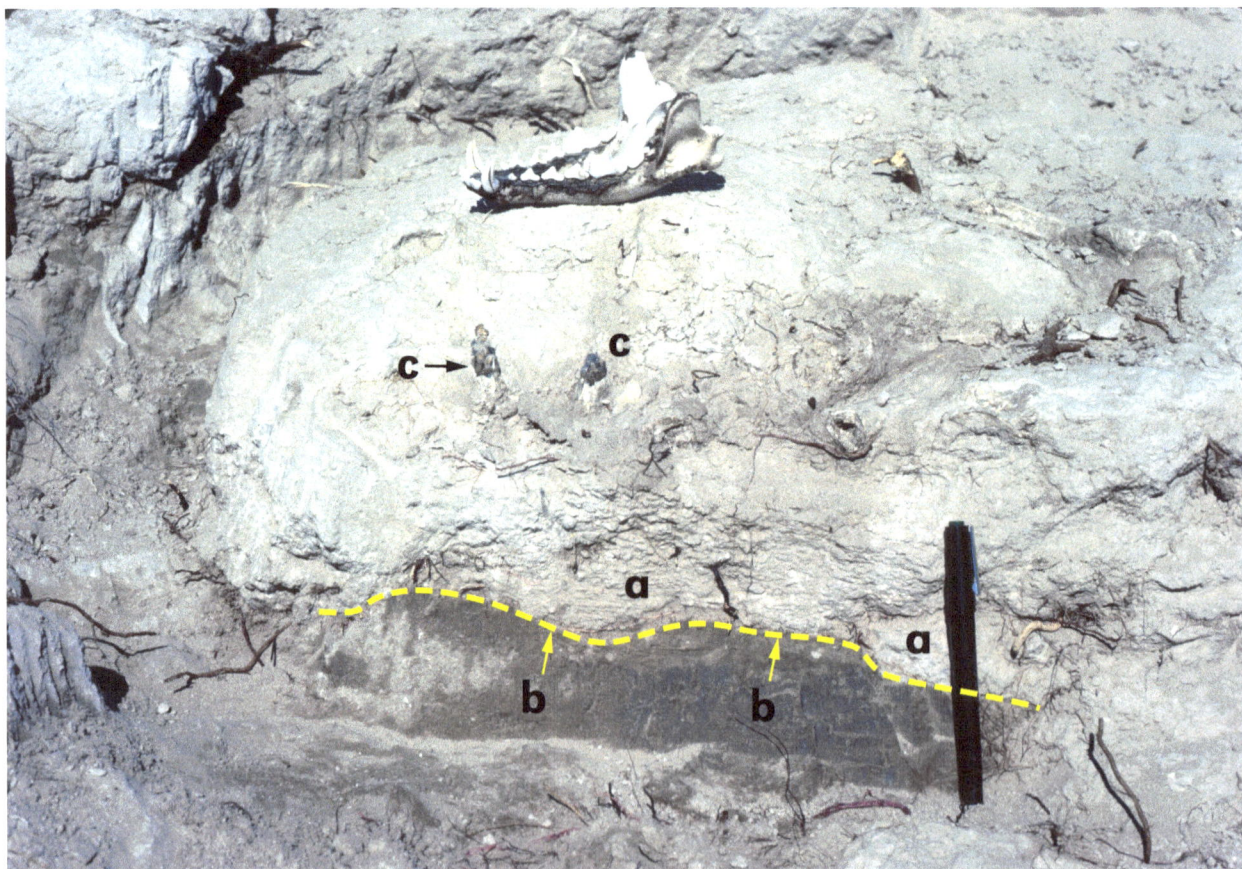

*Initial exploration of Den 3 revealed a pebbly laminated gray sand (**a**) resting with irregular relief on a compact floor (**b**). Emerging from the sediment ~10 cm above the floor can be seen the teeth and lower jaws (**c**) of the male Daphoenodon within the burrow fill. Plant roots invaded the uppermost sediment in the burrow, destroying the laminated bedding. The lower jaws of a coyote (Canis latrans) are included for scale.*

The linear alignment of the disarticulated bones suggested that the skeleton had been scattered along a burrow runway.

A fossil soil permeated with fragmented bone discovered 15 cm above the humerus in meter D2 suggested leftovers of a meal. Surrounding the fragments and extending down to the level of the beardog skeleton were fine-diameter fossil grass roots (*rhizoliths*)—the proximity of this grassland soil to the skeleton suggested that the old beardog had died near the land surface.

This fossil soil identified at Den 3 happens to lie at the same elevation in the quarry as the fossil soil above Den 1—together they establish the location of the vegetated land surface that occurred above

the dens. The old beardog in Den 3 was found within a foot of this fossil soil whereas the floor of nearby Den 1 with its adult female and juvenile male *Daphoenodon* skeletons was nearly 4 feet below the ground. This difference in elevation of the skeletons tells us that the old male of Den 3 could have been close to a den entrance, whereas as can be seen by the intact profile of the entrance tunnel and chamber of Den 1, its two *Daphoenodon* skeletons were deep underground.

In Den 3 we also first encountered siliceous crusts on bones that made it difficult to distinguish bone from the encasing sand. At the interface between bone and sediment, a resistant rind of very thin silica had developed around several limb bones of the

Excavation of the Den 3 Daphoenodon: A large, aged male whose skeleton was scattered within a poorly defined burrow—a partial forelimb is visible to the left of the yellow 30-cm scale; the lower jaws and other bones are protected by the white plaster field jacket.

Jaws of Daphoenodon from Quarry 3 showing a difference in size by gender and age: On the upper left, the juvenile male cub; in the center, the adult female found with the cub in Den 1; and below them the large, aged adult male from Den 3. Only the teeth of the large male are heavily worn. This wear pattern is like that seen in older gray wolves.

Den 3 *Daphoenodon*. The permeable ash-rich sediment that filled a burrow opening on the grassland is subject to the chemical action of plant roots and carbonic acid from rainfall. The soluble volcanic ash and unstable minerals in the sediment over time may have supplied the silica to a skeleton that was buried near a burrow entrance.

The considerable size of the jaws and teeth of the Den 3 male *Daphoenodon* when compared with those of the adult female and juvenile male in Den 1 led us to conclude a marked size difference existed between the sexes. These three skeletons of *Daphoenodon superbus* from Quarry 3 represent the only known instance in which young, mature, and aged individuals of the species have been found together (juvenile male, CM1589A; adult female, CM1589; aged male, UNSM 700-82). The young male cub by now had erupted much larger canines and cutting carnassial teeth relative to those of his presumed mother. His young age is evident from the absence of wear on all his teeth and by the crowding of the misaligned premolars toward the front of the jaw, which would have straightened as the jaw increased in length as he matured. The male cub is estimated to have been from 6 months to 1 year in age at time of death.

Den 4

Excavation in October 1982 led to the discovery of Den 4. As we cleaned meters to bedrock, a carnassial tooth (P4) of *Megalictis simplicidens* was found in loose gray sand at the margin of a small well-defined burrow in meters F4–G4. At first no other sign of burrows appeared as we worked north to northwest into meters G–J, 3–4. As cleaning continued, a vertebra and foot bone of *Daphoenodon* in meter H3 stimulated a more careful search. We realized that a large burrow difficult to recognize was centered in meters H–J, 3–4. Little by little a floor and walls could be identified. Undisturbed laminated fine gray sand en-

tirely filled the interior of the burrow tunnel in meter H–J, 3.

The den is shown here shortly after its discovery. Not until later was it realized that the shallow floor of the burrow in meters H4 and J4 included small lobe-like extensions much like those found in pupping chambers common in the dens of the larger living canids and hyenas. Only three bones of *Daphoenodon* were found here within the burrow, and a small foot bone of a neonatal gazelle-camel, *Stenomylus*, was screened from the surface. Because the burrow fill was intended for future study, the layered sand within the burrow tunnel was not excavated.

← Datum elevation
Meter H1

Den 4 was not recognized until the surface of the quarry had been carefully cleaned, revealing the floor and walls seen in this photograph. Laminated gray sand fills the burrow tunnel entering the hill to the left of the white 30-cm scale.

Den 4 after the completion of excavation: The burrow tunnel seen in cross-section is filled with ~50 cm of laminated light gray sand that contained a few beardog bones. The runway emerges from the sediment-filled tunnel and then continues to the bottom of the photograph to end as several small cavities interpreted as pupping chambers.

Spotted hyena cub at its African den with adult. The cubs excavate small terminal chambers in the dens that adults enter only with difficulty. (Photo by Janet Davis)

1983 Survey and Mapping

Survey and mapping of the quarries on Carnegie Hill and University Hill were completed at this time.

1984 Excavation

The first indication that burrows continued beyond Dens 1, 2, and 4 to the northwest was the discovery during the opening of the quarry in 1984 of a partial *Daphoenodon* humerus sieved from loose sand in meters L2–L3. However, rows L and K eventually proved to be mostly barren, emphasizing that bone in the quarry should be expected primarily in and near recognized burrows.

On the fifth day, gray sand filling a possible burrow appeared in row O—its margins were not clear but we soon realized that this was our first encounter with the perimeter of the Den 5 complex. The quarry was then gradually extended northwest to row Q; no defined burrows appeared at first but many small bones and fragments hinted at what eventually would be discovered in rows O, P, and Q. We continued screening as far as row R, then to rows S and T. We found many unidentifiable fragments and foot bones of the oreodont *Merychyus*; the lack of epiphyses on many of these bones showed juveniles were present.

By the end of the second week, burrow outlines became more defined in the northern half of the quarry. In particular, Den 6 stood out in relief in rows Q–R–S, 1–4. In meters Q3–Q4, removal of the fine gray sand revealed a runway leading to a deep pit that suggested a terminal chamber. The floor and sides of the runway displayed parallel linear grooves like those made by the claws of an animal excavating a burrow—the scratch marks of a former occupant. The narrow grooves matched those seen today in burrows of the North American badger, *Taxidea taxus*.

Discovery of Den 6 in the north part of Quarry 3: The blue Estwing hammer marks the termination of the as-yet unexcavated burrow in meters Q2, 3, 4 and R2, 3. Below: The runway floor (**a**) of Den 6 after excavation showing claw marks (**b**) leading into a possible terminal chamber (**c**) in meters Q3 and Q4.

Den 6 in the north quarry (after cleaning of the floor) and terminal chamber in meter Q3–Q4: Claw marks appear on the burrow wall to the left of the yellow 30-cm scale. The large Den 5A-Den 5B complex can be seen in the upper half of the photograph.

Despite the richness of bone in row P, at this time we had only limited success in locating the margins of Dens 5A and 5B. By comparison, the cleaning of meters in rows M and N turned up much less bone, mostly fragmented. Here however, from meters N3–4,

a lower jaw and pelvic bone of a large subadult *Daphoenodon* were found 5 cm above a burrow floor in cross-stratified laminated gray pebbly sand. Nearby were other broken limb bones, caudal vertebrae, and phalanges of these beardogs.

1985 Excavation

Exploration of meters in the north half of the quarry was emphasized in both 1984 and 1985. The area from meters L–T, 1–6 was covered in 1984. In 1985 we worked to the east beyond row 1 in the M–N–O–P–Q–R meters. This extended the excavation into Beardog Hill. The unanticipated discovery of bone in these eastern rows hence fell beyond the established grid network. Consequently these additional meters were designated during fieldwork by superscripts (for example, P^0, P^{00}) as excavation continued to the east into the hill.

A few days after opening the quarry in June 1985, the first mustelid carnivores appeared: a weathered skull of *Megalictis simplicidens* was discovered in the eastern portion of Den 5A, the only skull of this species known. Peterson had found a lower jaw and partial skeleton of a mature *Megalictis* adult in the southern quarry in 1905; however, our skull, that

of a young adult, told us that two individuals of this wolverine-like carnivore had been present in the dens. In meter P1, an upper jaw with teeth identified the small species *Promartes olcotti*, a carnivore unrecognized by Peterson at Quarry 3. Additional bones of this mustelid were concentrated in Dens 5A–5B and surrounding area; this species occurred only in the northern half of the quarry. Here we found narrow trenches, ~15 cm in width and of similar depth, some filled with loose brown sand and others with a more compact laminated gray-brown sand. On the floor of one of these small trenches in meter P1 was a lower jaw of a very old adult *Megalictis*, the teeth heavily worn from chewing hard material, such as bone. The jaw established the presence of a third individual of this large mustelid species in the quarry. As excavation proceeded, a complete innominate bone of *Daphoenodon superbus* was found on a burrow floor in meter P2—it is the largest known anywhere for the species, presumably a sizeable male.

The skull of the mustelid Megalictis simplicidens found in 1985 in the northern half of Quarry 3 compared with the skull of a living male wolverine Gulo gulo from Alaska. Despite its size, teeth recovered with the fossil skull showed it to be a young animal. The skull of the fossil species was the first to be discovered in North America.

The lower jaw of the mustelid Megalictis when discovered on the floor of a small burrow in meter P1. Its robust and worn teeth show that it could crush hard items in its diet such as bone and other resistant foods. It was found only 2 m from the skull of the young Megalictis in meter P^{00} but the jaw turned out to be from a much older adult.

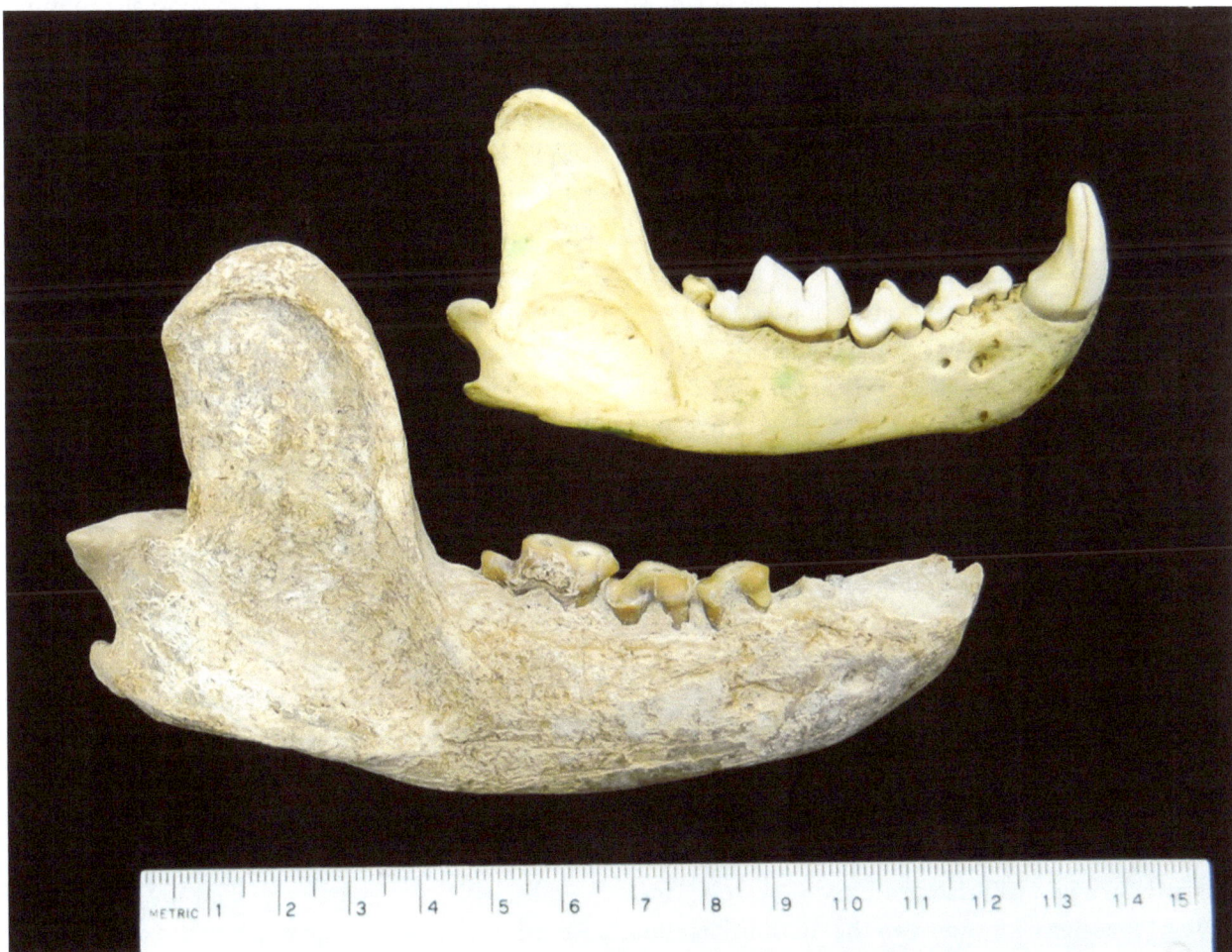

The lower jaw of Megalictis from meter P1 compared with a jaw of an adult male Alaskan wolverine. Megalictis possessed a massive jaw with a more developed musculature, and its worn teeth from eating tough, resistant foods are evident.

1989–1990 Excavations

Following the conclusion of the 1985 excavation, it was decided to review the work accomplished and to prepare and curate the material so far discovered. In the intervening years before reopening Quarry 3 in 1989, the National Park Service provided the opportunity to investigate the relationship of the den site to the waterhole bonebed on Carnegie Hill. Consequently, in 1986 all quarries on Carnegie Hill were opened and explored using test excavations, and the results were presented to the National Park Service in 1988 (University of Nebraska Paleontological Excavations 1985–1986—Agate Fossil Beds National Monument, CA-6000-5-8032, 60 pp., 16 figs., 1 plate). It was then that we realized that the bones had accumulated over time at a waterhole in an abandoned stream channel probably during severe drought—the carnivores had excavated their dens at the margin of the waterhole.

By 1989 there was evident concern that slope erosion on the west face of Beardog Hill might continue to damage the dens and for that reason the decision was made to reopen the den site and to renew excavation. At the conclusion of the 1985 effort, the area had shown considerable promise of additional relict burrows. Were the dens limited to Quarry 3 or were burrows distributed over a much larger area? On July 2 we removed vegetative overgrowth that had accumulated since 1985 and began the work.

The temperature exceeded 100°F. during the first week with time in the quarry restricted to the morning hours. An extended metric grid was established that added rows U, V, and W to the quarry to learn how far the dens might continue to the north in the direction of Carnegie Hill. After screening and finding a few relict bones in rows S and T, inspection of rows U, V, and W yielded no evidence of burrows and only a few fragments of bone. Additional test exploration directed farther north toward Carnegie Hill also produced no result. However, that dens continued to the east into Beardog Hill in the north half of the quarry seemed plausible given evidence of bone as meters were explored in that direction—the burrow identified as Den 5C discovered at this time was better defined than the easternmost vague perimeters of what we had called Den 5A and included foot bones of *Daphoenodon*, *Promartes*, and a molar of the canid *Cormocyon*. In the southern half of the quarry, increasing overburden would not allow continued excavation to the east into Beardog Hill; it was not possible at that time to trace the Miocene land surface and the burrows of the south quarry into the hill.

Dens 5 and 6

Excavation continued in 1990 with the aim of exploring the Den 5 to Den 6 area not yet thoroughly prospected. On June 11–13 we marked off the areas of the quarry for detailed work centered on meters N, O, P, and Q, rows 1, 2, 3, and 4, eventually continuing for up to 4 m into the hill to the east. Screening produced many isolated bones; others were embedded in laminated gray sand burrow fill. Additional bones of the mustelids *Promartes* and *Megalictis* were found in Dens 5A and 5B but also bones of *Daphoenodon*, now known to be ubiquitous throughout Quarry 3.

Den 5 was complex in plan, rich in bones, with apparent cross-cutting of the burrow by later re-excavation. In particular, Den 5B included an unusual concentration of bones at its terminus in meters P2–P3. There at the junction of meters O2 and P2 a mass of fragments and bones of the small canid *Cormocyon* represented the remains of a scavenged meal that included articulated ligament-bound fore and hind feet—the missing toes perhaps had been removed by the scavenger (see the section in this chapter Bone-Processing by Carnivores).

Den 5C was the final burrow discovered during the 1990 work and the only one recognized at the eastern margin of the quarry before the abrupt rise in slope of the hill. We think exploration if continued into the hill to the east could result in discovery of additional dens. Dens are unlikely to be found to the south of the present quarry because of the absence of burrows or bone in test trenches excavated in that area during the initial search for Quarry 3 in 1981.

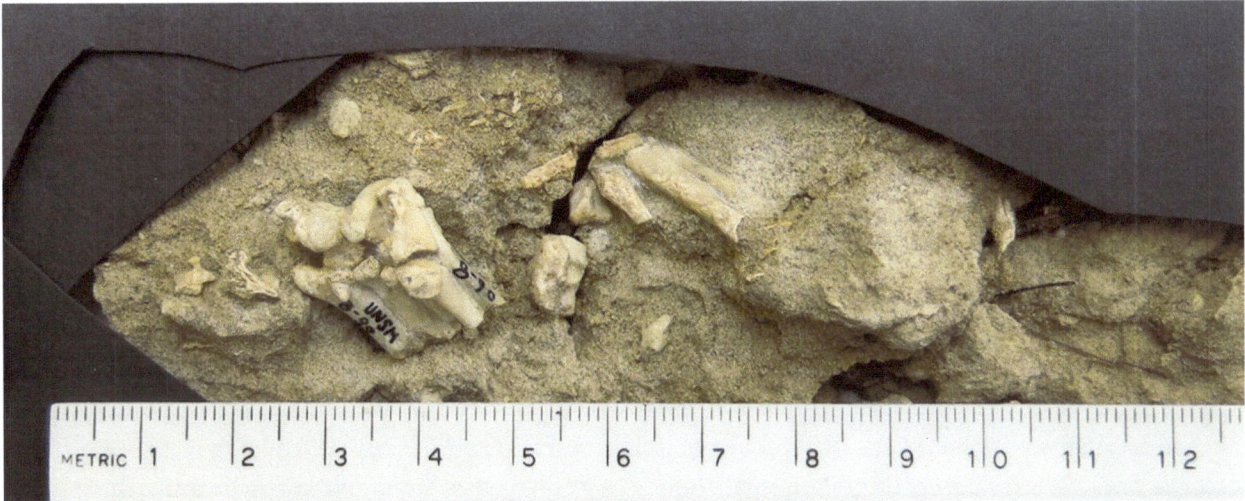

Remains of the scavenged feet of a small canid found in sand filling a burrow in Den 5B. The articulated upper parts of the feet were still bound by ligaments when buried in the den.

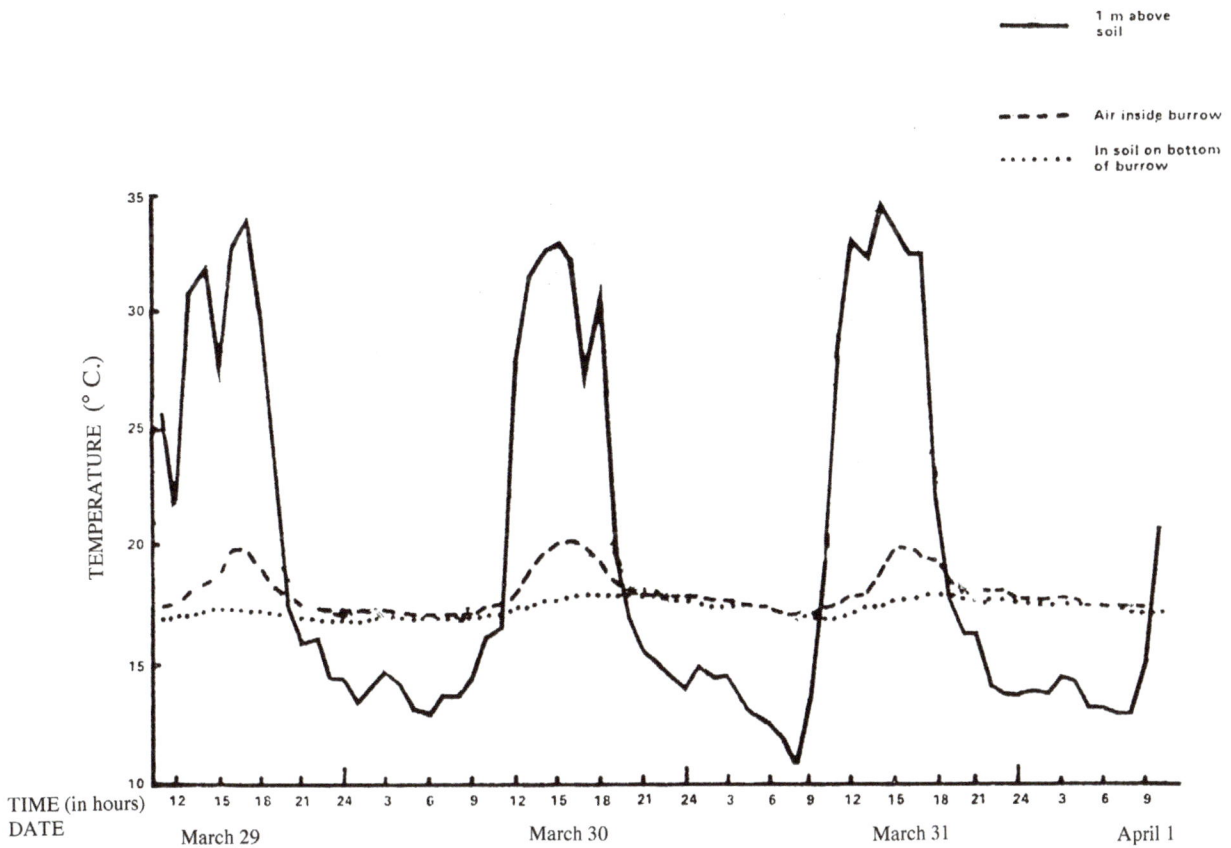

A comparison of the diurnal temperature fluctuations inside and outside an East African warthog burrow. Solid line, temperature 1 m above ground surface; dashed line, air temperature inside the burrow; dotted line, temperature in the soil on the bottom of the burrow. (Modified from Bradley, 1971)

Considerable evidence by now had built our interpretation of the site. For example, the diverse carnivores (*Daphoenodon, Megalictis, Promartes, Cormocyon*) discovered in the northern portion of the quarry during our work were surely at times burrowers or burrow occupants by comparison with living carnivores, and the numerous bones of ungulates found by us in the northern burrows and the few ungulate bones found by Peterson in 1905 in the south quarry not only all belonged to very few species but also belonged to the *same* species now understood to occur throughout Quarry 3. Moreover, the ungulates at Quarry 3 were limited to small vulnerable species (oreodont, camel, cervoid)—the logical preferred prey of the larger beardogs. Most ungulate bone from the quarry came from fore and hind feet, a common byproduct of scavenging. These facts began to lend credibility to interpretation of the quarry site as a den complex arrested at a moment in time.

At the conclusion of work, the burrows were buried under 4- to 8-mil sheet plastic for protection from the elements. The UNSM excavation of Quarry 3 ended on July 13, 1990. Excavation during 1989 through 1990 yielded an additional 230 specimen lots.

Dens of Living Carnivores

The modern carnivores that compare in size and body form to the beardogs found at Quarry 3 are facultative (not obligate) burrowers, and their dens—sometimes excavated by them and often not—serve a three-fold purpose: as protection from enemies, as relief from heat, and to ensure the care and survival of the young. Individual or multiple earthen dens, often structurally complex, come into use during the birthing time and then can be abandoned soon after. Sometimes a single location serves as a long-enduring focal point for a social clan that congregates at a communal den. Dens 1, 2, and 4, where size and internal dimensions can be measured in the quarry, probably served these functions and unmistakably approximate those of living large canids and hyenas.

In a study of burrow form (White, 2005) that included 42 species of semifossorial mammals (those that construct burrow refuges but forage above ground), among them the canids *Canis lupus, Canis latrans,* and the hyaenid *Hyaena brunnea,* a strong allometric relationship was found between body mass relative to burrow cross-sectional area and nest chamber volume. We decided to use this relation between den size and body mass for comparison with the den dimensions and body size of the beardog *Daphoenodon superbus.* Here, as a proxy for body mass, we use the shoulder height of several living canids and hyaenids (from Nowak, 1991) that excavate or reoccupy earthen dens to compare with this measurement from the beardog *Daphoenodon* at Quarry 3. Shoulder height of *Daphoenodon superbus* was measured from the Quarry 3 adult female CM1589 (~55 cm at the shoulder, scaled proportionally to ~70 cm for an adult male). The adult female and juvenile male in Den 1 and the presence of this species throughout the quarry suggest it was a principal occupant and probably, in parallel with living large canids and hyenas, also a remodeler of existing burrows if not occasionally the primary excavator.

Dens of the gray wolf (*Canis lupus*) often occur in sandy ground with entrances large enough for adults. They will dig their own earthen dens and also enlarge abandoned burrows: there may be several entrances that continue through a narrow passage for 1.2 to 1.8 m and then open to a chamber large enough to accommodate adults (Young and Goldman, 1944). Mech (1970) described a typical den: an oval entrance (~35 to 64 cm in diameter) entering a tunnel of similar to slightly larger size that continued for ~1.8 to as much as 4.3 m, ending in a chamber for pups. Elbroch (2003) reported a den measuring 51 to 76 cm in height and 64 to 89 cm in width where the den tunnel descended gradually for 4.6 m to a large chamber ~1.2 m in diameter. Some tunnels have reached a length of 5.5 m. In northern Canada the entrance to a wolf den excavated for pups was usually smaller than 50 × 50 cm with the entrance tunnel extending 1.8 up to 2.5 m to a den chamber (Lopez, 1978). Wolf dens are often located near water and said to be clean and well maintained; mothers with pups will remove any debris and faeces from

Dimensions of den tunnels and chambers of living hyaenid and large canid carnivores compared with measurements from the Miocene tunnels and chambers of the den community found in Carnegie Quarry 3

Species	Length	Diameter	Height	
Canis lupus				
Tunnels	1.2–5.5 m	64–89 cm	51–76 cm	
Chamber	Holds 2 adults	1.2 m		
Crocuta crocuta				
Tunnels	1.5–7 to 8 m	< 30–50 cm	30–50 cm	
Chamber	76 cm	61 cm to 2 m	30 cm to > 2 m	
Hyaena brunnea				
Tunnels	> 3.6 m	30–80 cm	75 cm	
Chamber		1.5 m	1 m	
Canis latrans				
Tunnels	2.4–8 m	23–28 cm	28–36 cm	
Chamber	91 cm	61–92 cm	61 cm	
Vulpes vulpes				
Tunnels	2.5–4.3 m	18–25 cm	~18–33 cm	
Chamber	76–91 cm	46–51 cm	—	

	Length	Diameter	Height	Meter Grid
Den 1				
Tunnel (B)	1.2 m[1]	30–43 cm[2]	—	B6
Tunnel (A)	> 76 cm[3]	—	23–45 cm	B5
Chamber	1.1 m	~1–1.5 m	38–52 cm	B,C 5,6
Den 2				
Tunnel	> 3.2 m[4]	70–85 cm	~30–50 cm	E4,5,6,7
Chamber	~80 cm	45 cm	—	E6,7
Den 4				
Tunnel	> 2.5 m[4]	95 cm–> 1 m	~60 cm	~H,J 2,3,4
Chambers	~70–90 cm[5]	~40–55 cm[5]	—	~H,J 4
Den 5B				
Chamber	~50–80 cm[6]	~40–45 cm	—	P3
Den 6				
Tunnel	~1 m[7]	~25–40 cm	—	Q,R 3
Chamber	~50 cm[7]	30 cm	—	Q3,4

[1] Measured from entrance descending vertically to chamber floor
[2] Measured where vertical tunnel enters den
[3] Length of hidden upper part of tunnel to entrance estimated at ~60 cm
[4] Upper part of tunnel enters Beardog Hill and cannot be measured
[5] Estimated dimensions of presumed pup chambers
[6] Estimated chamber length—the tunnel lengths of Dens 5A, 5B are uncertain
[7] Dimensions of tunnel and chamber in meters Q3–Q4

Burrows often used by spotted hyenas, commonly excavated by aardvark and/or warthog in Nairobi National Park, Kenya, as seen in plan view and vertical profile. (From Bradley, 1971)

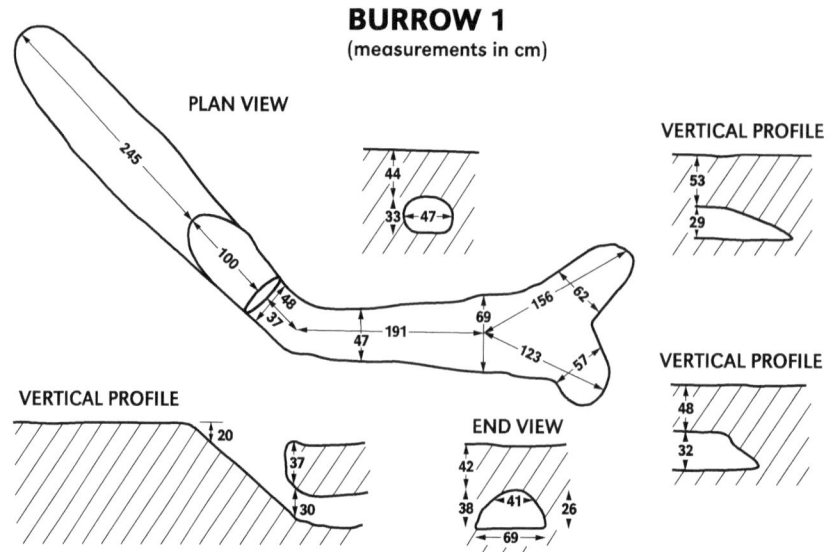

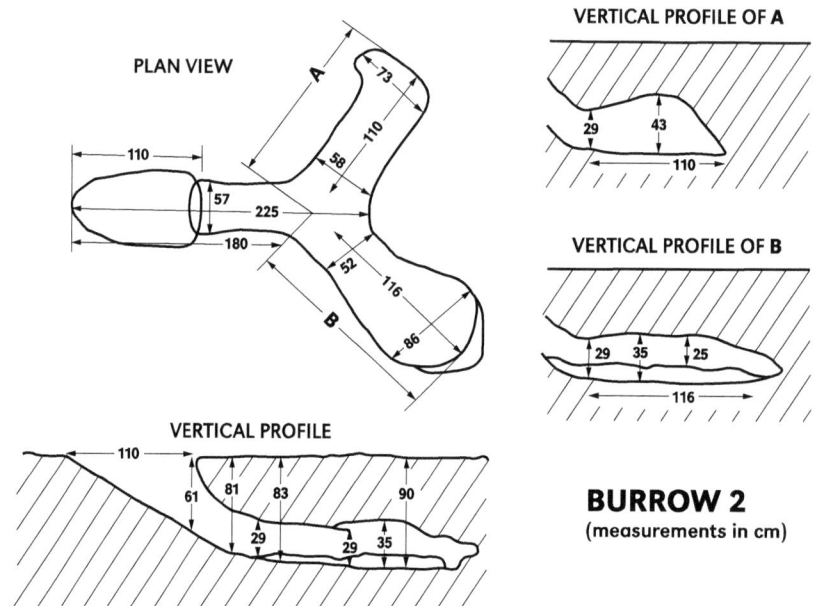

BURROW 1
(measurements in cm)

BURROW 2
(measurements in cm)

their dens. The same den may be used for several years (Mech, 1970).

The coyote *Canis latrans* (Gier, 1975; Bekoff, 1982) will den in stream banks and sandy hillslopes often with many entrances and interconnecting tunnels. Dens of other mammals are frequently used, and the species regularly occupies abandoned dens of badgers (*Taxidea taxus*). A den may be in use over several years (Bekoff, 1982). The length of a den of a California coyote mapped in 1920 measured ~5.5 m. From the entrance, the tunnel extended for 1.8 m, then branched into a lower passage 3 m in length, which ended in a slightly expanded terminal chamber (the width of this tunnel throughout its length was ~30 cm). The upper passage was more meandering with a length of 2.4 meters ending in 4 to 5 small chambers probably for coyote pups. The width of their terminations was ~20 to 22 cm, and the

Burrow of the North American red fox (Vulpes vulpes) with a terminal chamber for pups. (From a drawing by Ernest Thompson Seton)

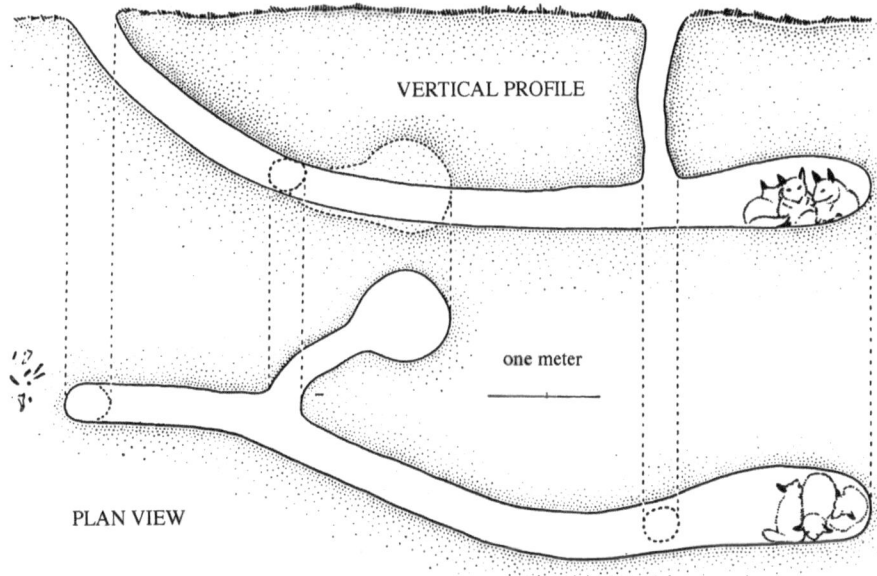

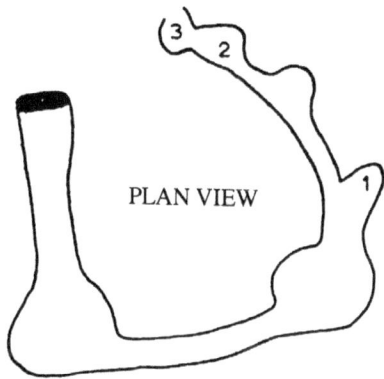

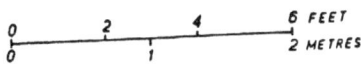

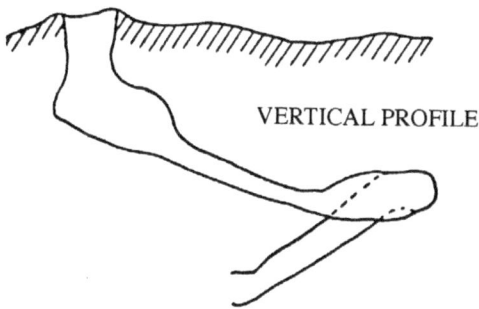

Burrow of a spotted hyena, Serengeti, Tanzania, that contained cubs: 1, two cubs; 2, one cub; 3, one cub. Numbers 1 and 3 each also held a three-quarters-grown hyena. (From Watson, 1965) The den was found in an old termite nest in the middle of a small, open plain surrounded by thorn thickets.

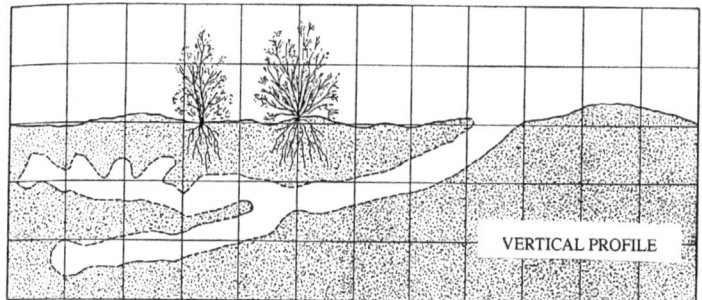

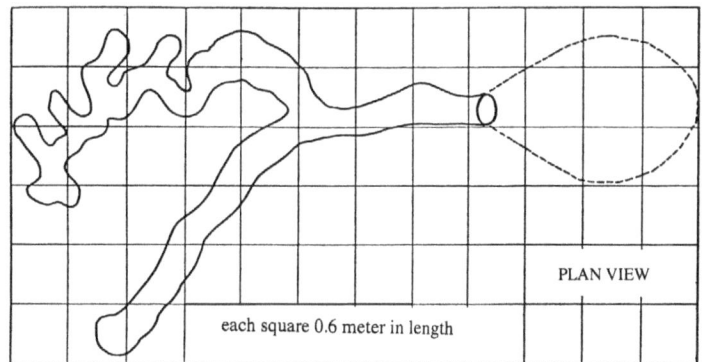

Burrow with multiple chambers of the California coyote (Canis latrans), in the San Joaquin Valley. (From Grinnell et al., 1937).

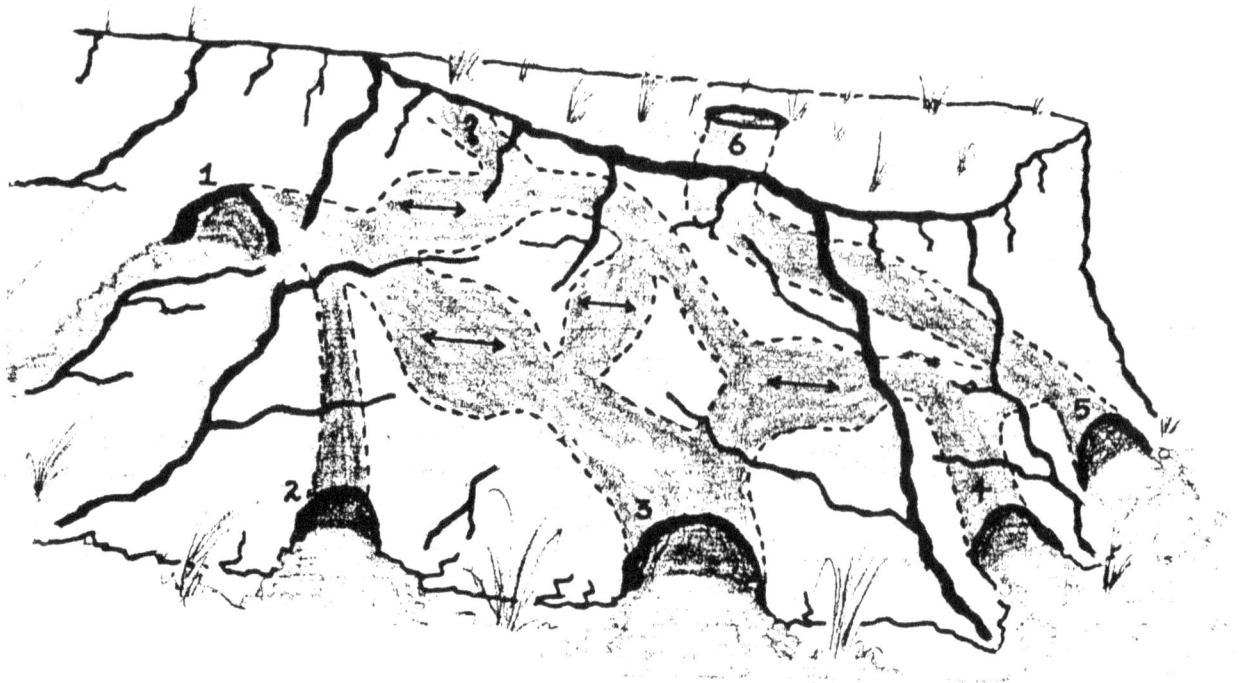

Field sketch of a complex den of Cuon alpinus with six entrances dug into a bank of a creek. Arrows indicate level chambers that are linked by interconnecting passageways. (Modified after Fox, 1985)

diameter of the tunnel itself varied from ~28 to 32 cm (Grinnell, 1937).

The red wolf (*Canis rufus*) of the southeastern United States is said to have dens averaging ~2.4 m in length with an entrance 60 to 76 cm in diameter (Riley and McBride, 1975). The dens did not descend below ~1 m and were either dug by the wolf or excavated by another animal.

The Australian dingo (*Canis lupus dingo*) uses enlarged rabbit-holes or adapts burrows of the large goanna lizard and the wombat (Corbett, 1995) for its dens. Some dens are known to have multiple entrances. Common to all dens is proximity to water; the prevalence of drought in Australia significantly influences the distribution of the dingo population.

Earthen dens of the spotted hyena (*Crocuta crocuta*) in the Serengeti are usually on flat ground and often have multiple entrances 0.5 to 1 m in width with passages decreasing to a diameter as small as 25 cm. These tunnels are about 0.5 to 1 m under the surface and are oval, wider than high, 1.5 to 3 m in

length (often extending much farther), and can lead to a large terminal chamber up to 2 m in diameter and of slightly lesser height, constructed from an abandoned burrow (Mills and Hofer, 1998; Kruuk, 1972). Along a streambed in Kruger National Park (South Africa), an earthen den of *Crocuta* co-opted by an aardvark continued for ~6.5 m and another within a termite mound for ~8 m (Skinner et al., 1986).

Large communal dens may be in use as needed for many years, whereas smaller dens have briefer occupancy, filling in or being occupied by other animals when the hyenas have left (Kruuk, 1972). Kruuk concluded from the dimensions of the narrow tunnels that, whereas adults do excavate, the cubs carry on most of the digging. On the East African savanna, burrows of this hyena once abandoned can fill in with sediment or collapse within several months to a few years after occupation (Pokines and Kerbis-Peterhans, 2007), then later undergo re-excavation.

The den of the brown hyena (*Hyaena brunnea*) has been said to differ from that of the spotted hyena

Communal den of the spotted hyena (Crocuta crocuta) at Masai Mara in East Africa. Hyena pups often enlarge and extend dens when creating small pupping chambers. (Photo by Suzi Eszterhas, Minden Pictures)

in revealing *H. brunnea*'s preference for a single hole in the ground with an entrance 30 cm in height and 50 cm in width (Mills and Hofer, 1998). The brown hyena can dig its own den but also uses abandoned aardvark burrows. Dens in the fossil sand rivers of Botswana studied by Owens and Owens (1979) were initially described with entrances that narrow to a vestibule 0.5 m in length (50–80 cm in diameter), continuing to an underground tunnel 30 to 35 cm in diameter, here size suggesting again that den excavation was chiefly by the cubs. However, Owens and Owens (1984) later discovered a communal den complex of this hyena with multiple entrances excavated in sand over a distance of ~14 m. One entrance entered a tunnel ~75 cm in height that continued for ~3.6 m, then turned and sloped gradually downward to a central chamber ~1.5 m in diameter and ~1 m in height where cubs were said to live. Three small tunnels and 2 larger tunnels went on from this chamber where depressions in the sandy floor were thought to be for the cubs. This large den had existed for at least three years. Brown hyenas form a clan, sharing food and territory, yet scavenge separately as a cooperative society (Owens and Owens, 1984). Food

is commonly taken to these dens so that processed bone accumulates.

African hunting dogs (*Lycaon pictus*) on the open savanna use abandoned dens of aardvarks and hyenas (Schaller, 1973; Nowak, 1991). The hunting dogs' dens then will be similar to those constructed by these other African savanna dwellers, sometimes with additional excavation by the canids.

Dens of the Asiatic wild dog *Cuon alpinus* were studied in southern India by Fox (1985). Their dens in the Nilgiri Valley ranged from some with a single entrance to others with multiple entrances associated with more than one den. A single earthen den located on the plains had a nearly vertical entrance with a sharp turn located 1 m or more down. This entrance tunnel in some dens opened into an antechamber from which one or more passages branched. A particularly complex earthen den used for many years had six entrances and at least 30 m of interconnecting tunnels with four large chambers (Fox, 1985). We reproduce here the field sketch by Fox (1985) of this den excavated in a stream bank; the chambers and connecting burrows extended for ~4.5 m along the stream.

The dens at Quarry 3 that are to some degree intact are Dens 1, 2, and 4. Measurements show that their size, shape, and dimensions are similar to those of several of the living carnivores we have reviewed here. In particular, obvious parallels exist in tunnel construction and dimensions, in the existence of both terminal and suggested pupping chambers, and in the periodic infilling and re-excavation of the tunnels. The beardog *Daphoenodon*, considered the principal occupant of the dens, is larger than the coyote, *Canis latrans*, whose den geometry is evident in the similar design of Den 2. In addition, the multiple dens of the Quarry 3 community seem to suggest the communal dens of the canid *Cuon alpinus* and the spotted and brown hyenas. We think that the parallels in den configuration and in the role of dens among these living canids, hyaenids, and *Daphoenodon* show a common denning habitus, evident in the use of dens for protection from environmental stresses, for birth and care of the young, and in possible social interaction within the Miocene den community.

In support, and perhaps at first not evident, is that the smaller carnivores found in the Quarry 3 dens also compare with species found in the dens of the living hyenas and large canids—for example, the mustelid *Megalictis* with the wolverine *Gulo*, and the small canid *Cormocyon* with the African black-backed jackal *Canis mesomelas*.

The tiny borophagine dog *Phlaocyon annectens* at Quarry 3 in its dryland habitat parallels the tiny fennec fox (*Fennecus zerda*) of arid North Africa, not only in size (~1 kg) but plausibly in the latter's dryland adaptations with a propensity for sheltering in burrows (several meters in length), its nocturnal habit, and its survival often without water (Bekoff, 1975; Nowak, 1991). The other small borophagine

Shoulder Height in Living Carnivores (from Nowak, 1991)

Species of Canid or Hyaenid	Shoulder Height (in cm)
Canis lupus	66–81
Canis latrans	53–61
Canis rufus	66–79
Canis lupus dingo	~50
Crocuta crocuta	70–91
Hyaena brunnea	64–88
Lycaon pictus	61–78
Cuon alpinus	43–56

Shoulder Height in the Beardog Daphoenodon at Quarry 3

Daphoenodon superbus	55–64

Daphoenodon superbus: Estimated Shoulder Height from Lengths of Forelimb Bones (in cm)

Element	Female[a]	Male[b]	% Female/Male
Radius	18.2	21.0	86.6
Scapula	16.5	18.0	91.6
Shoulder Height	55[c]	60 to ~64	

a. Holotype of the species (CM1589)

b. Evidenced by exostosis of the distal radius (UNSM 700-82)

c. Measured from the complete forelimb of the female holotype

Percentages of Identifiable Skeletal Elements of Species (NISE) of Carnivores and Ungulates Collected by UNSM from 1981 to 1990 at Quarry 3

Skeletal Elements	Carnivores and Ungulates		Carnivores		Ungulates	
	N	%	N	%	N	%
Skulls and jaws	17	5.7	15	7.5	2	2.0
Teeth	40	13.3	31	15.7	9	8.8
Vertebrae, sacrum, ribs	38	12.7	31	15.7	7	6.9
Fore and hind limbs*	54	18.0	39	19.7	15	14.7
Feet: podials-metapodials	88	29.3	48	24.2	40	39.2
Feet: phalanges	63	21.0	34	17.2	29	28.4
Totals	300	100	198	100	102	100

* Does not include the feet. The 151 bones of the fore and hind feet (podials, metapodials, phalanges) make up 50.3% of the identified elements found during the UNSM excavations.

Cormocyon from Den 5B shares not only size but arguably a similar ecology with the swift fox (*Vulpes velox*), who occupies burrows of other mammals in semiarid grasslands of the Great Plains. Its diet includes lizards, rodents, and birds, and its tunnels have reached 3.5 m in length with a chamber 1.5 m below ground, similar to dens at Quarry 3.

That the mustelid *Megalictis simplicidens* in Quarry 3 might have excavated in the dens is suggested by discovery of one of its large elongate claws found ~1 m from its skull in the north quarry and the deep parallel grooves cut into the floor and walls of the terminal passage of Den 6. The grooves are too large for the claws of a beardog pup, and the passage appears too small to accommodate a beardog adult.

The partial skeleton of *Megalictis* found by Peterson in 1905 in the south part of Quarry 3 and the skull, jaw, ulna, and claw discovered later in the northern area compare in anatomical detail with the skull and skeleton of the living wolverine, *Gulo gulo*. However, the skull, jaw, and limb bones of *Megalictis simplicidens* are larger and more massive than those of most male wolverines, and its foot bones and claw are more robust. The wolverine inhabits caves or uses the burrows of other animals and is said to have a diet of mostly carrion and rodents, although larger prey have been taken (Banfield, 1974; Nowak, 1991).

The presence of *Megalictis* together with *Daphoenodon* in the dens may not indicate shared occupancy, yet we know they were in occasional use by *Megalictis* because of the three individuals of different ages found in the dens. However, of interest is that interactive behavior between the living gray wolf and wolverine has been reported: Bueler (1973) described wolverine (*Gulo gulo*) foraging at the dens of gray wolves, who are known to kill wolverines (Mech, 1970). The several individuals of the wolverine-like *Megalictis* when visiting the dens perhaps met an untimely end.

Numbers of Identifiable Skeletal Elements (NISE) from Species of Carnivores and Ungulates Collected by UNSM from 1981 to 1990 at Quarry 3

Skeletal Elements	Carnivores	Ungulates	Combined
Axial	81%	19%	100%
Skull parts	5	1	6
Lower and upper jaws	10	1	11
Teeth	31	9	40
Vertebrae and sacrum	24	6	30
Ribs	7	1	8
Appendicular	59%	41%	100%
Forelimb			
Scapula-clavicle	1	1	2
Humerus	3	5	8
Radius	10	2	12
Ulna	4		4
Hind limb			
Pelvis (innominate)	3		3
Baculum	3		3
Femur	5	3	8
Patella	2	3	5
Tibia	6	1	7
Fibula	2		2
Forefoot			
Carpals	6	4	10
Metacarpals	9		9
Hind foot			
Tarsals			
Calcaneum	7	4	11
Astragalus	5	11	16
Other	7	5	12
Metatarsals	12		12
Metapodials (partial)	2	16	18
Phalanges: Fore or hind foot			
Proximal	23	20	43
Median	7	6	13
Ungual	4	3	7
Totals	198 (66%)	102 (34%)	300 (100%)

Note: These data compiled from Table 2 include all UNSM skeletal elements identifiable as either carnivore or ungulate. In addition to the 300 identified skeletal elements (NISE) reported here, screening and excavation of the burrows by UNSM from 1981 to 1990 yielded 1,184 unidentifiable bone fragments from in and near the dens. The partial skeleton of *Daphoenodon superbus* from Den 3 is not included in this table.

Accumulation of Bones at Dens

Listed above are the 300 identifiable skeletal elements (NISE) from carnivores and ungulates found in and near the dens at Quarry 3. If carnivores are compared to ungulates, the former account for two-thirds (N = 198, 66%) and ungulates for one-third (N = 102, 34%). Feet are well represented because of their lack of food value when carcasses are scavenged, and because the compact durable bones of the wrist and ankle resist physical and chemical damage. Bones of the fore and hind foot make up ~50% of all recovered identifiable elements; here percentages for bones of carnivore (54%) and ungulate (46%) feet were similar. Toes (the proximal, median, and ungual phalanges) alone compose 21% of all identified bone in contrast to remains of limb bones at 18%.

In addition to identified skeletal parts, the burrows from 1981 to 1990 yielded 1,184 unidentifiable bone fragments: mostly small sharp angular pieces, the probable result of scavenging and then reworking during surficial weathering. Much of this bone comes from the northern half of the quarry but was also evident to the south. The southern half of the quarry preserved a less disturbed part of the den complex that featured Dens 2 and 4 and especially the burrows and chamber of Den 1, where we reason the female adult and juvenile male *Daphoenodon* were found.

Do bones found at Quarry 3 compare with bone found at dens of several of the larger living carnivores? Whether living carnivores accumulate bones in or near their dens has been investigated for a number of the species whose size and ecology seem to parallel the beardogs found in the Quarry 3 dens. Among the most prolific accumulators of bone at dens today are the three species of living Old World hyenas (Owens and Owens, 1979; Skinner, Davis, and Ilani, 1980; Hill, 1989; Kerbis-Peterhans and Horwitz, 1992; Lansing et al., 2009): the spotted hyena (*Crocuta crocuta*), the brown hyena (*Hyaena brunnea*), and the striped hyena (*Hyaena hyaena*). Bones of prey dominate these accumulations, while those of carnivores are scarce. The lowest carnivore per-

centages occur at dens of the spotted hyena (0–9%) and the striped hyena (0–16%), but are more varied (16–69%) at dens of the brown hyena (Lacruz and Maude, 2005; Lansing et al., 2009).

The massive jaw muscles and formidable premolars of the spotted hyena are singularly adapted for breaking up even large limb bones at the kill site and at their dens. They achieve nearly complete reduction of a carcass at the kill—the adult hyena often tears the limbs from a carcass and will carry these to the den for cubs. However, cubs rely on their mother's milk for at least 4 to 6 months and are not weaned until 12 to 16 months (Kruuk, 1972). Once cubs can accompany adults they join them in feeding and thereafter are not regularly supplied with food at the den.

At communal dens of the East African spotted hyena at Masai Mara, Kenya (Lansing et al., 2009), the skeletal remains identifiable to species over a decade of observation were primarily from their large ungulate seasonal prey: migratory wildebeest (27%), zebra (11%), and the small resident gazelles and impala (14%). Unidentified bones made up 41% of skeletal parts at these earthen dens. Infrequent carnivore remains (jackal, bat-eared fox, hyena cubs) fell at < 1%, as did a few bones of bird, tortoise, and catfish. Bones accumulated slowly at the Masai Mara earthen dens; the rate of bone accumulation averaged only ~60 per year over the decade of the study and only ~1% of bone was seen carried into a den (Lansing et al., 2009). This low rate was influenced by the often temporary occupation of earthen dens. Many communal dens were moved monthly, and the longest continual residence was reported to be ~8 months (Boydston et al., 2006; Lansing et al., 2009).

The brown hyena in the fossil river valleys of Botswana accumulates bones and other food items at a communal den (Owens and Owens, 1984). These hyenas bring food to the den for cubs—including prey killed by other predators and even remains of a jackal, *Canis mesomelas* (Owens and Owens, 1979). The hyena cubs pulled apart and fed on this small canid; perhaps the canid *Cormocyon* scavenged in Den 5B at Quarry 3 represents a similar outcome. At one

During excavation at Quarry 3, we continued to find evidence of scavenging of the small ungulates and predation on juveniles:

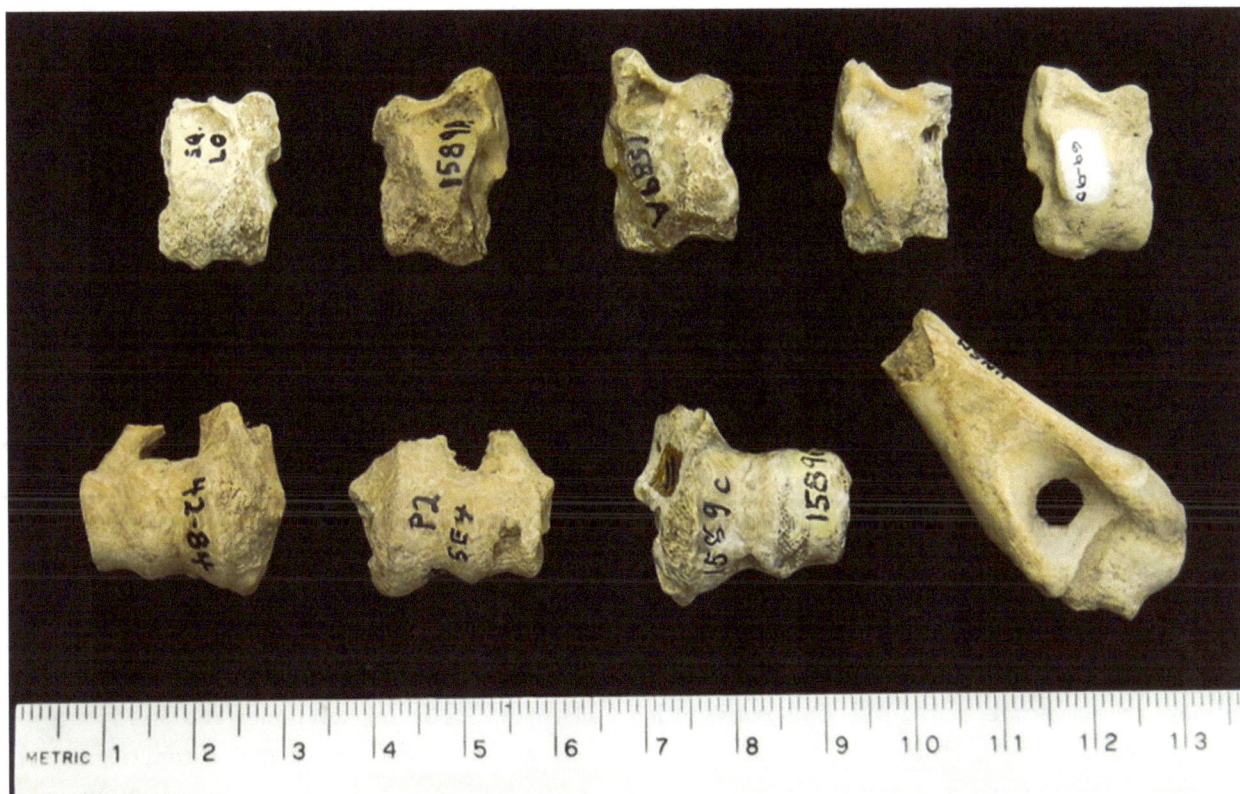

Gnawed foot bones (upper row: 5 astragali) and scavenged limb bones (lower row: 3 distal humeri) of the oreodont Merychyus. At the lower right is a scavenged humerus of a young gazelle-camel Stenomylus; note the separation of the epiphysis from the shaft.

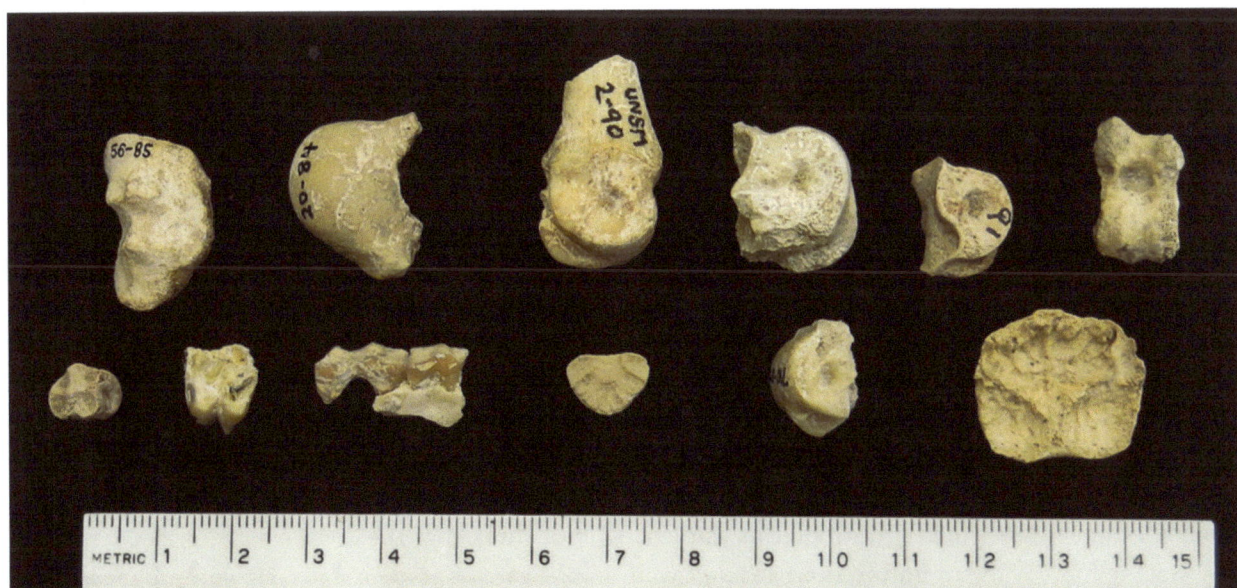

Bone fragments of juvenile animals from the burrows. Upper row: 2 epiphyses (tibia, humerus) of Merychyus, 2 epiphyses (both metapodials) of Oxydactylus, metapodial epiphysis of dromomerycine cervoid, gnawed moschid astragalus. Lower row: metapodial epiphysis of Merychyus, milk teeth of Merychyus (DP4, dp3-4), vertebral epiphysis of small mammal, metapodial epiphysis of Stenomylus, vertebral epiphysis of Daphoenodon.

communal den, food items that incorporated bone made up ~77% of food eaten by the cubs over a week: 43% of those items were from bovid antelope (the small springbok *Antidorcas marsupialis* and gemsbok *Oryx gazella*) and the remaining 50% was unidentified bone. Owens and Owens (1979) observed a small cub eating bone splinters, the result of an older cub gnawing large bones, showing that faeces of cubs as well as those of adults can contain bone fragments.

Somewhat smaller than the brown hyena, the striped hyena is a known scavenger that carries food to its den. Bones can accumulate in enormous amounts: an occupied cavern in the Negev of Israel was littered with a thick mass of bones of the domestic animals preyed upon by these hyenas that had accumulated bones in the cavern for several decades. Bones were found scattered over the floor of this cavernous den and continued into side passageways. A study (Skinner et al., 1980) that sampled 2 m^2 of the floor of the cavern recovered 267 bones representing 57 individuals ranging in size from dogs and goats to camels. Later Kerbis-Peterhans and Horwitz (1992) sampled 16 m^2 of the densest part of this bone deposit where, because of the arid climate, some bones had been preserved with tissue still attached. Of the recovered and identified bones from the cavern, 96% were from the domestic animals with a few bones of a small wild gazelle (*Gazella*). Bones of unidentified canids, the striped hyena, and a fox (*Vulpes vulpes*) composed another 2%. The remaining ~2% was made up of birds, diverse small mammals, and single bones of two lizards and a snake, groups also found at Quarry 3. The minimum number of individuals represented by this dense bone pile was estimated at ~200 for the 16 m^2.

Bones reported at dens of the larger living canids are usually not as numerous as those collected by hyenas. When bringing food to their dens for the pups, canids most often regurgitate this as meat. Receiving food by regurgitation from an adult wolf is critical for the pups: a litter of five pups four months of age requires ~11 pounds of meat per day (Bueler, 1973). In North America, the prey of

the gray wolf (*Canis lupus*) consists mostly of large ungulates—deer, moose, elk, caribou, and Alaskan Dall sheep. Wolves do not routinely collect large numbers of the bones of these ungulates at dens but instead consume most of the prey at the kill site, often returning later to finish it or gnaw the bones (Mech, 1970). Wolves on occasion will carry prey items and bones a distance (4–6 km) to the den; there the limbs and vertebrae will be gnawed by pups (Young and Goldman, 1944).

The den of the gray wolf is usually kept quite clean, although dens that are reoccupied over several years will have some bones strewn nearby (Lopez, 1978). At a den on Isle Royale (Michigan), Peterson (1977) observed bones of six beaver, a muskrat, and an adult and calf moose scattered around the den. Similarly, biologists working in the North Cascades (Washington) discovered bone, bone fragments, and faeces "littering the ground" outside a burrow (Moskowitz, 2013). Broken bones and bone fragments can accumulate at some distance from the den when older pups now living above ground congregate at "rendezvous" sites where adults continue to bring them food (Packard, 2003; Moskowitz, 2013). Because the molars of the wolf can crush bones, wolf faeces often include swallowed bone fragments from prey. The pronounced wear seen on molars and carnassial teeth of older wolves as the result of gnawing and bone cracking can also be seen on these same teeth in the aged beardog *Daphoenodon* at Quarry 3.

The Asian dhole (*Cuon alpinus*) of southern India (Fox, 1985), a canid slightly smaller than Quarry 3 *Daphoenodon*, constructs dens in which the tunnels and chambers of both active and abandoned dens were clean and free of carrion and bone. In three of five denning areas, a few bones were found near the den entrances. Although possibly related to how close to the den a kill was made, Fox (1985) did not think that the dogs usually carried large pieces of a carcass to their dens. However, bones of fawns of the small spotted deer (*Axis axis*) were found in dhole faeces, including tarsals, carpals, and phalanges; epiphyses of long bones; and bone fragments

(Fox, 1985: figs. 5.3, 5.4). These are the same elements common at Quarry 3; bones of the small camel *Stenomylus*, the size of the spotted deer, and those of the other small ungulates would not be unexpected in beardog faeces. Dholes in India take a broader size range of prey: sambar, a large deer (*Cervus unicolor*), and less frequently, based on their scarcity in faeces, the barking deer (*Muntiacus muntjak*) and the very small mouse deer (*Tragulus meminna*). The latter two are reminiscent of the cervoids at Quarry 3.

Adults of the African hunting dog *Lycaon pictus*, perhaps somewhat larger than Quarry 3 *Daphoenodon*, hunt in packs of 10 or more individuals—this social clan isolates and kills mammals as large as zebra on the African savanna. Thomson's gazelle and wildebeest are the preferred prey on the Serengeti plains (Schaller, 1973); wildebeest when present make up 57%, mostly calves, whereas the small gazelles compose 24%. When migratory wildebeest are absent, gazelles then become 79% of the dogs' diet. Schaller (1973) reported the practiced killings of a zebra foal and later a wildebeest calf, observing that their carcasses were devoured at the site. Carcasses are rapidly reduced by the pack. Meat and occasionally some parts are taken to the birthing dens where, as with wolves, *Lycaon* regurgitates meat for its pups. However, evidence of bone accumulating at or near their dens is minimal.

There can be considerable variation in the behavior of the living larger canids and hyaenids that influences the accumulation of bone at their dens. These predators differ in their preferred prey—in its availability, seasonal or continual; in prey size relative to that of the predator; and because of the predator's role either as a solitary hunter or as a member of a pack or clan. The amount of bone found at their earthen dens will also be determined by the amount of time of either continuous or irregular den occupation; by the role of single or communal dens in the life of a species; by the use of transient or more long-lived dens; by the need to bring food to a birthing den; and whether bone is or is not brought to the den because of different styles of processing prey at a kill site. These factors are reviewed in the study of the spotted hyena clan living in open grasslands of the Masai Mara, Kenya, by Lansing et al. (2009). Whereas these authors found a very low annual rate of bone accumulation at the communal earthen dens of Masai Mara, their concurrent review of ~15 additional field studies of spotted hyena dens (e.g., earthen, rock cave, or in calcrete) from 1954 to 2007 throughout East and South Africa showed considerable variation in bone accumulation: from dens without bones or with very few to those with hundreds to several thousand bones collected at the den. Lansing et al. (2009) emphasized that the amount of time represented by bone accumulation at a den is often the unknown factor—a large bone pile may have developed over a brief interval or a small concentration may be the residue of hundreds of years.

The amount of time necessary to create the bone assemblage at Quarry 3 we think was not considerable. Mixing of mammal bone from faunas widely separated in time that might occur at a fossil site existing over millennia is not seen at Quarry 3. Yet relative to bone accumulations at modern dens, the proportion of carnivore to ungulate bone at Beardog Hill is atypical—the dens of living hyena and canid usually only contain bones of ungulate prey or very little bone at all. Of significance is that the Quarry 3 ungulates belong to a very few small species predictable as the common prey of the associated beardogs, due not only to their size but because their recovered bones represent the expected discarded residue from scavenged carcasses. If ungulate bone composed the only remains at the dens, Quarry 3 might compare to dens of some living carnivores, but the disproportion of the beardogs, mustelids, and canids to ungulates is out of the ordinary compared to modern dens and implies that this "unbalanced" bone accumulation is uncharacteristic, presumably even for its time. The occurrence of partial skeletons of several youthful beardogs in their prime in the dens supplies further evidence of an unusual and perhaps catastrophic death event.

Bone-Processing by Carnivores

The teeth of several Quarry 3 carnivores show they were capable of bone-processing. The semicursorial beardog, *Daphoenodon superbus*, possessed skull, jaws, and teeth sufficiently comparable in form and function to those of the wolf to suggest a similar feeding mode. Although not the equivalent of the far-ranging gray wolf, the beardog was certainly capable of running down the small camels and oreodonts found in the quarry dens, particularly *Merychyus*, whose bones made up more than half of all bones of prey. Bones of this oreodont exhibit ample evidence of gnawing, gouging, and breakage. The absence of bones of the large mammals known at the waterhole, such as chalicotheres and dicerathere rhinoceros, and the presence in the dens of only the few durable bones of small adult and juvenile ungulates, tells us that these smaller carcasses were preferred and could be thoroughly processed by the predator.

That the carnassials and molars of the beardog *Daphoenodon* and the gray wolf show a similar pattern of tooth wear in older individuals, and that wolves break and gnaw bones during processing of carcasses, argues that *Daphoenodon* and the wolf share a capability to crush and fragment bone. Moskowitz (2013) investigating elk carcasses in the Salmon River Mountains (Idaho) found collections of fragmented bone that indicated wolves were processing the skeletons, breaking and consuming the bones.

Peterson and Ciucci (2003) pointed out this need for bone: "Bones from prey are required by wolves as a major source of calcium and phosphorus for the maintenance of their own skeletons; single wolves, which often scavenge to stay alive, may not see a fresh kill for weeks, yet they maintain themselves on a diet of bones from old kills." The undigestible bone and hair commonly end in wolf faeces, and often unidentifiable angular bone fragments in the quarry are identical to the sharp jagged pieces of broken bone observed in scats of the gray wolf and the dhole *Cuon*, and at the dens of hyenas. At Quarry 3 a proportion of this fragmented bone must come from processing of the small ungulates by *Daphoenodon*, perhaps mostly by pups. This bone-processing ability was shared with other carnivores in the dens: the beardog *Delotrochanter* in Den 2 has molars and premolars specialized for crushing, and the teeth in the jaw of *Megalictis simplicidens* found in Den 5A are heavily worn from a diet of hard, resistant food including bone. It was surprising to discover that both beardog species at the quarry as well as the large mustelid could not only process meat but also bone and tough connective tissues.

Among the carnivore bones found in the quarry, those belonging to the two tiny canid species were puzzling. Eventually the explanation for the fragmented remains of these two small borophagines (*Cormocyon* and *Phlaocyon*) in the dens was suggested by reports of small canids found in the modern dens

Spotted hyena (Crocuta crocuta) and black-backed jackal (Canis mesomelas), Serengeti, Tanzania—the jackal on occasion ends as the unfortunate prey of the larger aggressive hyena (André Gilden/Alamy photo).

of African brown and spotted hyenas. The brown hyena, primarily a scavenger in the Kalahari region of Botswana, on occasion has hunted the small bat-eared fox (*Otocyon megalotis*) and black-backed jackal (*Canis mesomelas*); remains of this jackal are known to have been carried by a female to a den and processed by the cubs (Owens and Owens, 1978; Owens and Owens, 1979). In the Kalahari the small carnivores, such as jackals and bat-eared foxes, are preyed on by all the large predators including the brown hyena (Ross, 1987). In Kenya at Masai Mara, dens of the Talek clan of spotted hyenas included carcass remains of jackal

and bat-eared fox (Lansing et al., 2009), yet carnivore remains overall were poorly represented at the Talek dens. It is interesting that jackals are among the animals that dig dens later used by the spotted hyena (Kruuk, 1972). By analogy it seems the scavenged canid *Cormocyon* in Den 5B may have been dragged in as food for cubs, or was a visitor surprised in the den.

The tiny canid *Phlaocyon* perhaps shared a similar fate in Den 1 at Quarry 3. Edentulous jaws of a few small unidentified juvenile carnivores found in the quarry possibly represent animals that met a similar end.

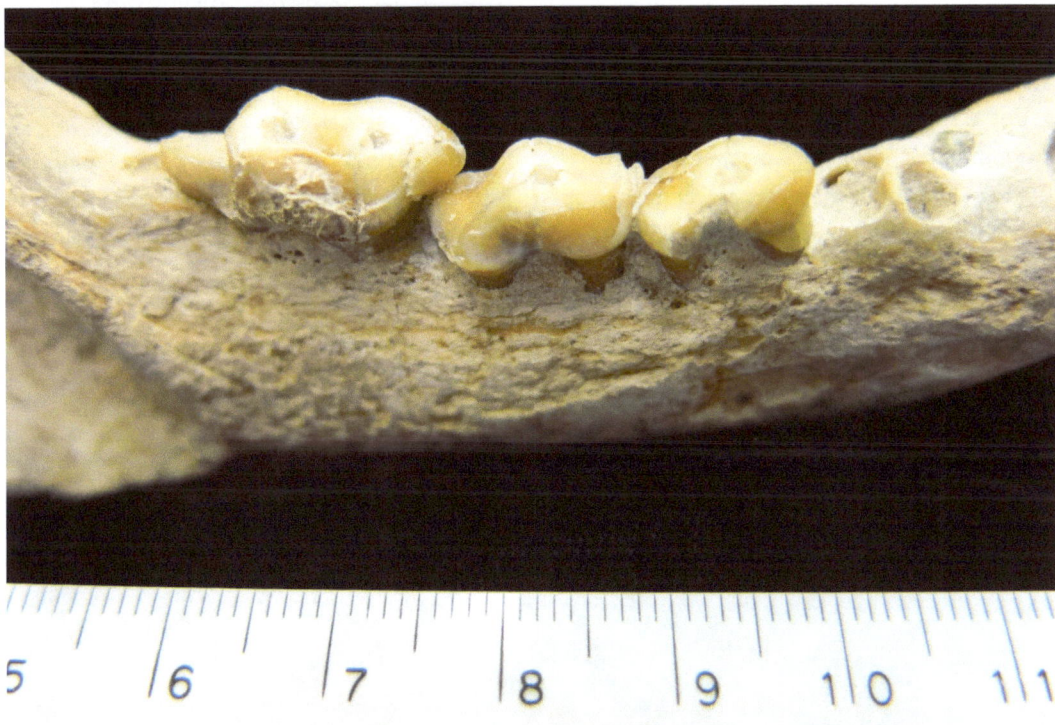

Teeth in the jaw of Megalictis worn flat by chewing hard tissues and bone—an extreme degree of wear has exposed the dentine cores of the molar and two premolar teeth.

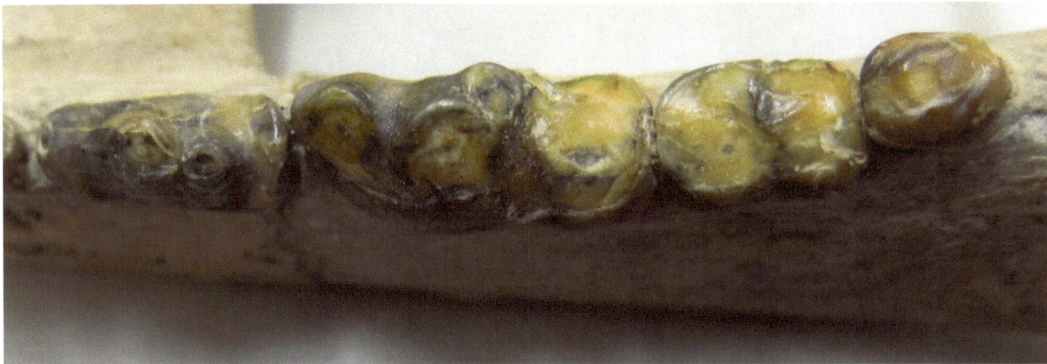

Teeth in the jaw of the very old male Daphoenodon in Den 3 also show pronounced dental wear from processing hard food items, as is evident in Megalictis above. Similar tooth wear is seen in the living gray wolf (Canis lupus), which gnaws and breaks bones.

Discovery of the "Bone Hash" Site

During excavation of Den 5B in July 1990, an unusual concentration of bone fragments appeared in thinly layered sand in the extreme southwest corner of meter O2. To preserve whatever associated skeletal parts might be present, the enclosing sediment was removed in a small plaster jacket and divided in the lab into two conjoined blocks each with an area of ~10 × 12 cm and thickness of ~2 cm.

Preparation of the first block (UNSM 59-90) revealed bones of an articulated forefoot of a small canid. A scavenged radio-ulna and two articulated phalanges were near the forefoot. As the foot emerged from the sediment, we realized that the lower part was missing, apparently bitten off, leaving only the carpals and upper parts of the metacarpal bones with the loss of the toes and distal metacarpals. During preparation, the skull bone of a small lizard (UNSM 8A-90) was discovered a few millimeters from and nearly in contact with the canid forefoot. Previously, a hind foot (UNSM 8-90) had been found near this forefoot in the adjacent southeast corner of meter P2. The hind foot included its articulated tarsal bones and upper parts of the metatarsals yet with toes and lower metatarsals also removed exactly as seen in the forefoot. The two feet evidently belonged to the same adult. Nearby ~50 cm from the hind foot was found an upper jaw with molars of the small canid *Cormocyon*, corresponding in size to the scavenged feet.

A "hash" of small, broken, sharp-edged pieces of bone began to appear in the second block (UNSM 54-90), patiently dissected by preparator Rob Skolnick. Among the mass of fragments was the scapula and a few phalanges of a small adult canid and what appeared to be parts of a crushed skull. Also present was the molar of a heteromyid rodent. Under these fragments we found the first evidence of a juvenile canid: a milk molar (DP4) of a very young pup, and nearby another milk tooth (dp4) and calcaneum. In addition to the "bone hash," other bones came from Den B: distal humeri and phalanges of *Merychyus* damaged by gnawing; scavenged bones of *Stenomylus*; an ulna, thoracic vertebrae, and canine of *Megalictis*; and several ribs, an innominate, and femoral epiphysis belonging to a large adult and to a juvenile *Daphoenodon*.

*The "bone hash" block (**a**) in Den 5B after removal from the dark area (**b**) in layered sand (**d**) that filled the den. A rib of Daphoenodon (**c**) can be seen in the burrow fill.*

The "bone hash," a collection of broken sharp-edged bone fragments from Den 5B, probably remains of scavenging, and perhaps a regurgitated mass. These fragments include the scapula of a small canid, teeth, and crushed skull pieces found together with a canid forefoot (see below).

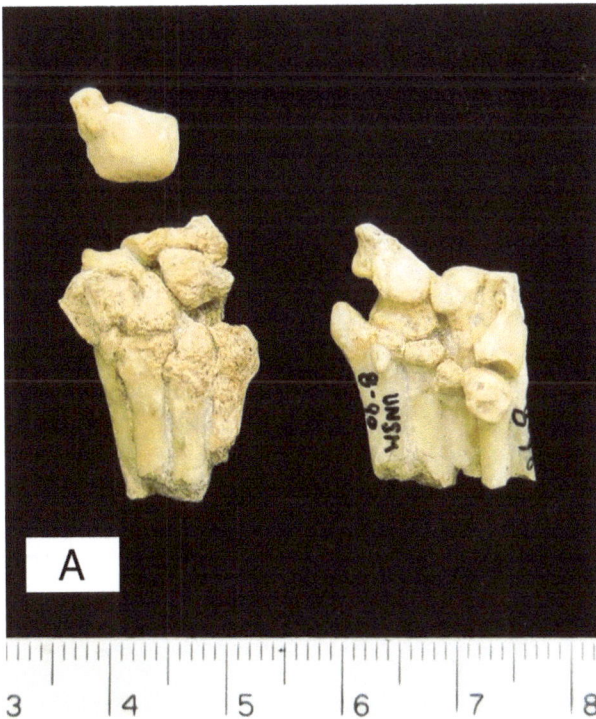

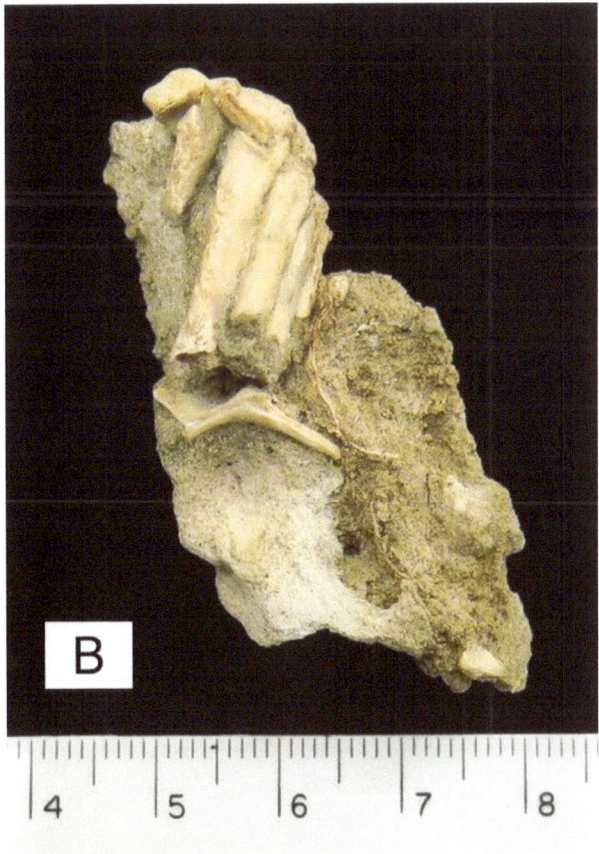

(**A**) Articulated forefoot (on left) and hind foot (on right) of small canid (Cormocyon) from Den 5B—both feet when buried in the den had toes bitten off with bones held together by ligaments and connective tissue. (**B**) The same canid forefoot (as in A, left) photographed at the time it was found in the burrow next to the skull bone of a small lizard.

The Carnivores and Their Dens: An Overview

The waterhole and its dens were an integral part of the history of a Miocene paleovalley similar to those of ephemeral sand-bed rivers known today in semi-arid East Africa and Australia. Water-dependent mammals rely on waterholes along such streams during a prolonged dry season or in severe drought. Although the use of waterholes and dens would not be unexpected in such situations, their burial and preservation in the Miocene is exceptional and came about through a fortunate intersection of climate, geographic location, and volcanic activity. The arid climate of a savanna grassland in the central Great Plains at this time coincided with westerly winds bringing fine sand, silt, and volcanic ash from erupting volcanoes 500 to 700 miles to the southwest. This sediment blanketed the land and today makes up the greater part of rocks of the Arikaree Group. Arikaree sediments of the Anderson Ranch Formation in western Nebraska and adjacent southeast Wyoming are a storehouse of evidence that documents the first fully realized savanna grassland ecosystem in North America, replete with a fauna of ungulates and predators occupying a land surface colonized by early grasses, dung beetles, colonial ants, and burrowing mammals, notably rodents and large carnivores.

Within this grassland ecosystem, the fossils found in Quarry 3 allow us to reconstruct and interpret the site. Even if burrows had not been preserved, the skeletal materials in aggregate point to a den complex. Consider (a) that the diversity of the carnivores, with more than a single individual of each species, suggests a place where carnivores congregated relative to their scarcity at the nearby waterhole;

(b) that a female adult and juvenile male beardog found together, likely a mother and her pup, parallel large living hyaenids and canids that require dens for shelter and care of their young; (c) that ungulate bones discovered in the quarry belong only to small vulnerable species, recognized as the probable prey of the larger fossil carnivores; and (d) that damaged ungulate bones and hundreds of broken fragments that survived in the quarry compare with bone from scavenged carcasses and/or faeces brought to the dens of living hyaenids and canids (the canid *Cormocyon* in Den 5B calls to mind a jackal brought into an African den by hyena pups). The identified skeletal elements and their number, condition, and distribution in the quarry not only establish the species present but also suggest their probable life roles within an integrated community, leading to prediction of their ecological relations. The eventual discovery of the burrows themselves completed the picture of a Miocene carnivore den community surviving today in the central Great Plains.

We do not know how long the dens were in use but believe that by analogy with denning behavior of the living hyaenids and larger canids the den complex would have been dedicated to annual care of the pups. The dens may have been in active use at different times, occasionally abandoned, or perhaps sometimes co-occupied by the predatory mustelids and beardogs; the small canids may have ended as food for cubs. Dens in the valley were either occupied for a season or over years as needed by the various carnivores, as beardogs and mustelids preyed on small mammals, the locally available small ungulates, and on young of the little rhinoceros *Menoceras*. Ungulate bone surviving in the dens shows that skeletal parts when carried into the den were gnawed, probably by pups, and that small mammals were scavenged there.

The role of earthen dens for protection and raising of young is nearly universal among the living African hyaenids and larger North American canids: the size and dimensions of their dens are determined by the terrain and size of the excavator. Our study of the Quarry 3 dens suggests that in the Miocene they shared a similar purpose and were constructed in much the same way. However, it was the discovery of skeletal remains of 6 different species of carnivores representing at least 21 individuals, found in the den complex with bones of small ungulates presumed to be prey, that is unusual and not reported elsewhere in the fossil record.

The beardog Daphoenodon superbus, the most common carnivore found in the dens at Quarry 3, was discovered in burrows with the small oreodont Merychyus, its preferred prey (from a mural by Jay H. Matternes).

Here we consider some situations that singly or in combination might lead to a decline of the den community and the deaths of occupants:

Flooding of the den—In semiarid grassland, brief yet heavy seasonal rainfall in the wide valley of the Miocene river at times could have flooded dens excavated along the watercourse, drowning unsuspecting occupants. In East Africa, flooding of a den of the hunting dog (*Lycaon pictus*) in the Serengeti during an intense rainstorm forced the female to carry her pups from the den; they reoccupied the den after the heavy rain but with the loss of several pups (Schaller 1972, 1973). Here also seasonal flooding of its savanna burrows led to the deaths of the African gerbilline rodent *Tatera robusta* (Senzota, 1984; Kinlaw, 1999). If an entrance tunnel descends at a steep angle to a chamber, as occurred at Den 1 at Quarry 3, the savanna den without another exit is at risk from heavy rain, slope wash, and wind-blown dust and sand.

Volcanic ash—There is no indication that the carnivores were killed by an ash-fall event. Although volcanic glass shards make up a significant percentage (22–35%) of the sediment filling the dens and in river sands that overlie and bury the den community, this amount of ash is found and frequently exceeded in the plains and stream environments recorded by Arikaree rocks of the national monument and throughout the region. The widespread distribution and uniformly fine-grained character of Arikaree rocks in the central and northern Great Plains supports a primarily eolian origin for this sediment (Darton, 1899; Stanley and Benson, 1979; Swinehart et al., 1985; Hunt, 1990). Ash from Oligocene and early Miocene volcanic centers in southwestern Utah and southern Nevada eventually settled within Rocky Mountain basins and on the adjacent plains of Nebraska, Wyoming, and the Dakotas (Larson and Evanoff, 1998). Transported by high-altitude winds to the midcontinent, the ash was then admixed and reworked by wind and ephemeral streams over thousands of years during the arid early Miocene.

Death from drought—If seasonal drought was common on the savanna grasslands of the early Miocene, dens in the region might respond in kind, serving as a final refuge from the prolonged heat and lack of water seen during the extended severe droughts like those that characterize the East African savanna today. Whereas Quarry 3 perhaps records such a moment in which resident beardogs and the mustelids sought shelter in the dens along with scavenged remains of their prey, we know of no directly comparable examples among living large Carnivora where such diverse skeletal remains of predator and prey have been found together in their dens. Although dens of several species of living hyenas and the large canids such as wolves show varied amounts of bone at the den mouth, these earthen dens themselves are usually quite clean. Bone when present at the entrance and outside the dens is almost entirely made up of the bones of prey with little evidence of carnivores unlike the surplus of carnivore bone at Quarry 3. If exceptional drought in the early Miocene was responsible for the numerous carnivores at Quarry 3, at present we lack the necessary substantive evidence.

Death in prime of life—The condition of the partial skeletons of the female *Daphoenodon* and her male pup found in what we believe was their den chamber is evidence of premature and possibly sudden death at Den 1. That the male pup's scavenged bones and the nearly untouched skeleton of the female adult were mostly undisturbed suggests they died together only a short time before they were buried in the den. Their skeletons together with that of the old male in Den 3 told us that they belonged to a sexually dimorphic species: this beardog probably birthed its young in dens where pups may have profited from maternal care beyond 6 months of age until nearly the size of an adult female. The pup, despite its apparent youth, was to become a very large male (its skeleton retained the baculum) based on the unfused epiphyses of its limb bones and its unworn carnassial teeth. These teeth were larger at this time in its young life than the worn carnassials of the much older mature male from Den 3.

Sediment filling dens—We know that sand, silt, and minor pebble-rubble was introduced gradually over time into burrows A and B at Den 1 by influx of water of low energy and by wind. Kruuk (1972) noticed that smaller temporary dens of the spotted hyena *Crocuta* filled in with sediment in this way once the animals had left, and that the canid *Lycaon* had been known to reexcavate abandoned hyena burrows (hyenas themselves reactivate old warthog and aardvark burrows). Episodic excavation in Den 1 was particularly evident where intervals of sedimentation were interrupted by re-excavation surfaces in burrow B.

The presence of bones and partial skeletons *within* the den fill at Quarry 3 and the evidence of re-excavation show that some sediment accumulated in the dens when they were in active use, as seen in the Serengeti. Some sediment was also surely introduced when wind-blown sand and debris entered abandoned dens, as observed by Kruuk (1972). However, final entombment of the den complex took place as 6 m of sand deposited by the Agate paleoriver eventually covered the dens.

Elephant crossing a sand-bed river in East Africa (photo by B. and J. Richardson).

The beardog Daphoenodon superbus confronts the scavenging entelodont Dinohyus hollandi.

The Carnivore Species

Fossils of the Order Carnivora found in the dens include members of three families: Amphicyonidae (beardogs), Mustelidae (wolverine and marten-like species), and Canidae (small foxlike forms). Throughout Quarry 3, the common carnivore is the beardog *Daphoenodon superbus*, discovered by Olaf Peterson (1907, 1909, 1910). The temnocyonine beardog *Delotrochanter oryktes* from Quarry 3 and also from Stenomylus Quarry is particularly rare and known only from Agate Fossil Beds National Monument.

Beardogs (Family Amphicyonidae)

Daphoenodon superbus

The fossils of *Daphoenodon superbus* from our excavation in Quarry 3 were primarily isolated bones and teeth, often broken, with surfaces gouged or punctured by scavenging. Those found by us and by Peterson included skull fragments (6), partial limb bones (41), innominates (7), podials (56), metapodials (52), phalanges (50), lumbar and caudal vertebrae (14), cervical and thoracic vertebrae (7), partial ribs (10),

Adult female Daphoenodon superbus (CM1589) found by Peterson at Quarry 3 in 1905 (holotype of the species).

81

and also some individual teeth (11). The scarcity of scapulae, proximal humeri, cervical and thoracic vertebrae, and most ribs may have resulted from scavenging of the forequarters. The ~243 bones and 3 partial skeletons of the young, mature and aged individuals from the quarry make up the only such sample of the species.

Daphoenodon superbus was the principal occupant of the dens—the skulls and jaws with teeth document at least seven individuals in Quarry 3:

Museum No.	Gender and Body Type	Dental wear stage*
CM1589 †	Female, small adult	2
CM1589A	Male, large juvenile	1
CM1589B	Male, largest adult	3
CM1589B, UNSM 723-82, CM1589D	Female, mid-sized adult	3
CM2774	Female, small adult	2
UNSM 92-84	Male, young adult	2
UNSM 700-82	Male, large adult	3

* Stage 1, minimal wear; 2, moderate wear; 3, well-worn molars
† For CM, USNM, and all institutional abbreviations, see p. 114.

Teeth of this beardog show that young, mature, and aged individuals were present in the quarry. This is confirmed dentally by wear on molars but also by the spacing of the premolars—the premolars are crowded in the jaw of a young beardog, but as the pup grows and the jaws increase in length, these teeth become spaced apart and properly aligned in the adult.

The youngest individual is the juvenile male (CM1589A) found together with the young holotype female (CM1589) by Peterson (1910) at Den 1. The young male's molar teeth are fully erupted yet unworn; its premolars are quite crowded in the lower jaw. The sutures of its skull remain open, which, with the crowding of the premolars, show the head will continue to grow and enlarge considerably. In addition, the epiphyses on all limb bones, metapodials, and vertebrae have not fused. A young gray wolf (*Canis lupus*) acquires all its adult teeth by 6 to 7 months, and the epiphyses of its limb bones have fused at about one year, a wolf reaching adult size at that time (Mech, 1970; Rausch, 1967). Whereas the beardog's growth rate need not closely match that of

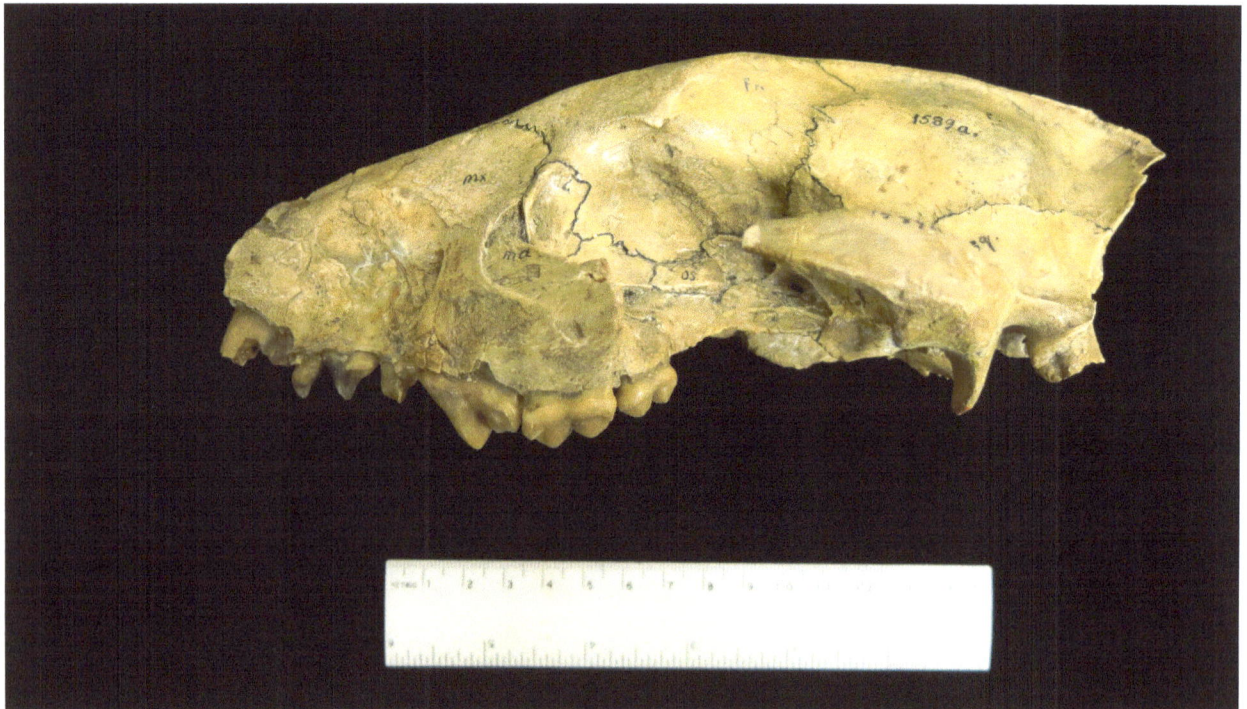

Skull of the young male Daphoenodon superbus pup (CM1589A) found with the adult female in Den 1.

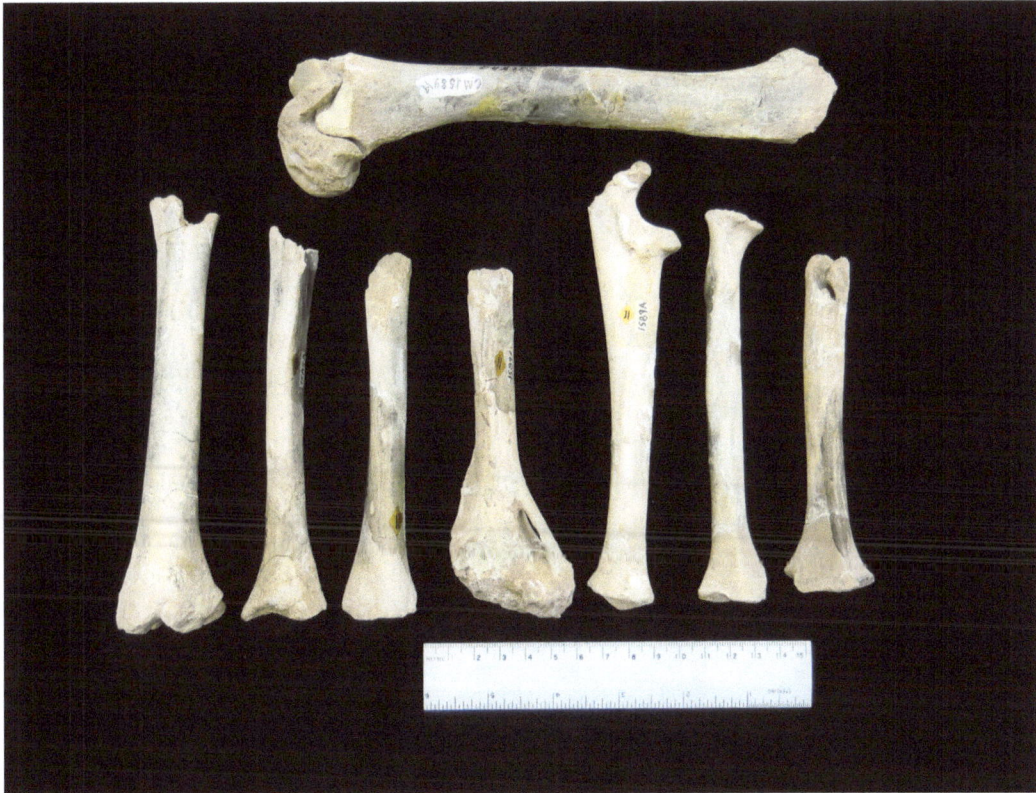

Scavenged limb bones of the young male Daphoenodon (CM1589A) from Den 1.

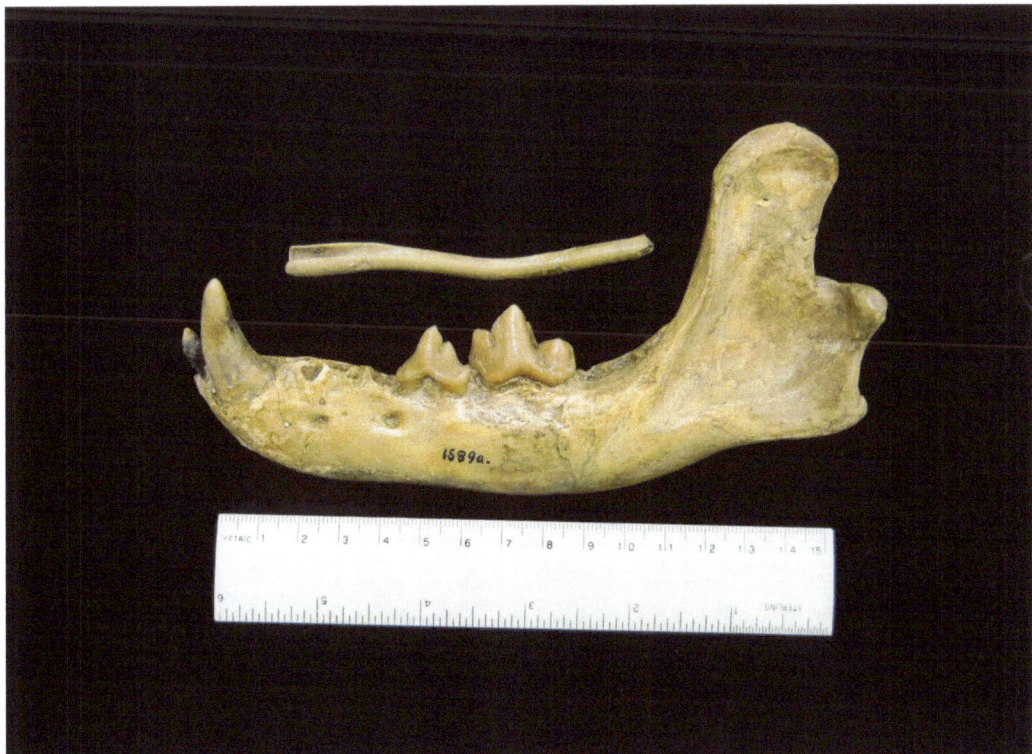

Jaw and baculum of the young male Daphoenodon (CM1589A) from Den 1.

the wolf, an age estimate using this comparison suggests the pup could be older than 6 months but not yet 1 year of age.

A second female (CM2774) of the same dental age as the holotype female is represented by an intact skull, jaw, and forelimb found by Peterson in 1908 but for some reason never described. Peterson's handwritten field label established that CM2774 came from "close to the place where the type skeleton of 'Amphicyon' superbus was found." The field label, the exceptional condition of the skull and jaw, and its reported proximity to the holotype female (CM1589) indicate CM2774 surely came from Quarry 3, and probably from a burrow, but no further mention by Peterson of this discovery has survived.

The only mandible of Daphoenodon from the northern quarry belonged to a large young adult male (UNSM 92-84) of an age similar to that of the two females (CM2774, CM1589); its premolars are aligned and in close contact but not crowded, indicating an animal somewhat older than the juvenile in Den 1 (CM1589A).

The three remaining D. superbus individuals are all dentally older adults. The best preserved, (a) UNSM 700-82 from Den 3, is a mature aged male with well-spaced premolars and pronounced wear on all molar teeth. Two jaw fragments with worn molars under CM1589B indicate the other two individuals: (b) a very large male represented by a mandibular fragment with an enormous m2, and (c) a probable female with a smaller, similarly abraded m2. An isolated worn m1 (CM1589D) and a worn m2 in a mandibular fragment, based on size and degree of molar wear, could both belong to this latter female.

We arrived at an initial minimum number of seven individuals of Daphoenodon at Quarry 3 from teeth (6 adults, 1 juvenile) and then, independently, reached the same number using the isolated postcranial bones from both UNSM and Carnegie excavations. The final estimate of nine beardogs resulted from bones of two additional juveniles found during the UNSM excavation—one, a metatarsal from the

laminated fill of Den 4 (meter H3). The second from the north quarry (meter O2) identified by a baculum (UNSM 23-90) and femoral epiphysis (UNSM 10-90) identical to these same elements in the juvenile male (CM1589A) in Den 1, showing that two male pups had been present in the dens.

The **Key to Mapped Distribution of Taxa** (hereafter **Map Key**, p. 108) lists the elements of *Daphoenodon superbus* found in Quarry 3, and their distribution is plotted on **Map C**.

Minimum number of individuals (MNI) of *Daphoenodon superbus* from the carnivore dens at Beardog Hill, Agate Fossil Beds National Monument, based on the isolated postcranial bones found at Quarry 3 during the UNSM and Carnegie excavations. It is the radius and astragalus that establish the postcranial MNI.

Element	UNSM	Carnegie	MNI
Scapula	1	3	4
Humerus	1	5	6
Radius	**4**	**5**	**7**
Ulna	2	5	6
Scapholunar	1	4	5
Magnum	1	2	3
Unciform	1	2	3
Carpal cuneiform	0	4	4
Metacarpals	3	23	6
Innominate	3	4	5
Baculum	1	1	2
Femur	1	4	4
Tibia	2	9	5
Fibula	1	2	3
Calcaneum	2	6	6
Astragalus	**2**	**6**	**7**
Cuboid	2	3	5
Navicular	1	3	4
Ectocuneiform	0	5	4
Mesocuneiform	2	3	5
Entocuneiform	2	4	5
Metatarsals	5	21	6
Phalanges	18	32	4
Vertebrae	9	12	2
Ribs	10	0	—
Total	75	168	

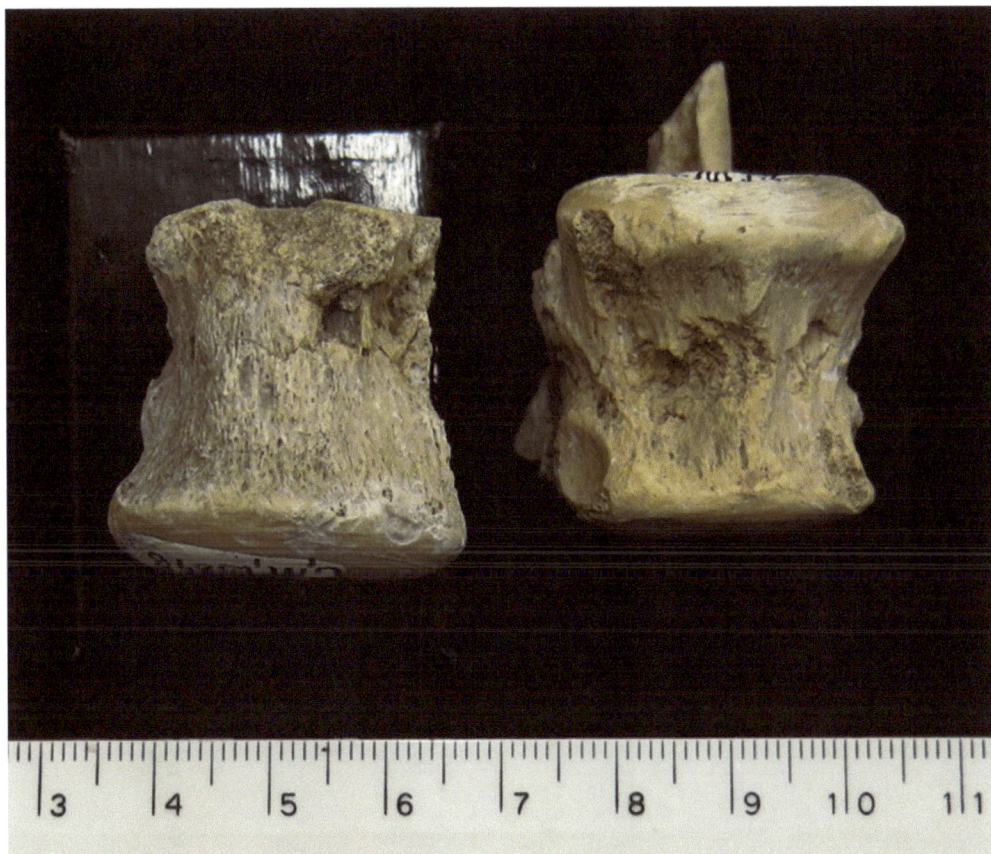

Scavenged thoracic vertebrae of Daphoenodon showing tooth puncture on the left centrum and tooth punctures and gouging on the right.

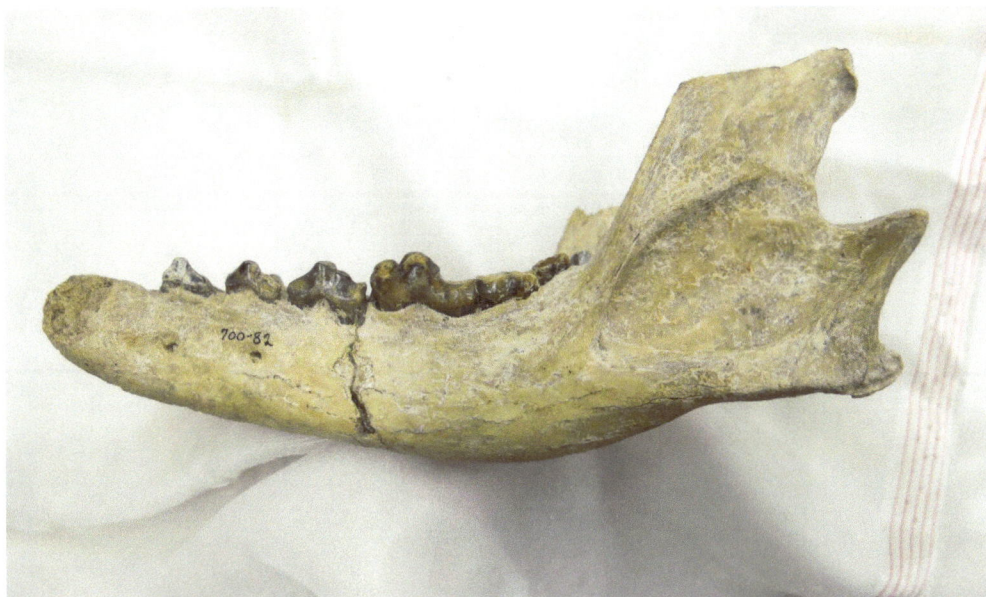

Jaw of the aged male Daphoenodon found by UNSM paleontologists in Den 3 in 1982.

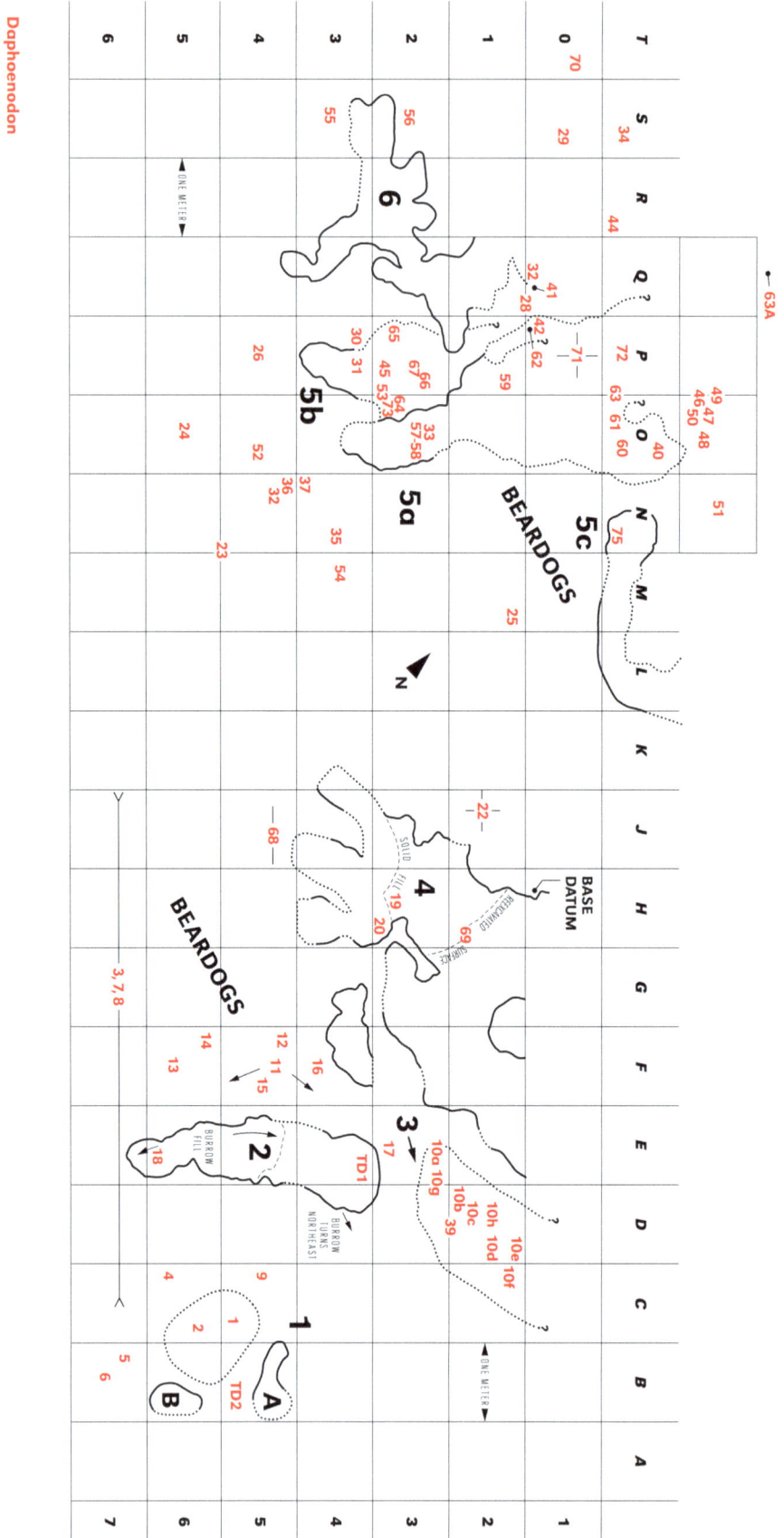

Map C. *Distribution of elements of Daphoenodon superbus found in Quarry 3.*

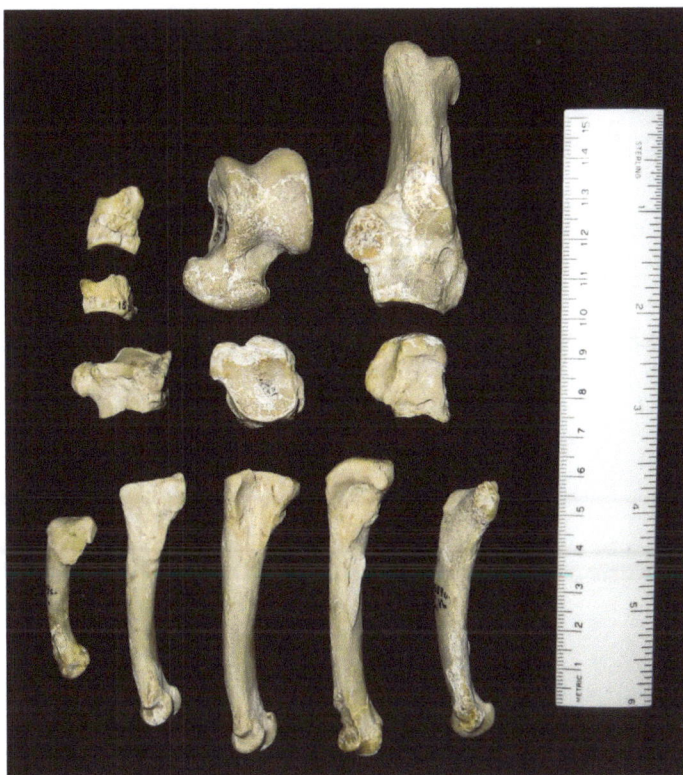

Hind foot of an adult Daphoenodon (CM1589C) found near Den 1—the bones are undamaged, preserved as if they had just come from a living carnivore.

Delotrochanter oryktes

Discovery

The temnocyonine beardog *Delotrochanter oryktes* was unexpected at Quarry 3. Temnocyonines are a subfamily of beardogs in which several species evolved unique cheek teeth adapted for processing hard food items—their large crushing molars are entirely different from those of *Daphoenodon*, whose molars and carnassial teeth are most like those of living wolves, best for cutting meat. *Delotrochanter* was first identified by a diagnostic molar fragment found in slightly consolidated sand at the future site of Den 2. Christened the "discovery molar" and found on September 14, 1981, it told excavators that a species of carnivore unknown to Peterson and his men might be present in the quarry.

With cleaning of the area, the margins of Den 2 began to appear. The runway of the den enclosed by white consolidated mudstone was packed with a few centimeters of gray sand that near its terminus contained only an astragalus and metatarsal of *Daphoenodon superbus*. However as the runway was traced upslope to the east, excavation of meter E4 revealed a 30-cm-thick burrow fill that with careful brushwork exposed the boundaries of a den and the maxillary toothrow and skull of the beardog. The skull (plotted on **Map C** as TD1) was found in the upper part of Den 2 and had been buried after sand had already begun to fill the den. The portion of the den with the skull in meter E4 was transported to the laboratory at the university. Here Rob Skolnick prepared the block, recovering not only the skull but also articulated bones of the fore and hind feet that showed the species had specialized as a long-footed runner adapted to pursue its prey over open terrain.

Additional evidence

In 1984 on the first day of excavation at Quarry 3, another foot bone (calcaneum, UNSM 3-84, plotted on **Map C** as TD2) of *Delotrochanter* was found near Den 1 where it had been deposited by slope wash. From a left hind foot, it was identical to this same bone in the left hind foot found with the skull in Den 2, proving two individuals of *Delotrochanter oryktes* had been present at Quarry 3. Fortunately, during our review of other large carnivores previously found at the national monument, we came upon a nearly complete skeleton, skull, and jaws of *Delotrochanter oryktes* (ACM 4804) in the collections of Amherst College in Massachusetts. The Amherst skeleton had been collected in 1908 by F. B. Loomis at Stenomylus Quarry almost as an afterthought while excavating skeletons of the small gazelle-camel *Stenomylus*. Although identified initially by Loomis (1910) as *Daphoenodon*, its teeth matched those of our *Delotrochanter* skull in Den 2, showing that it represented a second adult of the same species. Because the Amherst skeleton was nearly complete, its lack of a baculum suggested it was probably a female. With the adult "female" (ACM 4804) at Amherst were found juvenile postcranial bones (ACM 4804A) mirroring those of the adult, hinting that the adult and juvenile beardog may have shared a burrow as mother and pup.

Several years after the discovery of *Delotrochanter* at Den 2, we visited Yale University's Peabody Museum (New Haven) to examine a section of the Agate waterhole bonebed (YPM-PU 12213) removed from Carnegie Hill by Princeton University in 1914. In mapping these bones, we recovered another temnocyonine calcaneum identical to the calcaneum from the hind foot of the Den 2 *Delotrochanter*—this beardog had not only been present in the dens but also at an earlier time at the waterhole.

The Amherst skeleton from Stenomylus Quarry, the Yale calcaneum from the bonebed on Carnegie Hill, and the two temnocyonines from Quarry 3 are the only known fossils of *Delotrochanter oryktes*, a hyena-like predator with teeth capable of crushing bone (Hunt, 2011). It lived at a time of beardog hegemony in midcontinent grassland plains of the North American early Miocene, together with the wolf-like *Daphoenodon superbus* and large lion-like amphicyonine beardog *Ysengrinia americana*. These three beardogs were the dominant large carnivores of their time.

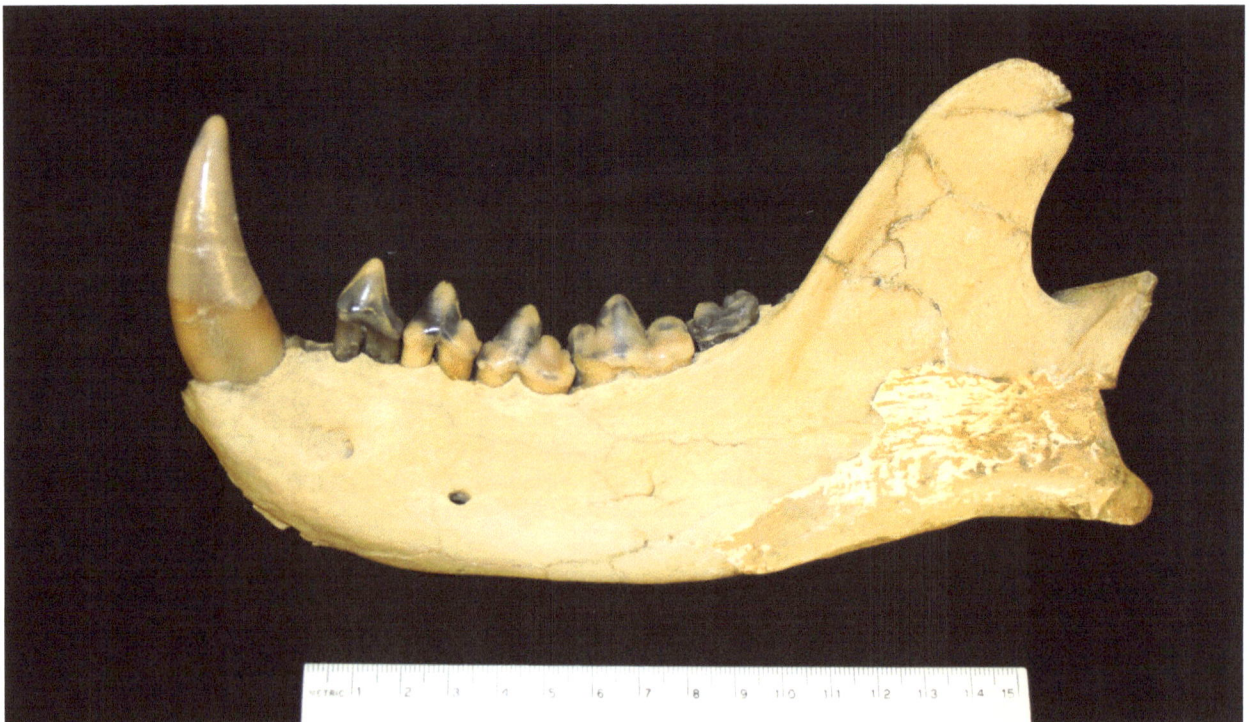

Jaw of Delotrochanter oryktes from Stenomylus Quarry, where this adult and its pup may have come from a den. The species was first recognized at Quarry 3, where the skull (UNSM 47800) and postcranials were recovered in Den 2 but without the lower jaw.

Mustelids (Family Mustelidae)

Megalictis simplicidens

Peterson (1910) found this large wolverine-like mustelid, *Megalictis simplicidens*, in Quarry 3 in 1905. He identified skull fragments, a lower jaw, femur, fibula, and a few fore and hind foot bones (CM2389) of a mature adult and named it *"Paroligobunis" simplicidens*. On a handwritten Carnegie Museum field label, Peterson established that *"Paroligobunis"* came from "talus below where type of *Amphicyon superbus* was found" and so would have come from the south half of the quarry near Den 1 or possibly from that den itself. Because we now know that Peterson's species

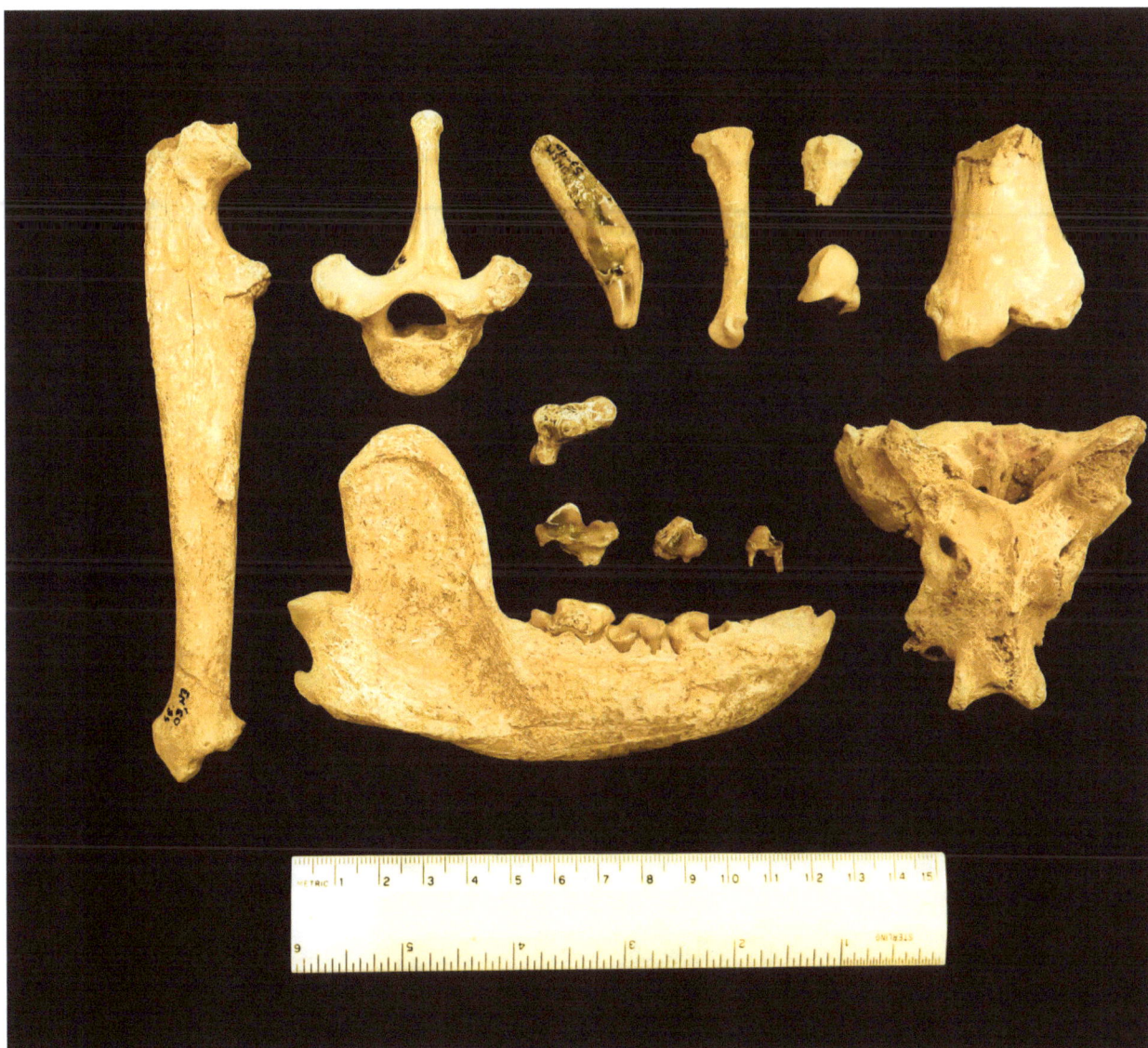

Jaw, teeth, and bones of Megalictis simplicidens* found during the UNSM excavations—most are from the north half of Quarry 3 and several probably represent the same adult individual.

* *The holotype of the species simplicidens is a lower jaw found by Harold Cook in 1905 at an unspecified locality "on the Agate Stock Farm." Cook had given the jaw to Peterson, but Peterson did not publish it until 1907, naming it "Brachypsalis" simplicidens. Curiously, in this publication Peterson never mentioned the jaw and partial skeleton (CM2389) of this mustelid that he had found in 1905 at Quarry 3 "in talus below where type of Amphicyon superbus was found" and that belonged to the same species as Cook's jaw. Peterson did not finally publish CM2389 (as "Paroligobunis" simplicidens) until five years after this large wolverine-like mustelid was collected at the quarry (Peterson, 1910).*

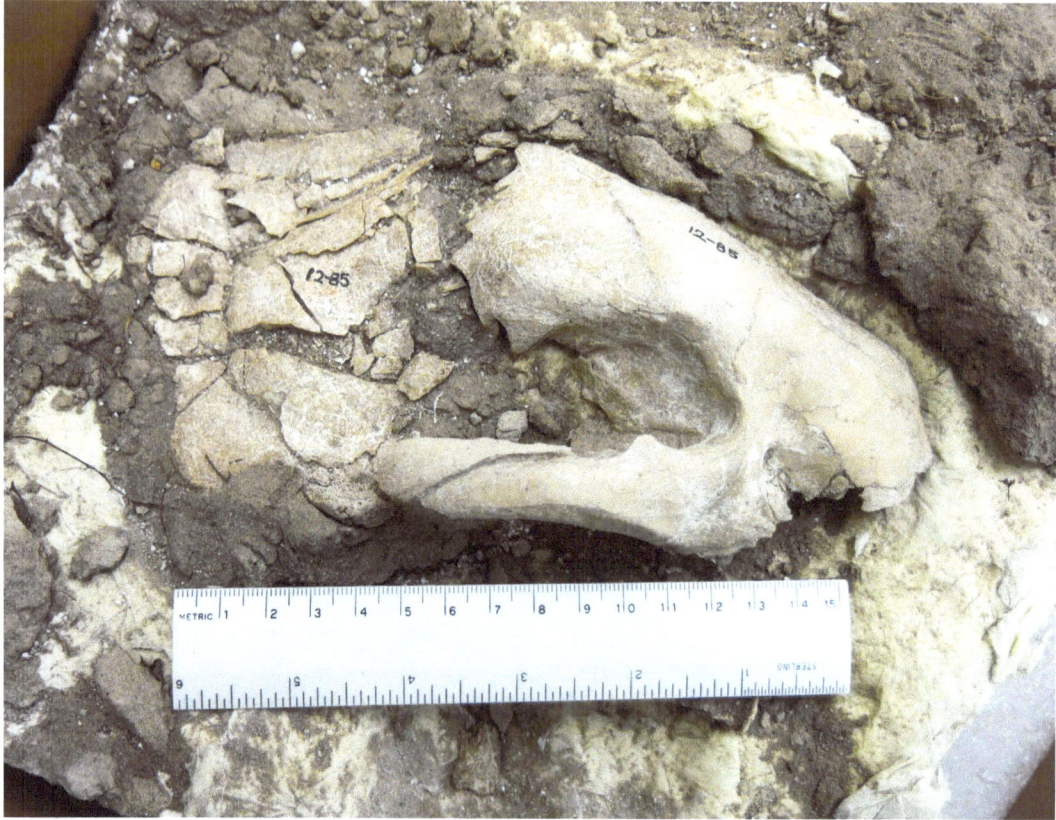

The skull of Megalictis (UNSM 12-85) during its removal from the north half of Quarry 3.

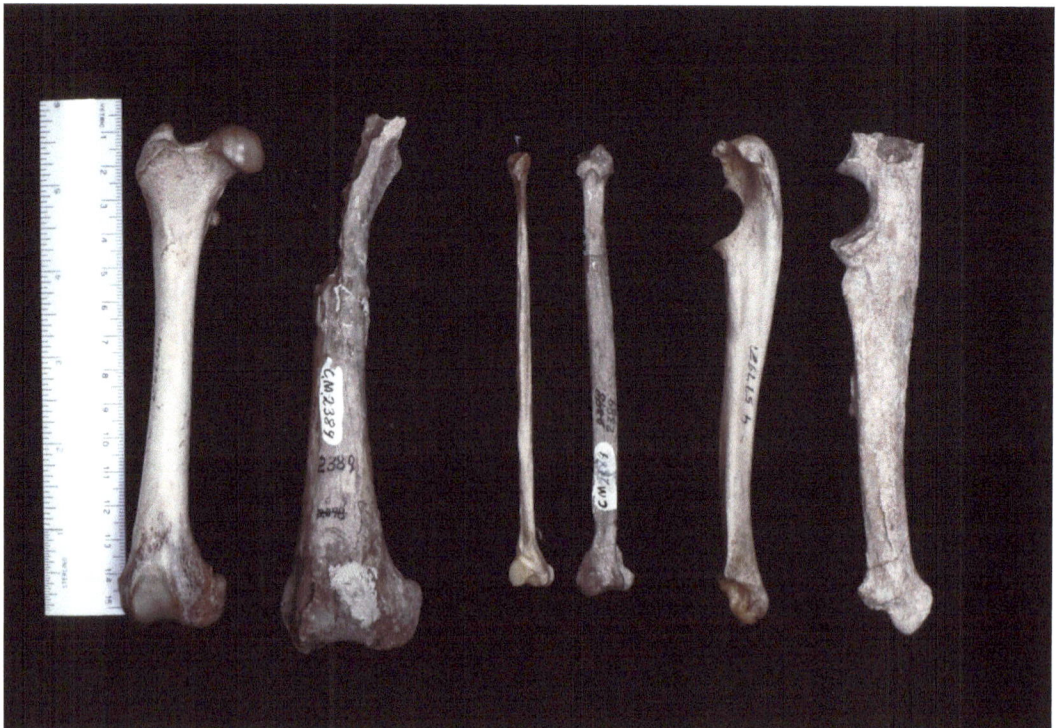

The femur, fibula, and ulna of the living wolverine Gulo gulo (left bone in each pair) compared with their more robust equivalents in Megalictis (CM2389) found at Quarry 3.

Grooves made by claws of a living badger in its den, like those discovered in Den 6.

was an early member of a group of large bone-crushing mustelid carnivores of the genus *Megalictis*, in which the lineage evolved to striking size, it has been placed in that genus: *Megalictis simplicidens* (Valenciano et al., 2016; Hunt and Skolnick, 1996).

We found bones of *Megalictis simplicidens* throughout the quarry. A partial skull of a young animal (UNSM 12-85) and a lower jaw of an old adult (UNSM 54-85), both from the Den 5A area, showed that at least two individuals were present in the north half of the quarry. Peterson's lower jaw and partial skeleton (CM2389) of his mature adult from the south quarry then established the presence of a third individual. From 4 to 6 m north of Den 1 also in the south half of the quarry we found a carnassial (P4), two metapodials, and a cervical vertebra.

The partial skull of *Megalictis* (UNSM 12-85) from within the Den 5A perimeter was the first known for this species. Unworn teeth found with the skull indicated a young adult. The lower jaw (UNSM 54-85) found ~2 m downslope from the skull belonged to a much older animal whose well-worn teeth showed it could process tough foods including bone. The re-

maining bones of *Megalictis* from the north quarry apparently migrated downslope from a breached den; included were an ulna, thoracic vertebrae, and canine in Den 5B and a complete sacrum in meter O4. These are elements missing from Peterson's partial skeleton (CM2389) but because they were found in the north quarry, they likely belong with the lower jaw of the old adult (UNSM 54-85).

Of particular interest was a large ungual phalanx 15 mm in length that would have been sheathed by a long keratin claw. It occurred ~3.5 m upslope from the terminal chamber of Den 6 (in meters Q3–Q4) whose walls display deep elongate furrow-like grooves similar to those made by the claws of living badgers when digging in earth. The forefeet and hind limb proportions of Peterson's *Megalictis* when combined with the massive sacrum, short robust ulna, distal tibia, and ungual claw from the north quarry let us reconstruct a strong fossorial mustelid capable of excavating an earthen burrow.

The **Map Key** lists the elements of *Megalictis simplicidens* found in Quarry 3, and their distribution is plotted on **Map D**.

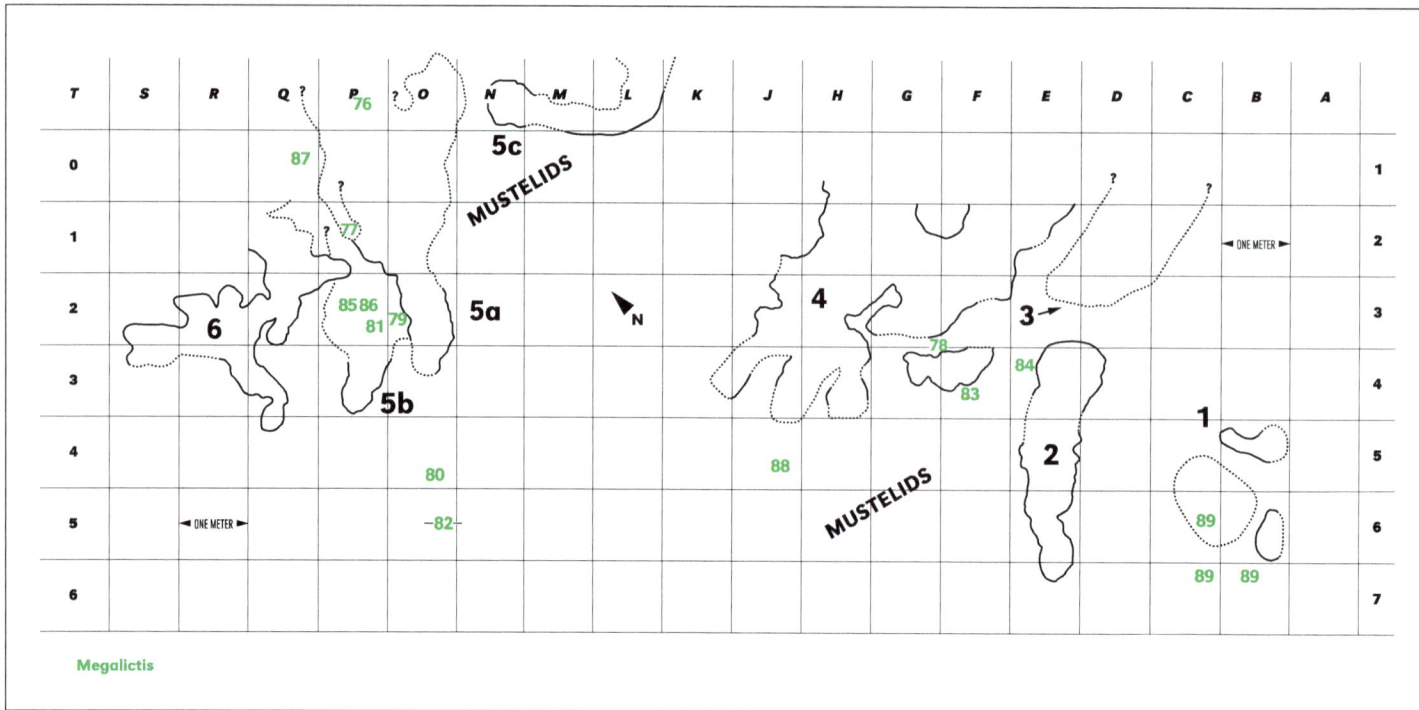

Map D. *Distribution of elements of Megalictis simplicidens found in Quarry 3.*

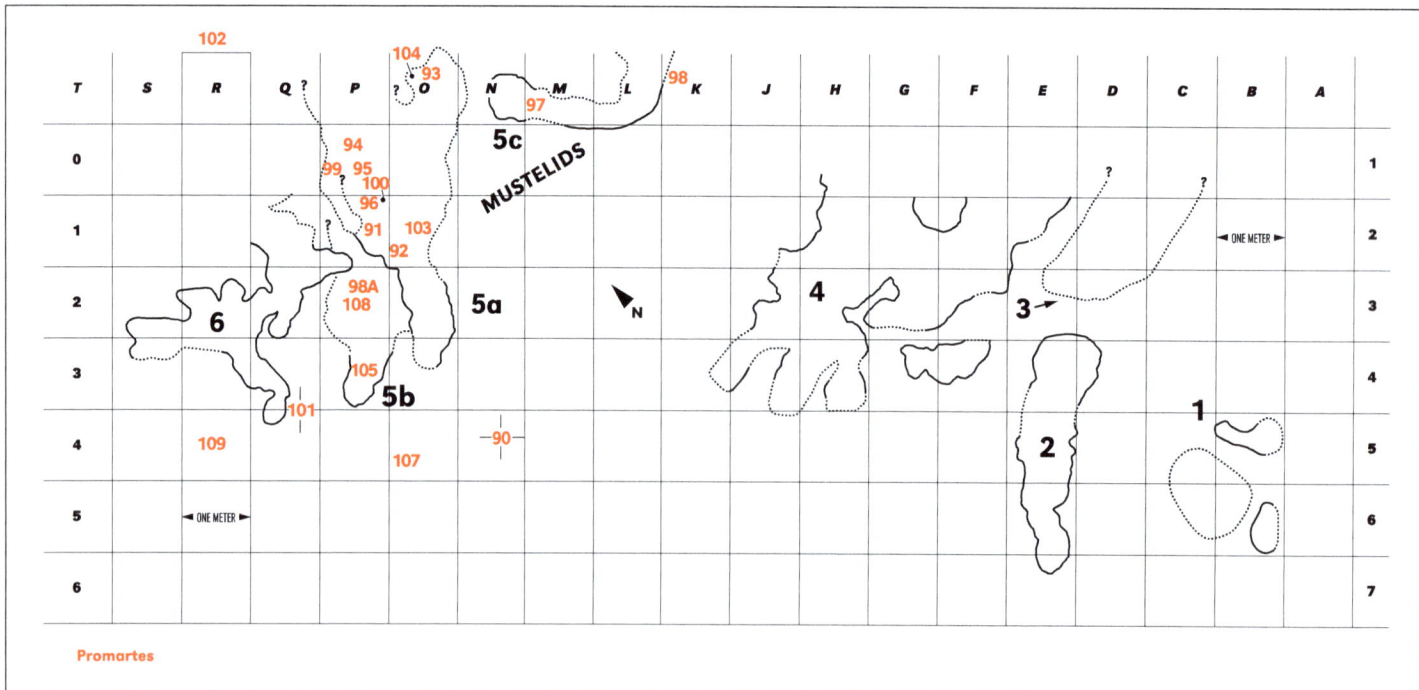

Map E. *Distribution of elements of Promartes olcotti found in Quarry 3.*

Promartes olcotti

The small mustelid *Promartes olcotti* was unexpected. Peterson had not found this species during his 1905 excavation. Entirely confined to the north half of the quarry, it was identified at first by a maxilla with defining P3-P4-M1, bones from the hind foot, and limb bone fragments. Although mostly confined to Dens 5A and 5B, other bones outside the burrows had been transported by slope wash.

Promartes olcotti is the size of a small male American pine marten, *Martes americana*. At Quarry 3, the teeth in the maxilla (UNSM 38-85) and an m1 (UNSM 58-85) told us an unrecognized mustelid carnivore had been present in the dens. Three adult individuals of *Promartes* are based on three distal right radii, and a fourth individual, a juvenile, was documented by a jaw fragment with milk tooth (dp4) in

Den 5B, a metacarpal in Den 5A, and a tibial epiphysis. Most limb bones were represented by broken articular ends. Postcranials included the radius, ulna, femur, and tibia, together with an astragalus, two calcanea, a 4th metatarsal, and lumbar and cervical vertebrae. The teeth in the maxilla closely match those in the holotype skull of *Promartes olcotti*, this species known to occupy a burrow. The use of burrows by small mustelids seems to have been commonplace: the *P. olcotti* holotype, a nearly complete skeleton, was found in the nesting chamber of the helical burrow of the beaver *Palaeocastor* (Riggs, 1945). Also found coiled in the upper portion of one of these burrows was a skeleton of the small mustelid *Zodiolestes* who had entered the burrow when it had already partly filled with sand (Riggs, 1942, 1945). Both of these little mustelids had been found

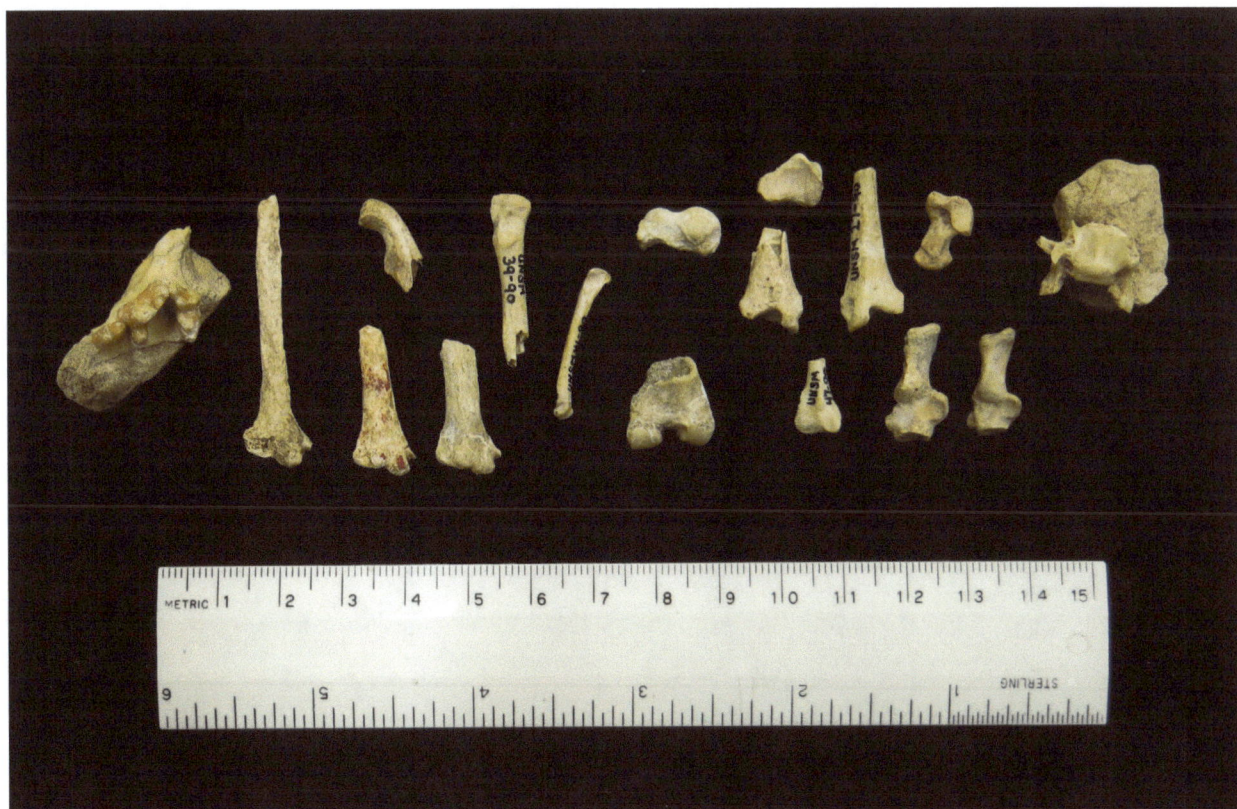

The maxilla with teeth, a cervical vertebra, and limb and foot bones of the small mustelid Promartes olcotti found in the north half of Quarry 3 by UNSM paleontologists. At least three adult individuals were present in the dens, demonstrated by the three lower limb bones (radius) to the right of the jaw with teeth. The Carnegie men did not encounter this small carnivore in their 1905 excavation.

in northwest Nebraska in exposures of the Harrison Formation, where prairie-dog–like colonies of these beaver burrows are common.

A quite small P4 of *Promartes* (UNSM 34-85) was found ~40 cm from the maxilla (UNSM 38-85) in Den 5A. This tooth corresponds in size to the holotype of *Promartes vantasselensis* (ACM 2099). Teeth of *P. vantasselensis* and *P. olcotti* differ only in size; their co-occurrence in Den 5A suggests that *P. olcotti* and *P. vantasselensis* may represent a single species, possibly male and female.

The **Map Key** lists the elements of *Promartes olcotti* found in Quarry 3, and their distribution is plotted on **Map E**.

Small Dogs (Family Canidae)

Cormocyon, Phlaocyon

The canids living when the dens were active were all small carnivores, almost none reaching the size of a coyote (*Canis latrans*). They are placed in the subfamilies Hesperocyoninae and Borophaginae (Wang, 1994; Wang et al., 1999). Two species of small borophagine canids were found in the dens: one approximately the size of the living swift fox (*Vulpes velox*, ~2.0–3.0 kg) of western North America and the other close in size to the fennec fox of Africa (*Fennecus zerda*, 1.0–1.5 kg), the smallest living canid.

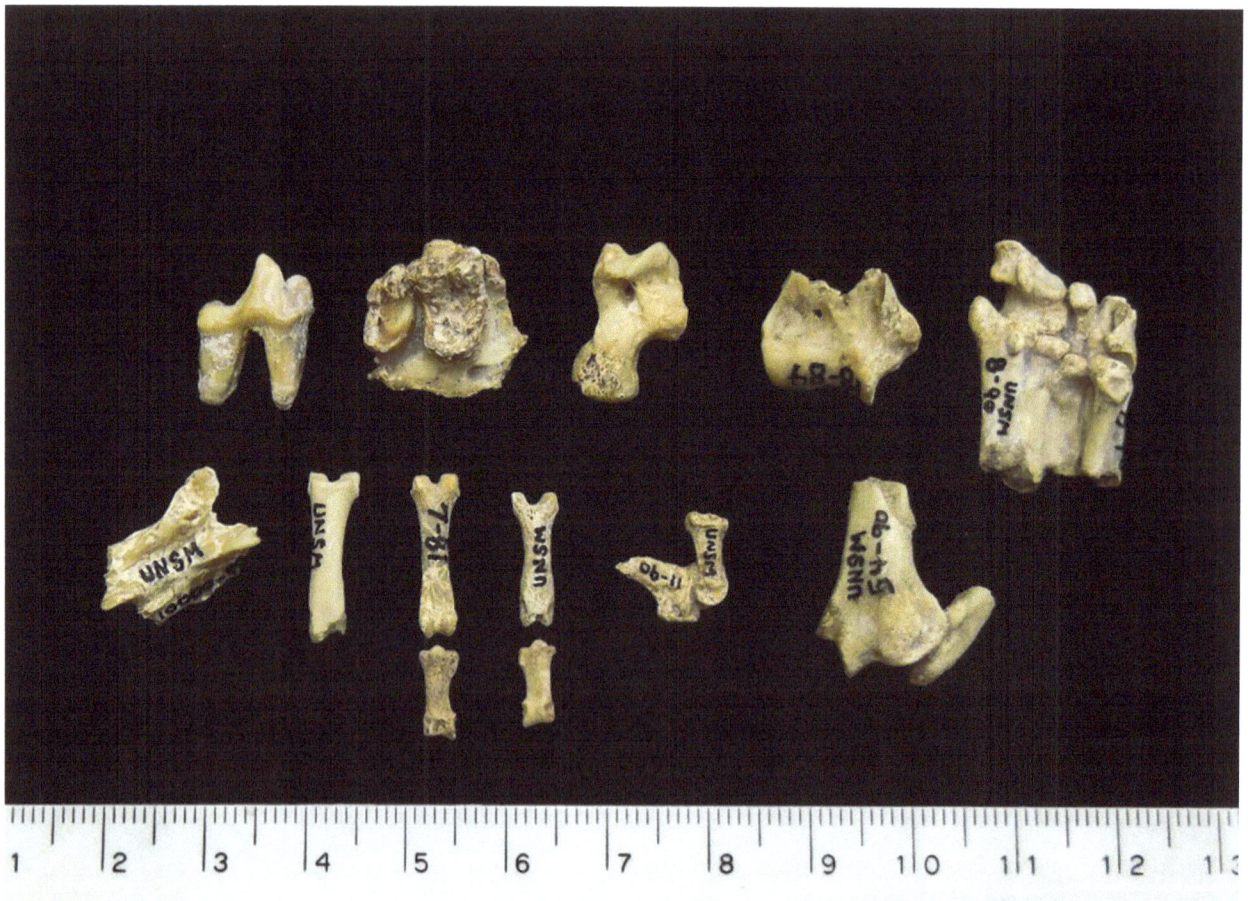

Remains of the foxlike canid *Cormocyon* discovered in the north half of the quarry. The maxilla with teeth, scavenged fore and hind feet, and pieces of limbs from Den 5B apparently belonged to a single individual. No bones of this canid were found by Peterson during his excavation of Quarry 3.

Borophagines are most easily identified by their teeth. The larger of the two species from the dens is most similar in its dentition to the borophagine species *Cormocyon haydeni-C. copei* (Wang et al, 1999). An adult individual is represented by a maxilla with M1-M2, a molar (m1), a scapula, distal humerus, a lumbar vertebra, an astragalus, and phalanges, and also from articulated bones in Den 5B—a radius and ulna, a median phalanx with its ungual, and nearly complete fore and hind feet. The conjoined bones of carpus and tarsus with their proximal metapodials had been held together by ligament and connective tissue at the time of burial in the den. The forefoot was discovered in a mass of comminuted small angular bone fragments (informally a "bone hash"), apparently the remains of a scavenged carcass or perhaps a regurgitated meal. An erupting milk molar (dp4, UNSM 64-85) and calcaneum (UNSM 75-85) found in Den 5B with the scavenged postcranials and a second tiny milk molar (DP4) from the "bone hash" show that a juvenile of the small canid, possibly a *Cormocyon* pup, occurred near the adult. Nearby in this same area were gnawed bones of *Merychyus* (2 distal humeri, phalanges, and a partial radius). A molar (m1, UNSM 46-90) found in Den 5C probably represents a second adult individual of *Cormocyon*.

Cormocyon was restricted to the northern half of Quarry 3, where it was not noticed until the 1990 UNSM excavation. Only a single phalanx occurred outside this area near the skull of *Delotrochanter oryktes* (Den 2). No fossils of *Cormocyon* were found by Peterson and his men, who probably did not screen sediment for the smaller mammals in the southern half of Quarry 3 in 1905.

Much scarcer is the even smaller borophagine *Phlaocyon annectens*. The holotype upper and lower jaws of this species (CM1602) with well-preserved teeth were found by Peterson (1907) "associated with the type of *Amphicyon superbus*" and initially described by him as *"Nothocyon" annectens*. When Peterson excavated the large block of sediment containing the *D. superbus* female and juvenile male at the south end of the quarry that we place in Den 1,

the block either included the jaws of *Phlaocyon annectens* or they were nearby. Unrecognized by Peterson, a second adult of this species was identified by a partial molar (m1) found by the Carnegie men at the south end of the quarry that had been included in a box of fragments under CM1589B.

The swift fox (*Vulpes velox*), which is similar in size to the species *Cormocyon haydeni* (Wang et al., 1999), depends on burrows for shelter and lives on small mammals, birds, lizards, and insects. Its burrow can extend to 3.5 m in length descending ~1.5 m to a den chamber (Nowak, 1991). The tiny African fennec fox (*Fennecus zerda*), the size of *Phlaocyon annectens*, also occupies burrows several meters in length; feeds on small rodents, birds, insects, and plants; and can live without water for long periods. Perhaps the borophagines paralleled these living small arid-land canids in their use of burrows and diet in a similarly dry climate.

The **Map Key** lists the elements of *Cormocyon* and *Phlaocyon* found in Quarry 3, and their distribution is plotted on **Map F**.

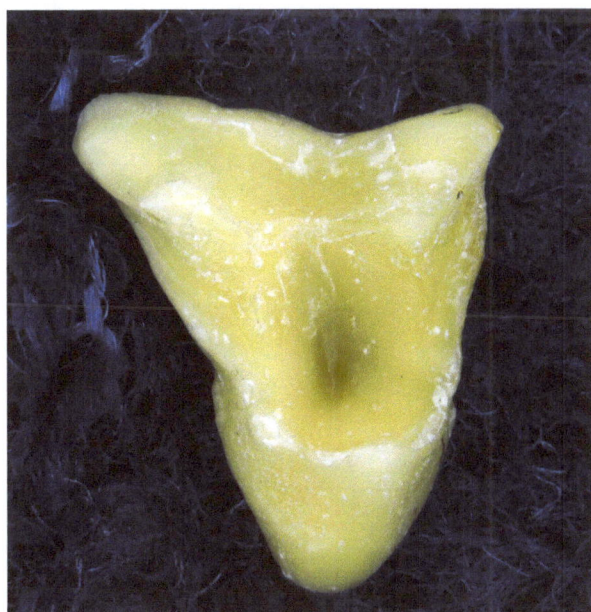

Milk molar (DP4) of Cormocyon pup found in the "bone hash" in Den 5B.

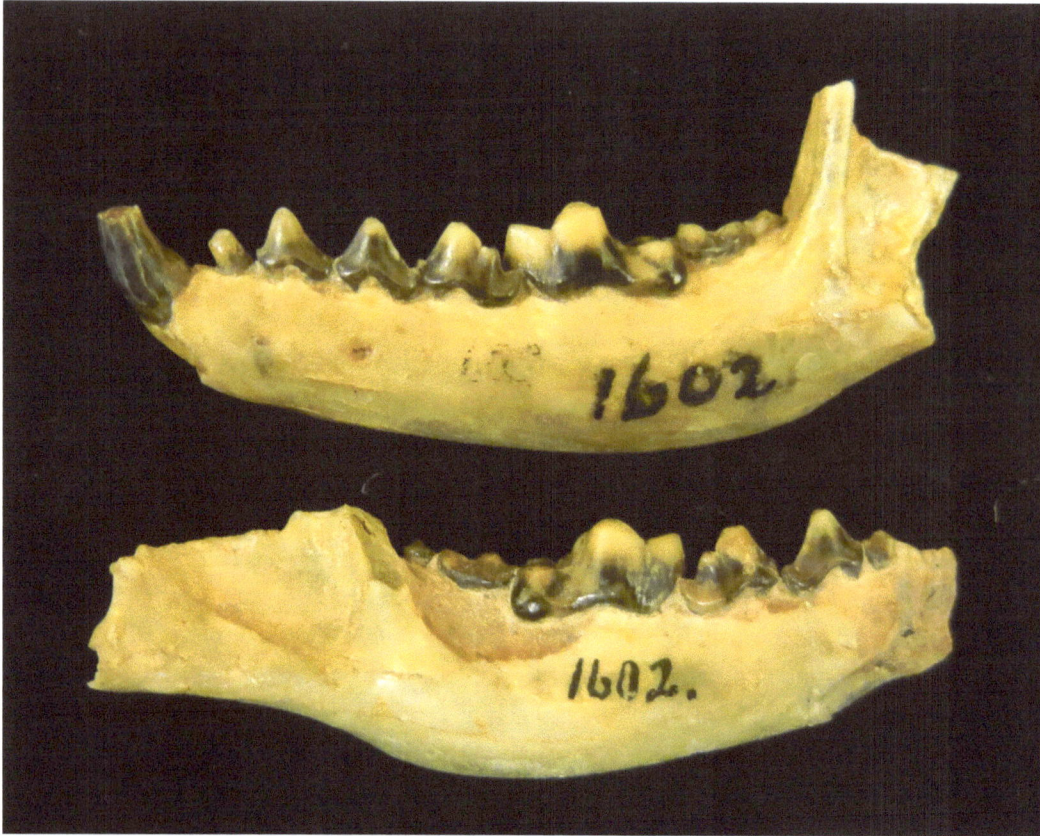

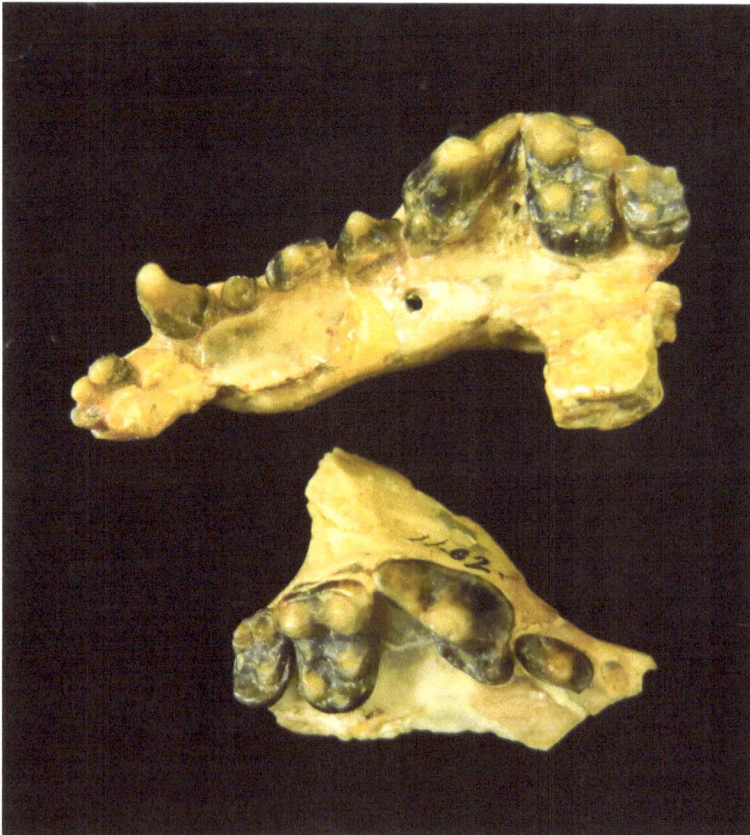

Holotype lower jaws (above) and upper jaws (below) of the Quarry 3 Phlaocyon annectens. Peterson (1907) wrote that on August 19, 1905, he "found associated with the type of Amphicyon superbus [Daphoenodon superbus]" the jaws of the little canid Phlaocyon, a carnivore the size of the smallest living canid, the tiny fennec fox of the African Sahara.

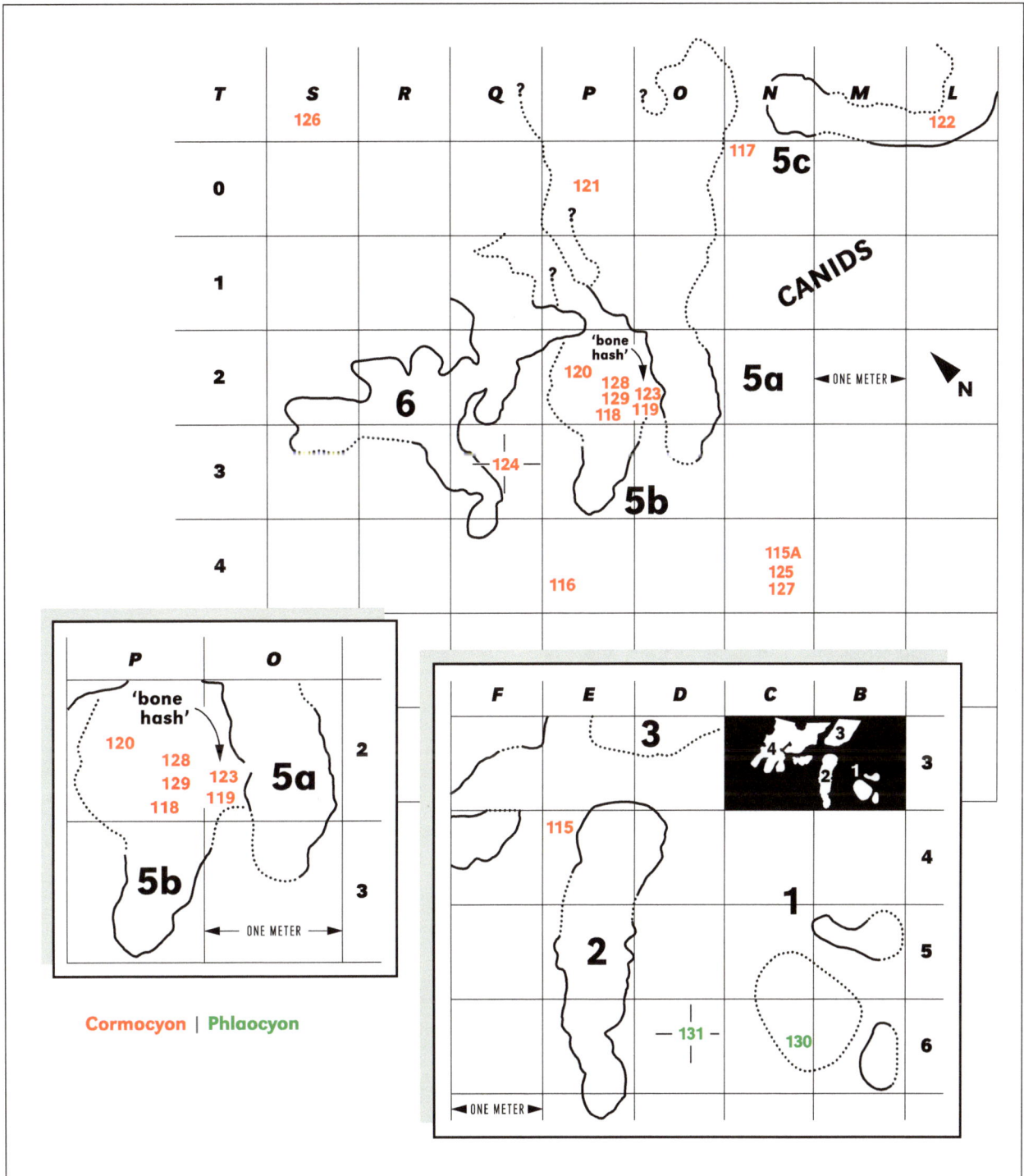

Map F. *Distribution of elements of Cormocyon and Phlaocyon found in Quarry 3.*

The Prey and Other Species

Approximately 30% of the fossils found in the quarry during the UNSM excavation were not carnivores (125 of ~415 specimen lots). The mammals other than carnivores found in Quarry 3 included small and vulnerable ungulates that soon emerged as probable prey of the den occupants: the oreodont *Merychyus*, the small gazelle-camel *Stenomylus*, a larger camel *Oxydactylus*, and two tiny deer-like cervoids. The most surprising was evidence of a neonatal calf of the rhinoceros *Menoceras*.

Other than the ungulates, the noncarnivoran bones in Quarry 3 came from a few very small unidentified mammals as well as from rare lizards, a snake, and birds, and also frogs, turtles, and a fish.

Fossils of *Merychyus* from Quarry 3

Bones of the small oreodont *Merychyus* were concentrated in the northern portion of Quarry 3 during our excavation. Most fossils were found in or near Dens 5A, 5B, and 6. We found only two foot bones of *Merychyus* in the south half of the quarry. However, *Merychyus* did exist in Peterson's Quarry 3 collection under his numbers CM1589A, CM1589D, and CM2774: two distal humeri, two astragali, two proximal phalanges, a median phalanx, and glenoid of a scapula. *Merychyus* then had probably been present in the southern dens, its bones not as common in Peterson's collection, perhaps because sediment was not

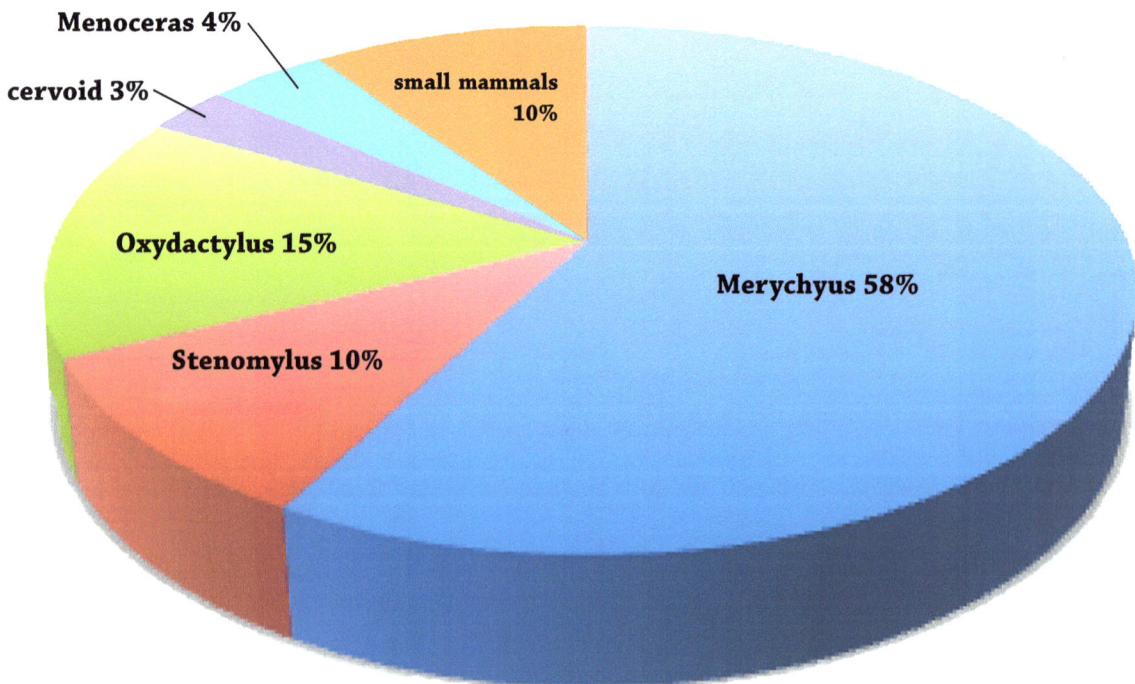

screened for the smaller bones. The *Merychyus* fossils found by Peterson proved to be the very same skeletal elements discovered by us in the northern area, these particular bones considered the most likely to survive from carcasses scavenged in the dens.

Merychyus was represented in Quarry 3 by 69 postcranial bones and 3 teeth and dental fragments—83% of the postcranials were bones of the feet. It was not unusual to find the astragalus (often gnawed), other durable podials, phalanges, fragments of metapodials, and parts of a scavenged forelimb (distal humerus, proximal radius). The pooled postcranials from the UNSM and Carnegie excavations gave these percentages: partial limb bones (14.5%), podials-metapodials of the fore and hind foot (43.5%), phalanges (39%), and vertebrae (3%). Of these bones, 65% were those of adults and 35% of juveniles, and the few teeth are deciduous (dp3-dp4, DP4). *Merychyus* is the most common ungulate at Quarry 3 making up ~58% of the noncarnivoran mammal bone sample. Many bones of *Merychyus* were found in Den 5B near the scavenged remains of the canid *Cormocyon*.

The **Map Key** lists the elements of *Merychyus* found in Quarry 3, and their distribution is plotted on **Map G**.

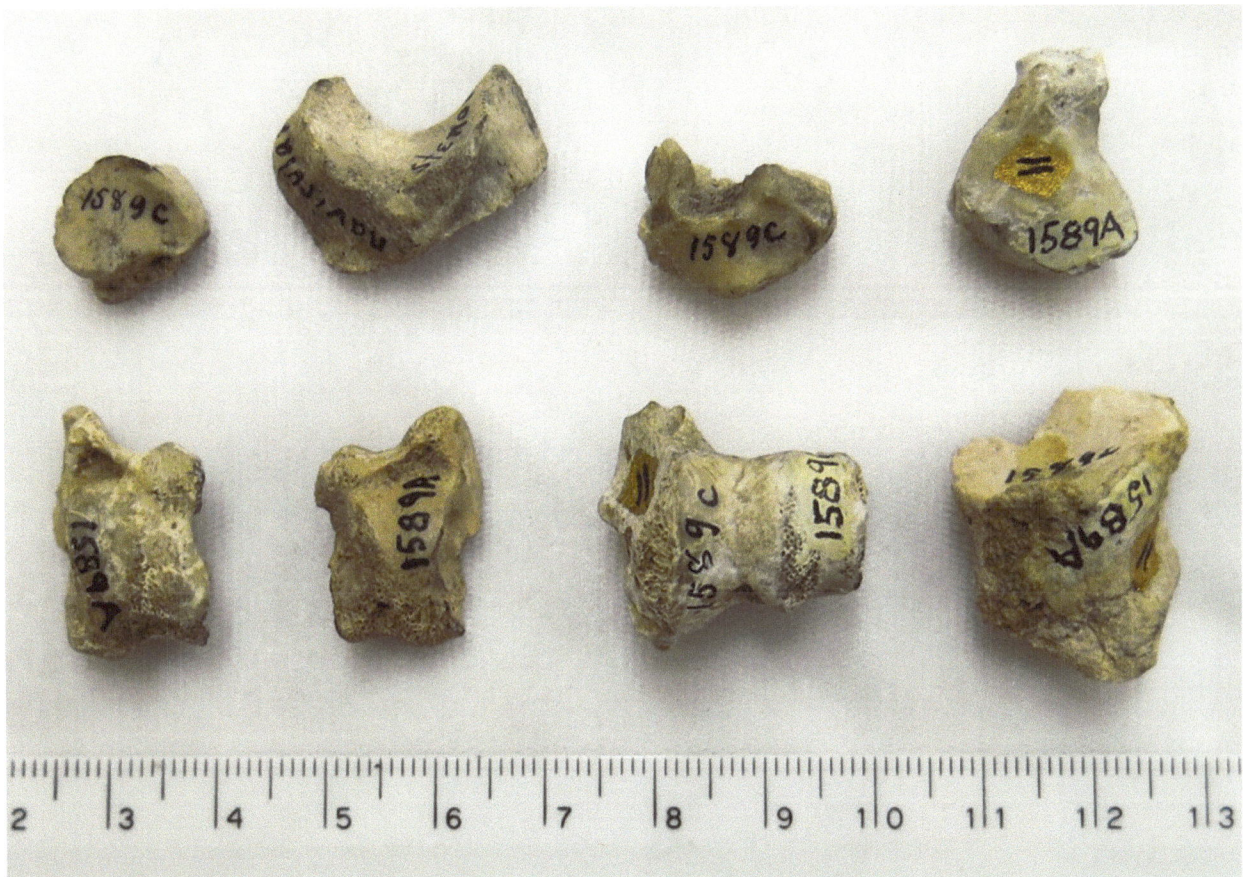

Bones of ungulate prey found with Daphoenodon in or near Den 1. Upper row, left to right: camel Oxydactylus (left ectocuneiform, left navicular, right unciform, and left magnum). Lower row, left to right: oreodont Merychyus (gnawed left and right astragalus and distal humerus), and rhinoceros Menoceras (proximal phalanx from side toe). These bones were collected by Peterson in 1905 and numbered as either CM1589A or 1589C; they were apparently recognized by him as ungulate bone but not identified.

Merychus

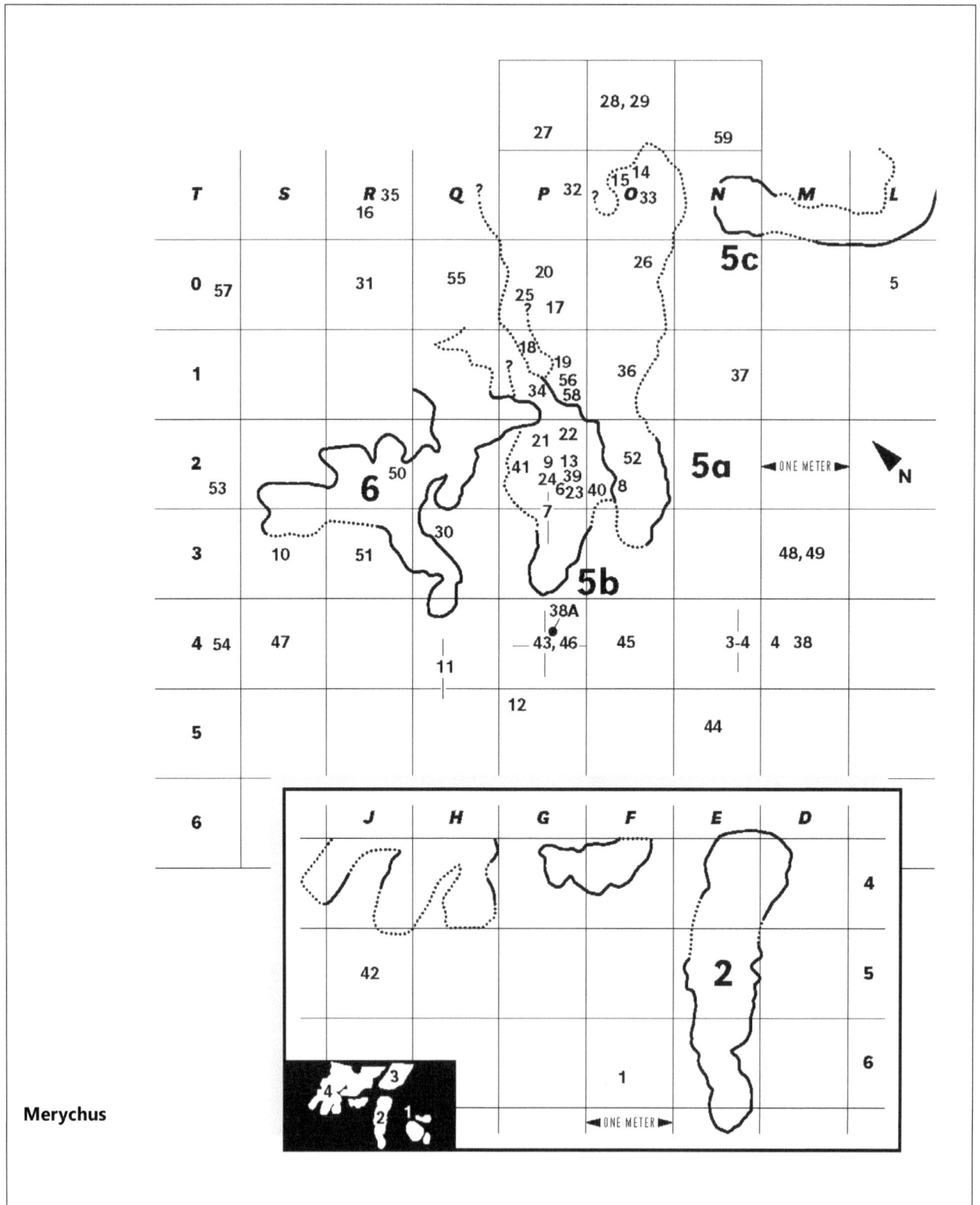

Map G. Distribution of elements of Merychyus found in Quarry 3.

Fossils of Small Camelids and Cervoids from Quarry 3

Camels were not common at Quarry 3, yet the 29 bones and tooth fragments of the two species of small camels found in the quarry, together with the 69 bones of the little oreodont *Merychyus*, had obviously been bitten and gnawed, these bones revealing that the less nutritious parts of a carcass, particularly feet, had been left as residue in the dens. Camel and oreodont made up nearly all (> 80%) ungulate bone from the den complex, and so provided "hard" evidence of the unmistakable fate of these small ungulates as preferred prey of the carnivores, most likely the beardogs.

The little gazelle-camel *Stenomylus* and the slightly larger species (*Oxydactylus* cf. *O. campestris*) each supplied about half of the camel bones from our excavations: a distal humerus, femur, podials, metapodials, phalanges, and a few vertebrae. About one-third of the camel bones found at Quarry 3 belonged to juveniles and two-thirds to adults.

In the north quarry, bones of *Stenomylus* with those of *Merychyus* and the scavenged canid *Cormocyon* occurred together in Den 5B.

From the south quarry, Peterson collected seven foot bones and a scavenged humerus of *Oxydactylus*, numbered either CM1589A, B, C, or CM1589D, but he did not identify them, several apparently coming from in or near Den 1. *Stenomylus* was scarce in the south half of the quarry; we found only four bones and Peterson only a single lumbar vertebra (CM2774). A podial of *Stenomylus* was the only ungulate bone found in Den 4 (with a calcaneum, lumbar vertebra, and juvenile metapodial of *Daphoenodon*), and a cuboid lay just outside the terminus of Den 2. The only ungulate bone from Den 3 was a gnawed astragalus of *Oxydactylus* found with the aged *Daphoenodon*; an unciform of this camel occurred near Den 1.

The presence of cervoids is even more infrequent, with only three bones discovered by us in the north half of the quarry. A small moschid "deer" is evidenced by a gnawed astragalus at Den 5A and a phalanx near the terminus of Den 5B; a large metapodial epiphysis (UNSM 37-84) from Den 6 comes from a juvenile dromomerycine cervoid comparable to *Barbouromeryx*. Likewise, a fragment of a tiny cervoid phalanx (CM1589B) was found in a tray of bone fragments of *Daphoenodon* collected by Peterson at Quarry 3 in 1905.

The **Map Key** lists the elements of camels and cervoids found in Quarry 3, and their distribution is plotted on **Map H**.

Fossils of *Menoceras* from Quarry 3

Although this small rhinoceros is represented by only three bones (and an edentulous section of lower jaw and tooth fragment), the presence of a young neonatal calf was evidenced by two proximal phalanges (from lateral toes) and a calcaneum lacking its epiphysis. The calcaneum was discovered in the south half of the quarry eroding from talus; the only other bone of *Menoceras* from the south quarry was a gnawed juvenile proximal phalanx collected by Peterson in 1905. This phalanx came from the large block shipped by Peterson to the Carnegie Museum in Box 17 and had been numbered CM1589A, the same number given to bones of the juvenile male *Daphoenodon* from Den 1. The second juvenile proximal phalanx (UNSM 7-90) was found by us ~10 to 15 cm from the scavenged bones of the canid *Cormocyon* in Den 5B, and the jaw fragment just beyond the terminus of that den. These few bones suggested that the young of this small cursorial rhinoceros sometimes fell victim to beardogs.

The bones of *Menoceras* are listed in the **Map Key** and plotted on **Map H**.

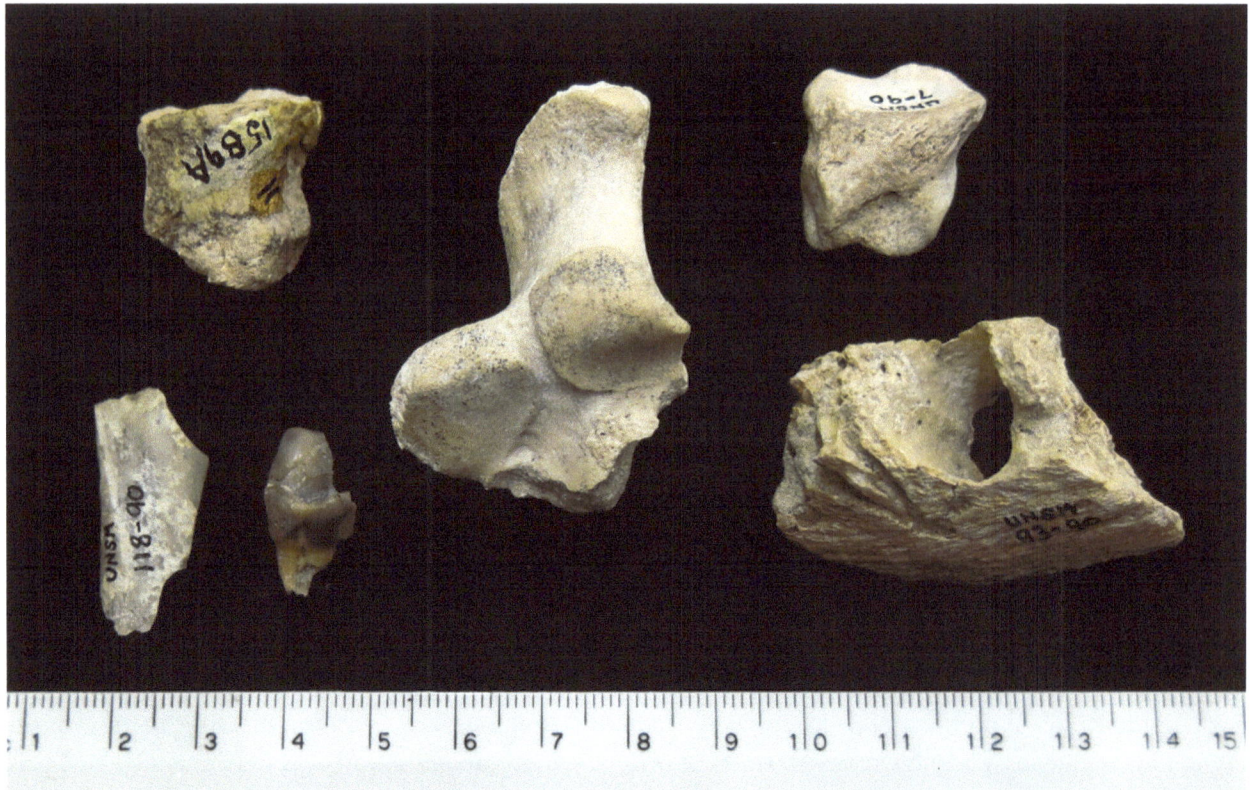

Bones and tooth fragment of the rhinoceros Menoceras arikarense from Quarry 3.

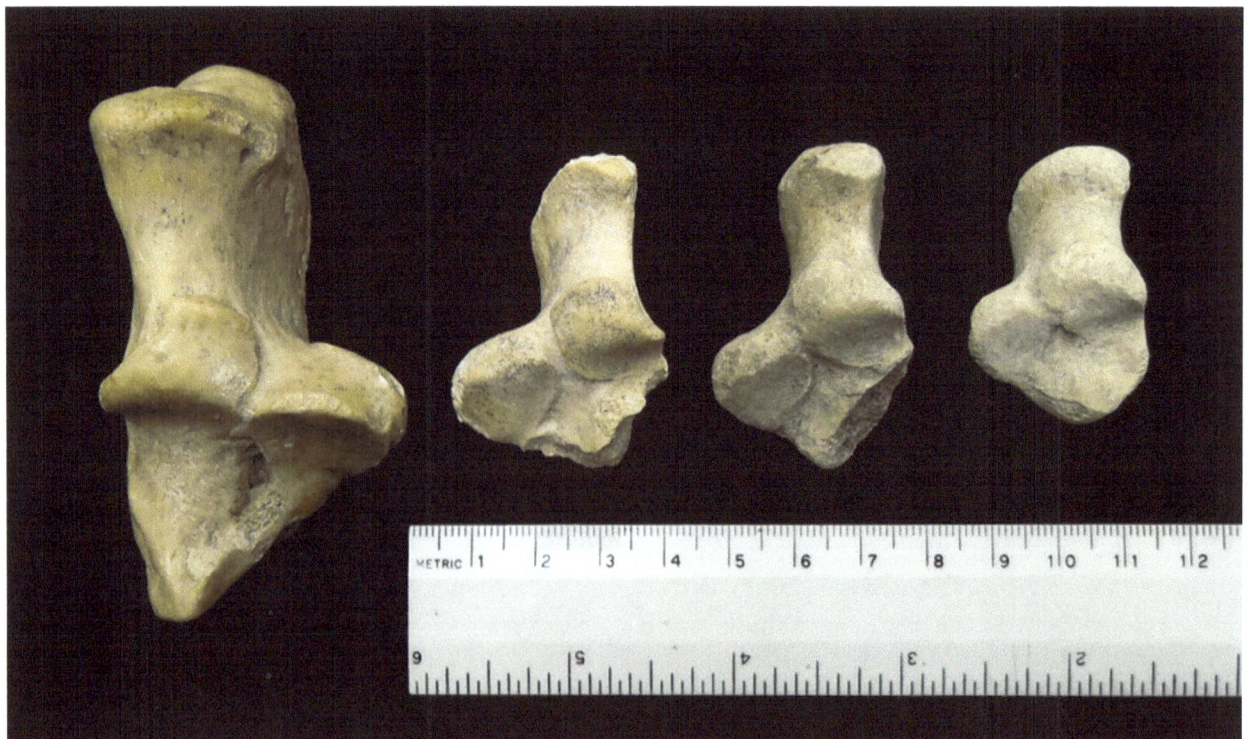

Calcanea of Menoceras. Left to right: An adult bone from the waterhole bonebed, the neonatal bone from the Quarry 3 dens, and a neonatal and a probable fetal bone both from University Quarry where remains of at least six calves were found in the bonebed.

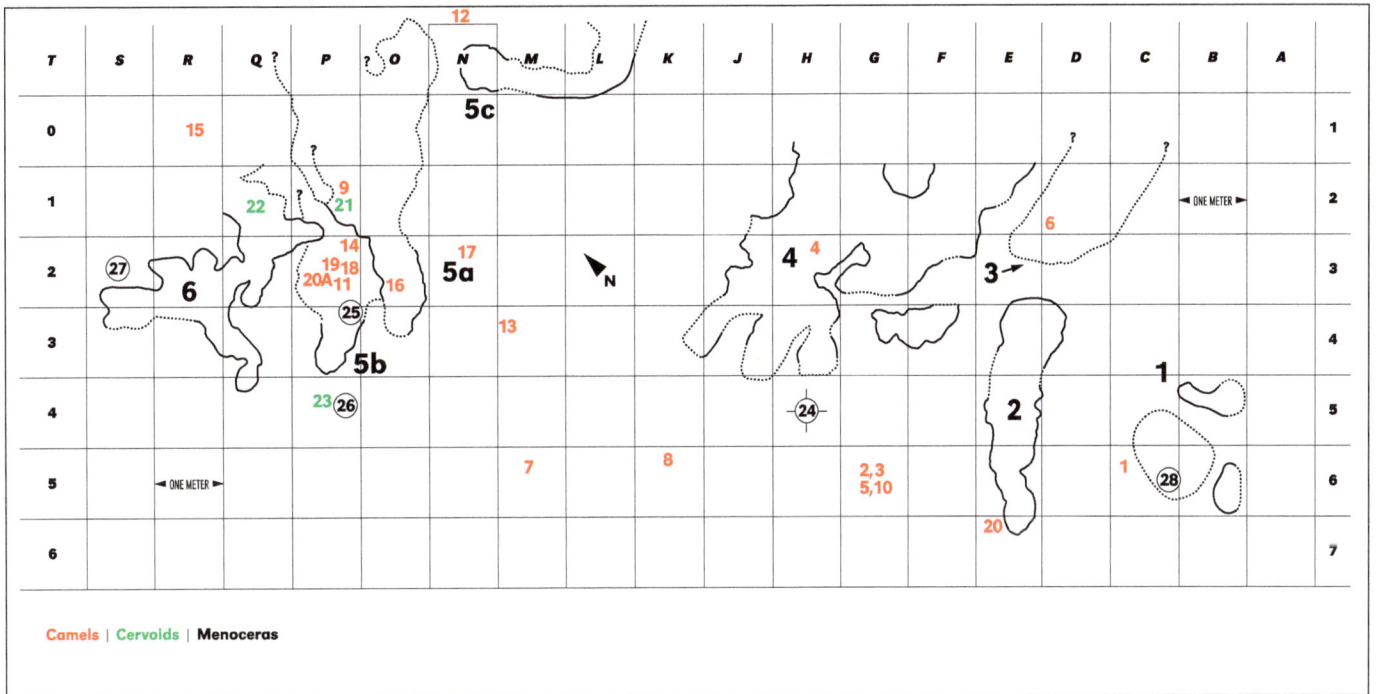

Map H. *Distribution of bones of camels, cervoids, and Menoceras.*

Fossils of Small Mammals from Quarry 3

Remains of unidentifiable small mammals amounted to a dozen bones of which one-third were from juveniles. The only tooth, a molar, belonged to a lagomorph. Because all are either damaged vertebrae or fragments of limb bones, none articulated or even complete, they too may have been scavenged bone within the dens. Whether these mammals on occasion occupied dens or were themselves prey is unknown. These fossils are not plotted on the den maps.

Fossils of Lower Vertebrates from Quarry 3

Remains of lizard, snake, and bird, and also of frog, turtle, and a fish were meager and inadequate for detailed identification, yet even this limited diversity in a small area such as Quarry 3 was unusual. Although a few birds have been found in other quarries within the national monument, lizard and snake are unreported and are unknown at the waterhole. However, these groups are known to occur in burrows of living carnivores in semiarid grassland and savanna; for example, near Arad, Israel, a bone accumulation in a striped hyena den (*Hyaena hyaena*) included remains of a few small mammals, lizard, snake, and birds (Kerbis-Peterhans and Horwitz, 1992). These were single bones thought to have come from decomposed hyena faeces. Brown hyena (*Hyaena brunnea*) faeces from the Kalahari also included remains of small mammals, diverse birds, and infrequent lizard and snake (Owens and Owens, 1978), and rare bird, tortoise, and catfish were found in spotted hyena dens in Kenya (Lansing et al., 2009). But the bones of frog, pond turtle, and a fish at Quarry 3 more probably came from ponded sediment seen in the north quarry where thin tabular lenses of a white silty calcareous mud are interbedded with gray stream-deposited fine sand. These aquatic vertebrates when living probably did not normally enter a burrow, yet their bones apparently became incorporated in burrow fill as the carnivores excavated their dens by digging through the pond sediment.

Lizard

Surprising and unexpected was a vertebra, limb bone, and multiple osteoderms of an anguid lizard sieved from sediment overlying Den 1. The clast of cemented gray sand enclosing this lizard appeared to have been reworked from a nearby burrow. A second anguid vertebra was found at the northeastern limit of our quarry excavation, and an identical vertebra came from Den 5A. In Den 5B, the skull bone of a small lizard (UNSM 8A-90) had been buried resting against the scavenged hind foot of the canid *Cormocyon* (UNSM 8-90).

Bird

Among fragments collected by Peterson at Quarry 3 was an unreported bird coracoid (CM1589F). A second coracoid was discovered in meter F4 north of the temnocyonine beardog near but not in a bur-

row. From the laminated sand yielding the lower jaw of *Megalictis* (UNSM 54-85) came a diaphysis of a bird's tibio-tarsus similar in size to that of a red-tailed hawk (*Buteo jamaicensis*), and on arriving at Quarry 3 in 1984 a bird talon from an owl or small raptor was found in surface talus.

Frog

Frogs were represented in the south quarry by a distal humerus sieved from sediment just outside of Den 2 not far from the skull of *Delotrochanter*. From the north quarry, a sacral vertebra was found below the terminus of Den 5B in meter P5, and a sacral vertebra with urostyle was sieved in meter R4 near Den 6. A skull bone (pterygoid) of a frog and other small bones were discovered with an ostracod in a block of white calcareous mudstone, once a pond mud, confirming the presence of frogs in pond sediment in the north quarry. The frog pterygoid compares in size and form with this element in an individual of *Incillius valliceps* (length, 8 cm), the living Gulf Coast toad. Some frogs construct burrows: fossorial members of the hylid genus *Pseudacris* burrow using their forelimbs (Brown and Brown, 2014).

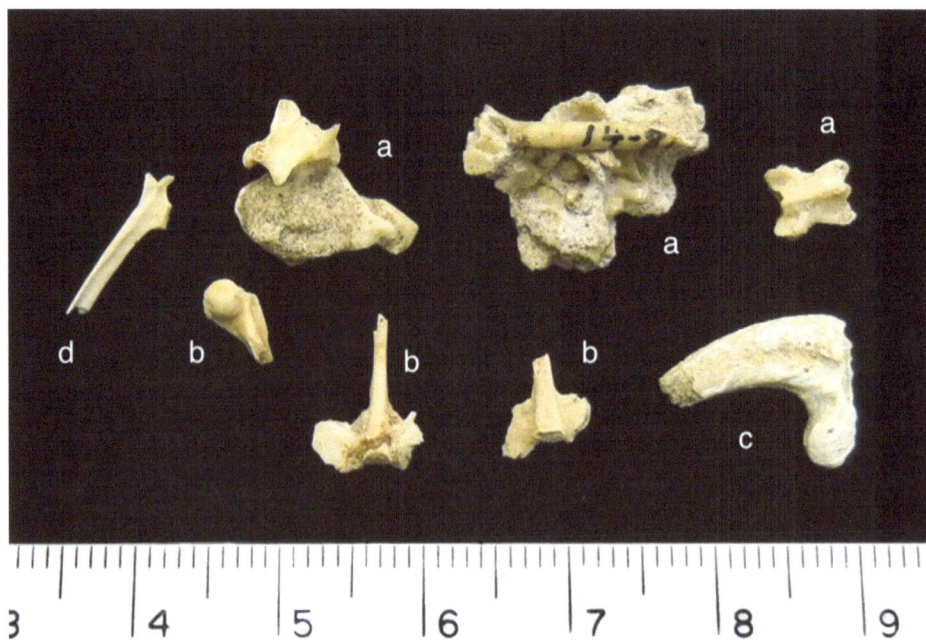

*Bones of (**a**) lizard, (**b**) frog, (**c**) bird, and (**d**) fish from the UNSM excavation of Quarry 3.*

Turtle

Carapace fragments from a small pond turtle were scattered through the north half of the quarry. These appear to be broken pieces of pleural or peripheral bones.

Fish

At the northern limit of the quarry a pectoral spine of a small fish was recognized among bones sieved from the area of interbedded pond and stream sediments—fish on occasion may have survived at the larger long-lived waterholes.

The **Map Key** lists the lower vertebrates found in Quarry 3, and their distribution is plotted on **Map I**.

A frog skull bone (pterygoid) found with fresh-water ostracods in white ponded sediment in Quarry 3.

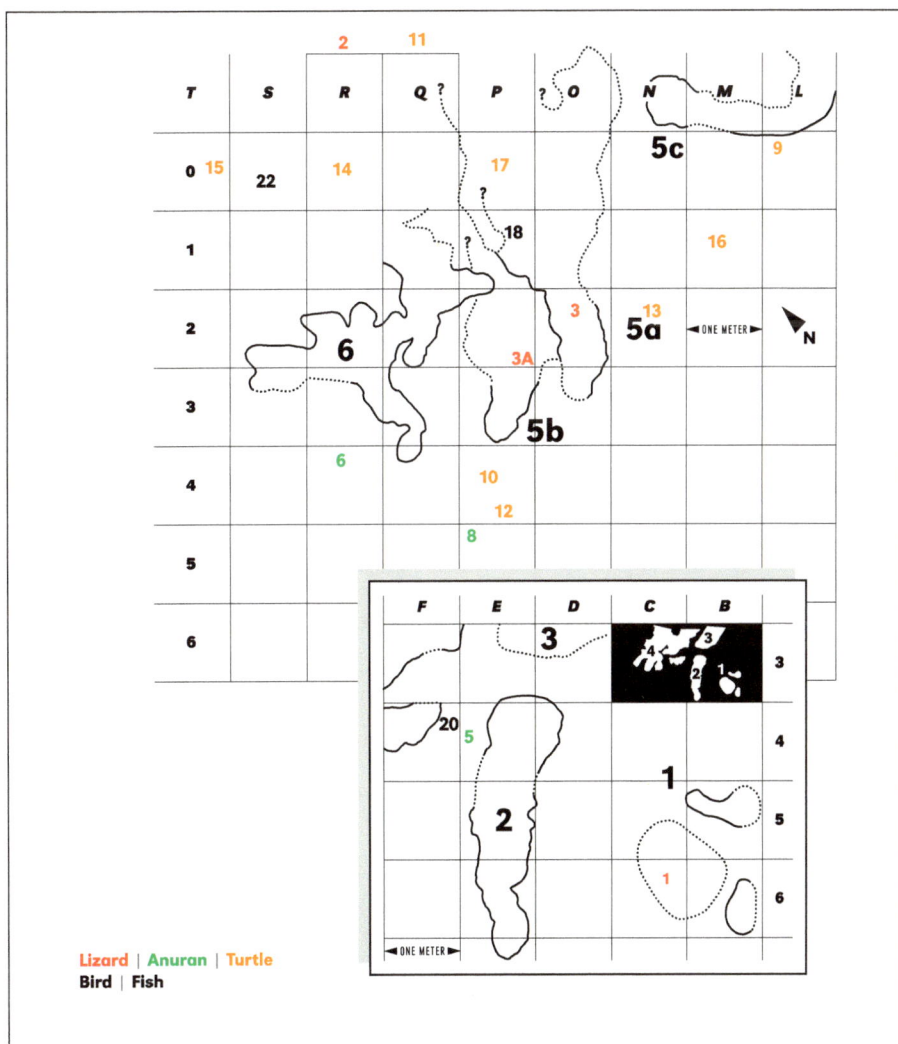

Map I. *Distribution of elements of lower vertebrates found in Quarry 3.*

Epilogue

Quarry 3 of the Carnegie Museum opened by Olaf Peterson in 1904–5 and extended by the University of Nebraska from 1981 through 1990 now covers ~160 m² on the west slope of Beardog Hill. Here on the hill the fossils and burrow perimeters discovered during our survey of the quarry were plotted on a metric grid to which were added the probable locations of Peterson's specimens, determined from his publications, field notes, and specimen labels conserved in the Division of Vertebrate Paleontology of the Carnegie Museum.

The dens on Beardog Hill had been excavated by the carnivores along the margin of the Agate waterhole where interbedded stream and pond sediments defined its southern perimeter. Peterson's Quarry 3 was discovered here at the edge of the waterhole from the precise fit of bone fragments collected by the Carnegie paleontologist in 1905 with several bones discovered by us in 1981. The importance of the site was recognized when excavation unexpectedly uncovered an unmistakable profile of a den with its entrance burrow. The den chamber (designated Den 1), beautifully outlined on the face of a low cliff, continued upward to an ancient land surface, a Miocene grassland, identified by a prominent fossil soil (paleosol). Identification of additional large burrows nearby soon explained why Peterson had found almost nothing but remains of carnivores at Quarry 3.

Mapping of the quarry showed that fossils were concentrated in two areas: (a) in or near burrows that we have considered as Dens 1, 2, 3, and 4 on the south and (b) in or near those designated Dens 5A, 5B, 5C, and 6 on the north. The absence of fossils in the intervening area and their proximity to only either the north or south dens told us by this distribution that even the fossils found outside a den had not strayed far from their host burrows. In the north half of the quarry, fossils came from both identified as well as unrecognized breached burrows. Peterson's records and papers made it possible to locate the majority of his fossils within the south quarry.

Based on the partial skeletons and scattered bones identified at Quarry 3, the dens held evidence of at least 22 carnivores representing six species (two beardogs, two mustelids, two small canids), remarkable considering the general absence of skeletal remains found within the dens of comparable living large canids and hyaenids. The isolated bones of at least 14 individual ungulates occurred with the carnivores: a minimum of six oreodonts, four small camels, two cervoids, and two neonatal rhinos. Much of this bone was scavenged, and juveniles were common. This disproportionate representation of carnivores relative to ungulates is not seen in the dens of the living canids and hyaenids. This and the atypical number of carnivores that were identified from bones and teeth found in the burrows we think suggests an unusual and likely catastrophic end to the community as opposed to a "normal" den complex in savanna grassland today.

Although Peterson found very few bones of ungulates at Quarry 3 in 1905, his unidentified fossils belonged to the same species discovered by us throughout the quarry—all were small ungulates (oreodont, camel, cervoid) belonging to the Miocene herbivore community of that time. The absence of these ungulates in the bonebed on Carnegie Hill and their relative ubiquity at Quarry 3 argued their presence was directly related to the abundant carnivores. That the ungulates were prey is shown by the scavenged remains left in the dens where only durable bones and those of least food value survived.

From Peterson's excavation of 1905, the quarry was extended to the limits of recognizable burrows on the hill. Beyond that area, we found no evidence of burrows to the north in the direction of Carnegie Hill or to the south of Beardog Hill. Excavation into Beardog Hill to the east was halted by increasing overburden—there undiscovered dens could continue into the hill. To the west of the quarry, erosion by the present Niobrara River dissected and long ago removed the waterhole sediments and whatever burrows might have been present.

Key to Mapped Distribution of Taxa

The paleontologist William Matthew had an almost religious veneration for every specimen,
no matter how small or unimportant in appearance . . . because he was constantly seeing
the value and meaning even of small fragments which had been carefully recorded
as to precise geologic level and locality.

—William King Gregory

Maps

The specimens numbered in these lists represent the species excavated and identified at Quarry 3 by the University of Nebraska from 1981 to 1990. The distribution of each species or group is plotted using these numbers on maps C, D, E, F, G, H, and I. Fossils collected by O. A. Peterson for the Carnegie Museum in 1904–5 in some cases could also be sited in the quarry. Fossils with an unspecified location are not plotted on the distribution maps.

Abbreviations
r, right; l, left; juv, juvenile

Map C

Remains of *Daphoenodon superbus* were present throughout Quarry 3 and were the most common mammal found.

Peterson's Collection from Quarry 3

1. Holotype skeleton of female *Daphoenodon superbus* (CM1589)
2. Partial skeleton of juvenile male *Daphoenodon superbus* (CM1589A)
3. A large male and small female *Daphoenodon* represented by multiple partial elements and fragments (CM1589B)[1]
4. Intact articulated left hind foot of *Daphoenodon superbus* (CM1589C)
5. Jaw fragment, limb, and foot bones of *Daphoenodon* (CM1589D)

6. "Ungulates" (CM1589E) reported by Peterson from talus near *Daphoenodon superbus* holotype skeleton
7. Microfauna (small carnivore, snake, owl, ?rodent) found by Peterson from Quarry 3 in summer 1905 probably from south area of quarry (CM1589F)[1]
8. Skull, jaw, and most of right forelimb of *Daphoenodon superbus* (CM2774)[1]

UNSM Fossils of *Daphoenodon superbus* from Quarry 3

	UNSM No.	Elements
9.	10 to 12-81[2]	Proximal tibia (juv); ulna and ischial fragments
10.	700-82[3]	Lower jaws (r, l), large aged male, and partial skeleton
11.	701-82	Proximal phalanx; distal tibia (r); distal fibula (l); rib; canine root; 2 limb diaphysis fragments
12.	702-82	27 fragments including 4 rib sections
13.	703-82	M1 (r)
14.	705, 707-82	Proximal phalanx, hind foot, digit I (r); glenoid of squamosal (r)
15.	713, 715-82	Lumbar vertebra, scavenged; rib
16.	719-82	Proximal phalanx
17.	723 to725-82	m2 (l) in jaw fragment; lingual M1 (r); p3 (l)
18.	730-82[4]	Astragalus (l); MT4 (l)
19.	733-82	MT2 (l, juv)

20.	734-82	Lumbar vertebra
21.	10-84	Lumbar vertebral fragment
22.	16-84	Distal humerus (l); astragalus (l)
23.	17-84	Proximal radius (l); proximal phalanx; caudal vertebra; caudal vertebral fragment; vertebral neural arch; 5 bone fragments
24.	24-84	Caudal vertebra
25.	26-84	Proximal MC1 (r)
26.	28-84	Entocuneiform (r)
27.	30-84	Incisor (I1 or I2)
28.	33-84	2 proximal phalanges
29.	43-84	Median phalanx, forefoot
30.	44-84	Cuboid (l), 5 bone fragments
31.	47-84	Astragalus (r)
32.	48-84	Innominate (r)
33.	50-84	Navicular (l, juv)
34.	51-84	Proximal phalanx
35.	83-84	Proximal phalanx
36.	84-84, 91-84	Distal radius and diaphysis
37.	92-84	Lower jaw (l) with m1
	113-84	canine and 13 bone fragments
38.	15-85	Patella
39.	18-85	Magnum (r)
40.	24-85	Unciform (l, juv)
41.	32-85	5th caudal vertebra
42.	41-85	MT4 (l)
44.	67-85	Mesocuneiform (l); caudal vertebral chevron
45.	70-85	Innominate (r)
46.	6715-89[5]	Zygoma (r); alisphenoid (r)
47.	6716-89	P4 (l)
48.	6717-89	Petrosal (l)
49.	6718-89	Maxilla fragment with P3 (r)
	6713-89	Patella
	6705-89	Vertebral epiphysis
50.	6719-89	I3 (l)
51.	6725-89	p1 (r)
52.	4-90	Radius (l), diaphysis
53.	6-90	Rib
54.	17-90	Entocuneiform (l)
55.	19-90	Proximal phalanx, forefoot, digit I (r)
56.	20-90	Proximal phalanx, forefoot, digit I (l)
57.	23-90	Baculum (p, juv)
58.	24-90	Mesocuneiform

59.	26-90	Proximal phalanx
60.	34-90	Cuboid (r)
61.	35-90	Median phalanx
62.	37-90	Terminal caudal vertebra
63.	40-90	i3 (r)
63A.	51-90	Median phalanx
64.	55-90	Rib, distal, with cartilage termination
65.	64-90	Complete rib (~11th)
66.	65-90	Distal tip of rib
67.	66-90	Scapholunar (l)
68.	70-90	Proximal MT4 (r)
69.	72-90	Calcaneum (l)
70.	152-90	Median phalanx, 4 bone fragments
71.	200-90	Caudal vertebra (p)
72.	201-90	Chevron bone
73.	10-90	Femur (l, juv), distal epiphysis
74.	55-85	Proximal phalanx
75.	35-85	Ungual phalanx

Notes

1. Peterson established that Nos. 3 and 7 were from Quarry 3; they were collected in the summer of 1905 when Peterson's excavation was likely restricted to the south half of the quarry. No. 8, a fine skull, jaw, and forelimb (CM2774), also probably came from there given that the intact better-preserved fossils were found in the southern dens. Nos. 21, 27, and 38 lacked a specified location and were not plotted.

2. This proximal tibia (UNSM 10-81) was found among bones on the surface of the west slope of Beardog Hill in September 1981—it perfectly fit a bone fragment collected by Peterson in 1905 that we discovered among fragments he had numbered as CM1589B. The two pieces were collected 76 years apart and demonstrated that the dens discovered by UNSM in 1981 were in fact where Peterson had initially collected his carnivore material at Quarry 3.

3. No. 10, a large aged male (UNSM 700-82) was distributed over a linear distance of 1.7 m in grid meters E3, D2, and C2. Elements of this skeleton were numbered: 10a, lower jaws; b, lumbar vertebrae and rib; c, humerus; d, associated radius-ulna, forepaw, and second ulna; e, radius with exostosis; f, metapodials; g, innominate; h, scapula.

4. The astragalus and MT4 of *Daphoenodon superbus* were found in place in the terminus of Den 2. The upper part of this den also contained the skull and postcranials of *Delotrochanter oryktes* (UNSM 47800). The two bones of *D. superbus* and articulated foot bones of *Delotrochanter* looked as if they had just come from a living animal.

5. Nos. 46, 47, 48, 49, and 50 are considered to belong to one individual.

Map D

Other than the *Megalictis* material described by Peterson (1910), these 13 specimens found during the UNSM excavation compose the *M. simplicidens* sample from Quarry 3. This large mustelid is scattered through the quarry. At least three individuals are represented.

UNSM Fossils of *Megalictis simplicidens* from Quarry 3

	UNSM No.	Elements
76.	12-85	partial skull, distal tibia, proximal femur
77.	54-85	lower jaw, p3-m1 (r)
78.	732-82	P4 (l)
79.	22-84	ulna (r)
80.	3-90	sacrum
81.	53-90	upper canine (l)
82.	211-90	unciform (l)
83.	9-84	proximal metacarpal 4 (r)
84.	7-81	metatarsal 2 (l)
85–86.	60, 61-90	two thoracic vertebrae
87.	25-90	ungual phalanx
88.	47801	cervical vertebra

	CM No.	Elements
89.	2389	lower jaw (l) and postcranials

Map E

No fossils of *Promartes* were reported by Peterson from Quarry 3. The specimens of *Promartes* found during the UNSM excavation represent at least four individuals, including a juvenile. Most of the sample comes from the area of dens 5A and 5B. Because of uncertain location, numbers 106 and 110 are not plotted.

UNSM Fossils of *Promartes olcotti* from Quarry 3

	UNSM No.	Elements
90.	18A-84	cervical vertebra
91.	49-84	calcaneum (r), incisor
92.	58-84	MC3 (r, juv)
93.	25-85	distal radius (r)
94.	26-85	calcaneum (r), astragalus (r)
95.	34-85	P4 (l)
96.	38-85	maxilla with P3-M1 (l)
97.	47-85	MC4 (l)
98.	58-85	m1 (l)
98A.	12-90	dp4 in jaw fragment (l)
99.	78-85	distal tibial epiphysis (l, juv), proximal ulna (l)
100.	27-90	distal tibia (l)
101.	30-90	distal radius (r)
102.	39-90	proximal radius (l)
103.	41-90	MT4 (l), podial
104.	43-90	distal tibia (r)
105.	47-90	distal fibula (l)
106.	74-90	MT3 (r)
107.	99-90	distal radius (r)
108.	112-90	2 lumbar vertebrae
109.	113-90	femoral head (l)
110.	207-90	vertebra
CM	1589	distal femur (r)

Map F

No fossils of *Cormocyon* were found by Peterson at Quarry 3. UNSM *Cormocyon* material was concentrated in the north half of the quarry. The articulated specimens (118, 119, 123) found in close proximity are probably the remains of a single individual. Distribution of fossils in the quarry and teeth indicate at least three individuals of *Cormocyon*, including a juvenile. Despite the scarcity of *Phlaocyon annectens*, the holotype and a partial m1 show that at least two adults were present in the quarry.

UNSM Fossils of *Cormocyon* and *Phlaocyon annectens* from Quarry 3

Cormocyon sp.

	UNSM No.	Elements
115.	7-81A	proximal phalanx
115A.	18-84	proximal phalanx, distal humerus (r)
116.	55-84	median phalanx
117.	21-85	median phalanx
118.	8-90	tarsus and proximal metatarsals, articulated (l)
119.	11-90	median and ungual phalanges, articulated
120.	16-90	maxilla with M1-2 (r)
121.	28-90	distal humerus (l)
122.	46-90	m1 (r)
123.	54-90, 59-90	distal radioulna (l), articulated carpus-metacarpus (l), "bone hash"
124.	126-90	proximal phalanx and limb bone fragments
125.	209-90	astragalus (r)
126.	156-90	proximal phalanx
127.	210-90	vertebra (1st lumbar, p, juv)
128.	75-85	calcaneum (r, juv)
129.	64-85	dp4 (deciduous carnassial, l)

Phlaocyon annectens

	CM No.	Elements
130.	CM1602	lower jaw (l) with canine, p1-4, m1-3, maxilla (l) with I1-3, C, P1-4, M1-2
131.	CM1589B	m1 (l)

Map G

Peterson did not mention fossils of *Merychyus* at Quarry 3, although a few bones (astragali, phalanges, distal humeri) of this animal were present in the Carnegie Museum collection from the quarry. The astragalus provides an estimate of the number of individuals (MNI, 6) in the north half of Quarry 3. Bones of *Merychyus* represent the residue from scavenged carcasses.

UNSM Fossils of *Merychyus* from Quarry 3

	UNSM No.	Elements
1.	704-82	astragalus (r)
2.	11-84	tooth fragment
3.	19-84	dp3-4 (r, juv)
4.	20-84	epiphysis, humerus (juv)
5.	25-84	astragalus (l)
6.	31-84	distal humerus (l)
7.	32-84A	proximal metapodial, distal epiphysis (juv)
8.	38-84	proximal phalanx
9.	41-84	proximal radius (–)
10.	42-84	distal humerus (r)
11.	53-84	lunate (r)
12.	57-84	proximal phalanx
13.	60-84	distal humerus (l)
14.	24-85	proximal phalanx
15.	25-85	proximal phalanx
16.	29-85	proximal phalanx
17.	39-85	proximal phalanx
18.	45-85	patella
19.	46-85	carpal cuneiform (–)
20.	50-85	ecto-mesocuneiform (l)
21.	56-85	tibial epiphysis (juv)
22.	68-85	patella
23.	71-85	proximal phalanx
24.	72-85	ungual phalanx
25.	78-85	ungual phalanx
26.	86-85	distal metapodial
27.	6703-89	proximal phalanx
28.	6707-89	calcaneum (l)
29.	6708-89	median phalanx
30.	18-90	proximal phalanx
31.	22-90	proximal phalanx
32.	33-90	proximal metapodial
33.	35-90	astragalus (r)
34.	36-90	proximal phalanx
35.	39-90	podial
36.	41-90	distal metapodial
37.	45-90	astragalus (r), medial phalanx
38.	48-90	DP4 (l, juv)
38A.	49-90	proximal phalanx
39.	57-90	proximal phalanx
40.	58-90	proximal phalanx
41.	63-90	proximal metapodial
42.	69-90	astragalus (l)

———

The location of the following specimens within a designated grid meter was approximate.

43.	94-90	median phalanx
44.	96-90	cuboid (l)
45.	100-90	proximal phalanx
46.	106-90	median phalanx, proximal metapodial
47.	115-90	median phalanx
48.	116-90	proximal metapodial
49.	117-90	centrum
50.	122-90	proximal metapodial
51.	125-90	tooth fragment
52.	133-90	distal metapodial
53.	136-90	proximal metapodial, vertebra
54.	144-90	proximal phalanx, tooth fragment
55.	149-90	proximal radius (r)
56.	150-90	proximal phalanx
57.	152-90	proximal metapodial
58.	158-90	astragalus (r), tooth fragment
59.	187-90	podial

Map H

Peterson did not mention either camels or cervoids at Quarry 3, although a few bones were unreported among the carnivores he collected under CM1589B. The presence of many scavenged bones of these small vulnerable species, including juveniles, favors their suspected identity as prey. In this they parallel the small oreodont *Merychyus*.

UNSM Fossils of Small Camelids from Quarry 3

	UNSM No.	Elements	Taxon
1.	13-81	unciform (l)	*Oxydactylus*
2.	709-82	distal metapodial	*Oxydactylus*
3.	710-82	distal metapodial	*Stenomylus*
4.	717-82	carpal cuneiform (l)	*Stenomylus*
5.	729-82	proximal phalanx	*Oxydactylus*
6.	731-82	astragalus (l)	*Oxydactylus*
7.	12-84	distal phalanx	*Stenomylus*
8.	8-84	rib head	*Stenomylus*
9.	49-84	distal metapodial	*Oxydactylus*
10.	15-85	distal calcaneum (–)	*Oxydactylus*
11.	72-85	distal phalanx	*Oxydactylus*
12.	6725-89	patella	*Oxydactylus*
13.	2-90	distal metapodial	*Oxydactylus*
14.	15-90	cervical vertebra	*Stenomylus*
15.	21-90	ungual phalanx	*Stenomylus*
16.	44-90	thoracic vertebra	*Oxydactylus*
17.	46A-90	incisor (i3)	*Stenomylus*
18.	56-90	median phalanx	*Stenomylus*
19.	62-90	distal humerus (r)	*Stenomylus*
20.	71-90	cuboid (r)	*Stenomylus*
20A.	87-85	distal femur (l)	*Stenomylus*

UNSM Fossils of Small Cervoids from Quarry 3

	UNSM No.	Elements	Taxon
21.	32-84	astragalus (r)	moschid
22.	37-84	metapodial epiphysis (juv)	dromomerycine
23.	55-84	phalanx	moschid

UNSM Fossils of *Menoceras* from Quarry 3

Few bones of this small rhinoceros were found at the quarry. The calcaneum of a neonatal individual of the species and the two phalanges represent juveniles considered probable prey of the beardogs.

	UNSM No.	Elements
24.	2-84	calcaneum (l)
25.	7-90	proximal phalanx
26.	93-90	jaw fragment
27.	118-90	tooth fragment
28.	CM1589A	proximal phalanx

UNSM Fossils of Small Mammals from Quarry 3

Bone from very small mammals are represented only by damaged fragments: a proximal humerus, two proximal ulnae, a cervical vertebra, two articulated trunk vertebrae, and an isolated trunk vertebra and centrum, all from adults; and a proximal radius, femoral epiphysis, and two centra from juveniles. A lagomorph lower molar is the only tooth. These specimens were not plotted on the den maps.

Map I

UNSM Fossils of Lower Vertebrates from Quarry 3

	UNSM No.	**Group**	**Elements**
1.	14-81	anguid lizard	osteoderms, vertebra
2.	38-90	anguid lizard	vertebra
3.	194-90	lizard	vertebra
3A.	8A-90	lizard	skull bone
4.	CM1589F	snake	vertebra
5.	15-81	anuran	distal humerus
6.	120-90	anuran	sacrum and urostyle
7.	23-84	anuran	pterygoid
8.	57-84	anuran	sacral vertebra
9.	49-85	tortoise	dentary fragment
10.	1-90	turtle	carapace plate
11.	39-90	turtle	carapace plate
12.	50-90	turtle	carapace plate
13.	145-90	turtle	carapace plate
14.	146-90	turtle	carapace plate
15.	152-90	turtle	carapace plate
16.	153-90	turtle	carapace plate
17.	168-90	turtle	carapace plate
18.	148-90	bird	diaphysis
19.	1-84	bird	phalanx (talon)
20.	726-82	bird	coracoid
21.	CM1589F	bird	coracoid
22.	151-90	fish	pectoral fin spine

Institutional abbreviations:

UNSM, University of Nebraska State Museum, Lincoln

CM, Carnegie Museum of Natural History, Pittsburgh

AMNH, American Museum of Natural History, New York

ACM, Beneski Museum of Natural History, Amherst

YPM-PU, Yale Peabody Museum of Natural History, New Haven

Introduction to the Tables

Table 1 lists the specimens found by O. A. Peterson and colleagues in Carnegie Quarry 3 together with his remarks discovered on field labels written during their excavation and later recorded in the Carnegie Museum archives. The remarkable partial skeletons of *Daphoenodon* discovered by Peterson in 1905 were described by him in his classic memoir "Description of New Carnivores from the Miocene of Western Nebraska" (Peterson, 1910). These two individuals were of particular value in identifying isolated bones found during our excavations in the den complex.

Table 2 lists the 415 specimen lots found at Carnegie Quarry 3 during the 1981–90 UNSM excavations at Beardog Hill. Included here are 300 identifiable skeletal elements and 1184 unidentified bone fragments. The date of collection in the table links each lot to more detailed information in the UNSM field notebooks. This table is the principal summary of craniodental and skeletal material recovered by UNSM.

Table 3 records all identifiable carnivoran post-cranial bones from the quarry, listing them under each skeletal element and then by taxon; here bones from both the UNSM excavation and from Peterson's Carnegie Museum collection establish skeletal representation in the quarry. Some carnivore bones are included that could not be assigned to taxon but could be identified to element. Where relevant, measurements provide comparative data on postcranial bones that may be of use in future investigations. Postcranials of the holotype skeleton of *Daphoenodon superbus* (CM1589) were measured except for phalanges, vertebrae, ribs, and sternebrae. Postcranials of the accompanying juvenile male (CM1589A) were for the most part incomplete; some appear in the table and are used in the MNI estimate for the species. Also listed are postcranials of *Delotrochanter oryktes* (UNSM 47800) from Den 2 and the partial skeletons of *Megalictis simplicidens* (CM2389) and *Daphoenodon superbus* (CM2774) collected by Peterson.

Table 4 lists all noncarnivoran specimens from the dens collected both by UNSM and by the Carnegie Museum. The species, chiefly small ungulates, and the particular skeletal elements that are represented, suggest that most of these fragmented remains represent scavenging by the carnivores. Lizard, snake, bird, and frog, turtle, and fish are also in evidence in minor amounts.

Tables 5–10 list craniodental measurements of carnivorans collected by both the Carnegie Museum and UNSM; they were essential to identification of the species that occupied the various burrows.

Table 1. Fossils Collected in Carnegie Quarry 3 by Olaf A. Peterson and a Carnegie Museum Party (1904–1905)

Carnegie Mus. No.	Taxon	Material	Stated Locality	Collector	Date	Remarks[1]
1589	*Daphoenodon superbus*	Partial skeleton	Qu. 3	Peterson	Summer 1905	This is the female genoholotype of *Daphoenodon* shipped in 1905 in Box 17.[2]
1589A	*Daphoenodon superbus*	Partial skeleton	Qu. 3	Peterson	Summer 1905	This is the juvenile male found with CM1589 in Box 17. "This specimen was found in the same block with the type."
1589B	*Daphoenodon superbus*	Many bones and bone fragments	Qu. 3	Peterson	Summer 1905	"Various bones and fragments found on the surface."
1589C	*Daphoenodon superbus*	Left hind foot	"Near Agate Spr. Quar."	Peterson & party	Aug. 11, 1905	"Left hind foot found close to where specimens in Box 17 was found" "Found near 1589 skeleton."
1589D	*Daphoenodon superbus*	"Limb and foot bones"	Qu. 3	Peterson	Summer 1905	"Note: These bones were found in the talus below where the type of Amphicyon superbus was found. And part of the specimen came from the same block as the latter."
1589E	"Ungulates"	"Various foot bones and sternebrae"	Qu. 3	Peterson	Summer 1905	"Various foot bones and sternebrae found in talus below where the type of Amphicyon was found."
1589F	—	Various bones and fragments	Qu. 3	Peterson	Summer 1905	"Various bones and fragments."
9645	Carnivore	Bone fragments	Qu. 3	—	Oct. 4, 1905	"These fragments belong with large block in Box 17 of 1905 . . . the fragments are from the surface."
2389	"*Paroligobunis*" *simplicidens* (*Megalictis*)	Left lower jaw, femur, fibula, and foot bones	Qu. 3	Peterson	Season 1905	"Note = Fragments found in talus below where type of Amphicyon superbus was found."
1602	"*Nothocyon*" *annectens* (*Phlaocyon*)	Upper and lower jaws	"Near Agate Spring Quarry"	Peterson	Aug. 19, 1905	"The specimen was found associated with the type of Amphicyon superbus . . . near the Agate Spring Fossil Quarry, in Sioux County, Nebraska." (Peterson, 1907, p. 53)
2774	*Daphoenodon superbus*	Skull, left lower jaw, ulna, proximal radius, MC3, carpal cuneiform, distal humerus, caudal vertebra, scapula, and rib fragment	Qu. 3	Peterson	1908	Acc. No. 3937 excavated by Peterson: Box 7 – "In this box are packed the skull, jaw & other bones of Amphicyon which were collected about 100 yards to the south of quarry no. 1 (Ag. Spr. Foss. Quarries) or close to the place where the type of Amphicyon superbus was found."

Notes

1. The entries under Remarks present verbatim quotations from O. A. Peterson's Carnegie Museum 1905 field labels and box lists that establish where individual carnivores were found in Quarry 3 and confirm critical associations of key specimens.

2. It is certain that the pair of articulated beardog skeletons (CM1589, CM1589A) collected in a single large block of sandstone from Quarry 3 in 1905 was shipped in Box 17. Thus, references to discovery of material close to or in association with the two beardogs in Box 17—the type of *Daphoenodon superbus* (CM1589) and the male pup (CM1589A)—indicate that such fossils came from Quarry 3 and were closely associated with the Box 17 beardogs.

    Box 17 and later boxes were packed and numbered after July 27, 1905, following Peterson's return to the field at Agate (based on notes in Leon Pepperberg's UNSM 1905 field diary recording the visit that day by Peterson and his wife); the first 16 Carnegie boxes (Box Nos. 1 to 16) of fossils were collected in Quarry 1 on Carnegie Hill during Peterson's absence by T. F. Olcott from April until the last week of July.

    The 1905 Carnegie Box List reported that 45 boxes (Nos. 1 to 45) were packed and shipped to the museum that year, of which almost all contained bone from Quarry 1 except for Box 17, which held only the two *Daphoenodon* partial skeletons. Box 22 according to Peterson did include inconsequential bone fragments that belonged to the Box 17 skeletons: "One small package of small fragments found by washing dirt. These belong with specimen in box 17."

TABLE 2. FOSSIL MATERIAL EXCAVATED AT BEARDOG HILL 1981-1990   117

Table 2. Fossil Material Excavated in Carnegie Quarry 3, Beardog Hill, Agate Fossil Beds National Monument, Nebraska (1981–1990). *Abbreviations:* r, right; l, left; p, partial; juv, juvenile; NI, indeterminate

UNSM No.	Taxon	Description	Date Collected
7-81	*Megalictis simplicidens*	metatarsal II (l)	9-15-81
7-81A	*Cormocyon*	proximal phalanx	9-15-81
8-81	*Delotrochanter oryktes*	skull (p), MC3-4 (l), proximal phalanx, 2 sesamoids, (UNSM 47800) magnum (l), calcaneum (l), MT 2, 3, 4 (l)[1]	9-14-81
9-81	*Delotrochanter oryktes*	MC5 (l) found with 8-81[1]	9-14-81
10-81	*Daphoenodon superbus*	proximal tibia (l, p, juv)	9-10-81
11-81	*Daphoenodon superbus*	ischial fragment (l, p)	9-10-81
12-81	*Daphoenodon superbus*	ulna fragment (r, p)	9-10-81
13-81	small camelid	unciform (l)	9-10-81
14-81	small lizard	osteoderms vertebra, and fragments	9-10-81
15-81	anuran	distal humerus	9-14-81
16-81	NI	tooth fragment	9-12-81
17-81	canid or mustelid	incisor	9- - -81
18-81	*Merychyus*	astragalus (r)[2]	9-14-81
700-82	*Daphoenodon superbus*	lower jaws (r, l), partial skeleton	7-12-82
701-82	*Daphoenodon superbus*	proximal phalanx, distal tibia (r), distal fibula (l), rib (p), canine root, 2 limb diaphysis fragments	7-12-82
702-82	*Daphoenodon superbus*	27 fragments including 4 rib sections (p)	7-12-82
703-82	*Daphoenodon superbus*	M1 (r) and bone fragment	7-13-82
704-82	*Merychyus*	astragalus (r)	7-13-82
705-82	*Daphoenodon superbus*	proximal phalanx, hindfoot, digit I (r)	7-13-82
706-82	NI	15 bone fragments	7-13-82
707-82	*Daphoenodon superbus*	glenoid of squamosal (r, p)	7-13-82
708-82	small mammal	distal metapodial	7-13-82
709-82	*Oxydactylus*	distal metapodial epiphysis (juv)	7-14-82
710-82	*Stenomylus*	distal metapodial (juv)	7-14-82
711-82	mammal	chevron from caudal vertebra	7-14-82
712-82	artiodactyl	astragalus, gnawed	7-14-82
713-82	*Daphoenodon superbus*	lumbar vertebrae (2)	7-14-82
714-82	small mammal	rib (p)	7-14-82
715-82	*Daphoenodon superbus*	rib (p)	7-14-82
716-82	NI	31 bone fragments	7-14-82
717-82	*Stenomylus*	carpal cuneiform (l), neonate	7-14-82
718-82	*Daphoenodon superbus*	imprint of m2-m3 in matrix	7-14-82
719-82	*Daphoenodon superbus*	proximal phalanx	7-15-82
720-82	NI	14 bone fragments	7-15-82
721-82	small mammal	vertebral epiphysis (juv)	7-15-82
722-82	small mammal	distal metapodial	7-15-82
723-82	*Daphoenodon superbus*	m2 (l) in jaw fragment	7-16-82
724-82	*Daphoenodon superbus*	lingual half of M1 (r)	7-16-82
725-82	*Daphoenodon superbus*	p3 (l)	7-16-82
726-82	bird	coracoid	7-16-82
727-82	amphicyonid	incisor	7-16-82
728-82	NI	55 fragments including ribs (p), sesamoid, and metapodial (p)	7-16-82
729-82	*Oxydactylus*	proximal phalanx	7-27-82
730-82	*Daphoenodon superbus*	astragalus (l), MT4 (l)	7-30-82
731-82	*Oxydactylus*	astragalus (l), gnawed (from Den 3)	10-17-82
732-82	*Megalictis simplicidens*	P4 (l)	10-17-82
733-82	*Daphoenodon superbus*	MT2 (l, juv) (from Den 4)	10-18-82
734-82	*Daphoenodon superbus*	lumbar vertebra (from Den 4)	10-19-82
47801	*Megalictis simplicidens*	cervical vertebra	7-6-83
1-84	bird	terminal phalanx (talon)	6-16-84
2-84	*Menoceras arikarense*	calcaneum (l, neonate)[3]	6-16-84
3-84	*Delotrochanter oryktes*	calcaneum (l, p)[4]	6-16-84
4-84	amphicyonid	distal metapodial	6-16-84
5-84	*Daphoenodon superbus*	labial half of M1 (l), distal metapodial	6-16-84
7-84	small carnivore	canine	6-18-84
8-84	*Stenomylus*	rib head	6-18-84
84	*Megalictis simplicidens*	proximal MC4 (r)	6-18-84
10-84	*Daphoenodon superbus*	lumbar vertebral fragment	6-18-84
11-84	*Merychyus*	tooth fragment	6-18-84
12-84	*Stenomylus*	distal phalanx (juv)	6-18-84
13-84	small mammal	podial?	6-18-84
14-84	small mammal	femoral epiphysis (juv) and fragments	6-18-84
15-84	mammal	patella (juv), sesamoid, 4 fragments	6-18-84
16-84	*Daphoenodon superbus*	distal humerus (l), astragalus (l, p)	6-18-84
17-84	*Daphoenodon superbus*	proximal radius (l), caudal vertebra, proximal phalanx, caudal vertebral fragment, vertebral neural arch, 5 bone fragments	6-19-84
18-84	*Cormocyon*	distal humerus (r), proximal phalanx, 13 bone fragments	6-19-84
18A-84	*Promartes*	cervical vertebra	6-19-84
19-84	*Merychyus*	dp3-4 (r, juv), 5 bone fragments	6-19-84
20-84	*Merychyus*	humerus (juv), proximal epiphysis	6-19-84
21-84	NI	19 bone and tooth fragments	6-19-84
22-84	*Megalictis simplicidens*	ulna (r)	6-20-84
23-84	anuran	pterygoid	6-20-84
24-84	*Daphoenodon superbus*	caudal vertebra	6-20-84
25-84	*Merychyus*	astragalus (l), gnawed	6-20-84
26-84	*Daphoenodon superbus*	proximal MC1 (r)	6-20-84
27-84	NI	sesamoid, podial, bone fragment	6-20-84

Table 2. (Continued) Fossil Material Excavated in Carnegie Quarry 3, Beardog Hill, Agate Fossil Beds National Monument, Nebraska (1981–1990). *Abbreviations:* r, right; l, left; p, partial; juv, juvenile; NI, indeterminate

UNSM No.	Taxon	Description	Date Collected	UNSM No.	Taxon	Description	Date Collected
28-84	*Daphoenodon superbus*	entocuneiform (r)	6-20-84	113-84	*Daphoenodon superbus*	canine (p) and 13	7-11-84
30-84	*Daphoenodon superbus*	incisor (I1 or I2)	6-20-84			bone fragments	
	small mammals	rib head, patella,		10-85	*Daphoenodon superbus*	proximal phalanx	6-25-85
		2 vertebral fragments,				and >19 bone	
		42 bone fragments				fragments	
31-84	*Merychyus*	distal humerus (l)	6-21-84	12-85	*Megalictis simplicidens*	skull (p) with M1,	6-27-85
32-84	moschid	astragalus (r), gnawed	6-21-84			P2-P4 (p), proximal	
32-84A	*Merychyus*	proximal metapodial,	6-21-84			femur, distal tibia,	
		distal epiphysis (juv)				numerous fragments	
33-84	*Daphoenodon superbus*	2 proximal phalanges	6-21-84	13-85	*Promartes vantasselensis*	edentulous lower	6-27-85
34-84	NI	rib (p), 2 femoral	6-21-84			jaw (l)	
		heads, 2 sesamoids,		15-85	*Daphoenodon superbus*	patella	6-25-85
		small calcaneum (juv)			*Oxydactylus*	distal calcaneum (p)	
35-84	NI	bone fragment (juv)	6-21-84	16-85	mustelid	m2 (r)	6-27-85
36-84	NI	15 bone fragments	6-21-84	17-85	NI	bone fragment	6-29-85
37-84	dromomerycine	distal metapodial	6-22-84	18-85	*Daphoenodon superbus*	magnum (r)	6-29-85
		epiphysis (juv)[5]		19-85	NI	cranial fragment	6-29-85
38-84	*Merychyus*	proximal phalanx (juv)	6-22-84			(cf. mustelid)	
39-84	mammal	large vertebral	6-22-84	20-85	NI	weathered bone in	6-29-85
		fragment				sediment	
40-84	mammal	sesamoid, 10 bone	6-22-84	21-85	*Cormocyon*	median phalanx	6-29-85
		fragments		22-85	NI	7 bone fragments	6-28-85
41-84	*Merychyus*	proximal radius and	6-22-84	23-85	NI	2 bone fragments	6-28-85
		18 bone fragments		24-85	*Daphoenodon superbus*	unciform (l, juv)	6-28-85
42-84	*Merychyus*	distal humerus (r)	6-23-84		*Merychyus*	proximal phalanx	
43-84	*Daphoenodon superbus*	median phalanx,	6-23-84	25-85	*Promartes olcotti*	distal radius (r)	6-28-85
		forefoot			*Merychus*	proximal phalanx,	
44-84	*Daphoenodon superbus*	cuboid (l), 5 bone	6-23-84			16 bone fragments	
		fragments		26-85	*Promartes olcotti*	calcaneum (r),	6-29-85
45-84	small rodent	proximal radius (juv),	6-23-84			astragalus (r),	
		femoral trochanter				16 bone fragments	
46-84	NI	6 bone fragments	6-23-84	27-85	*Megalictis simplicidens*	p2 (r, p), 128 bone	6-27-85
47-84	*Daphoenodon superbus*	astragalus (r)	6-23-84			fragments	
48-84	*Daphoenodon superbus*	innominate (r, p)	6-22-84	28-85	small mammal	neural arch, 13 bone	6-25-85
49-84	*Promartes olcotti*	calcaneum (r), incisor	6-25-84			fragments	
	Oxydactylus	distal metapodial		29-85	*Merychyus*	proximal phalanx (juv),	6-25-85
50-84	*Daphoenodon superbus*	navicular (l, juv)	6-25-84			17 bone fragments	
51-84	*Daphoenodon superbus*	proximal phalanx	6-25-84	31-85	*Daphoenodon superbus*	thoracic vertebra (p, juv)	7-1-85
52-84	NI	sesamoid,	6-25-84	32-85	*Daphoenodon superbus*	5th caudal vertebra	7-1-85
		5 bone fragments		33-85	NI	vertebral epiphysis (juv)	7-1-85
53-84	*Merychyus*	lunate (r, juv)	6-25-84	34-85	*Promartes olcotti*	P4 (l)	7-2-85
54-84	NI	2 bone fragments	6-25-84	35-85	*Daphoenodon superbus*	ungual phalanx	7-2-85
55-84	moschid	phalanx (juv), proximal	6-25-84	36-85	small canid	baculum	7-2-85
	Cormocyon	median phalanx		37-85	small mammal	vertebral centrum (juv)	7-2-85
56-84	NI	cortical bone with	6-25-84	38-85	*Promartes olcotti*	maxilla (l) with P3-M1	7-2-85
		plant roots		39-85	*Merychyus*	proximal phalanx	7-2-85
57-84	*Merychyus*	proximal phalanx	6-26-84	41-85	*Daphoenodon superbus*	MT4 (l)	7-3-85
	anuran	vertebra		42-85	NI	11 bone fragments	7-3-85
	NI	limb bone (p, juv)		43-85	NI	vertebral fragment	7-3-85
58-84	small mustelid	MC3 (r, juv)	6-26-84	44-85	NI	rib (p), 2 bone fragments	7-3-85
59-84	small carnivore	tooth fragment	6-26-84	45-85	*Merychyus*	patella	7-3-85
60-84	*Merychyus*	distal humerus (l)	6-26-84	46-85	*Merychyus*	carpal cuneiform	7-3-85
61-84	NI	29 bone fragments	6-26-84	47-85	small mustelid	MC4 (l)	7-2-85
62-84	NI	podial?	6-26-84	48-85	NI	femoral head	7-2-85
83-84	*Daphoenodon superbus*	proximal phalanx	7-9-84	49-85	tortoise	dentary fragment	7-2-85
84, 91-84	*Daphoenodon superbus*	distal radius and	7-9,10-84	50-85	*Merychyus*	ecto-mesocuneiform (l)	7-2-85
		diaphysis			small mammal	rib head	
92-84	*Daphoenodon superbus*	lower jaw (l, p) with m1	7-10-84	51-85	small mammal	carpal (p)	7-2-85
92A-84	NI	12 bone fragments	7-10,12-84	52-85	NI	3 bone fragments	7-2-85

TABLE 2. FOSSIL MATERIAL EXCAVATED AT BEARDOG HILL 1981-1990   119

Table 2. (Continued) Fossil Material Excavated in Carnegie Quarry 3, Beardog Hill, Agate Fossil Beds National Monument, Nebraska (1981–1990). *Abbreviations:* r, right; l, left; p, partial; juv, juvenile; NI, indeterminate

UNSM No.	Taxon	Description	Date Collected	UNSM No.	Taxon	Description	Date Collected
53-85	lagomorph	lower molar	7-2-85	6717-89	*Daphoenodon superbus*	petrosal (l)	7-15-89
54-85	*Megalictis simplicidens*	lower jaw with p3-m1 (r)	7-5-85	6718-89	*Daphoenodon superbus*	maxilla fragment with P3 (r, p)	7-15-89
55-85	*Daphoenodon superbus*	proximal phalanx	7-5-85	6719-89	*Daphoenodon superbus*	I3 (l, p)	7-15-89
56-85	*Merychyus*	proximal tibial epiphysis (juv)	7-5-85	6720-89	NI	2 bone fragments	7-15-89
	carnivore	tooth fragment		6721-89	NI	26 bone fragments	7-15-89
57-85	NI	vertebral fragment	7-5-85	6722-89	NI	numerous weathered bone fragments	7-15-89
58-85	*Promartes olcotti*	m1 (l)	7-5-85	6723-89	NI	numerous weathered bone fragments	7-15-89
59-85	NI	7 bone fragments	7-5-85				
60-85	NI	3 bone fragments	7-5-85	6724-89	NI	3 bone fragments	7-15-89
61-85	NI	3 bone fragments	7-5-85	6725-89	*Daphoenodon superbus*	p1 (r)	7-15-89
62-85	NI	bone fragment	7-5-85		*Oxydactylus*	patella	
63-85	small carnivore	MT5 (l)	7-6-85	6726-89	small carnivore	proximal phalanx (p)	7-15-89
64-85	*Cormocyon*	erupting dp4 (l, juv)	7-6-85	6727-89	NI	3 bone fragments	7-15-89
65-85	NI	bone fragment	7-6-85	6728-89	NI	bone fragment	7-15-89
66-85	NI	2 bone fragments	7-6-85	6729-89	NI	2 bone fragments	7-15-89
67-85	*Daphoenodon superbus*	mesocuneiform (l)	7-6-85	6730-89	NI	bone fragment	7-15-89
	Daphoenodon superbus	chevron from caudal vertebra		6731-89	NI	3 bone fragments	7-15-89
	amphicyonid	sesamoid		1-90	turtle	carapace plate	6-12-90
68-85	*Merychyus*	patella (juv), 9 bone fragments	7-6-85	2-90	*Oxydactylus*	distal metapodial (juv)	6-13-90
				3-90	*Megalictis simplicidens*	sacrum	6-13-90
69-85	NI	8 bone fragments	7-6-85	4-90	*Daphoenodon superbus*	radius (l, p), diaphysis	6-13-90
70-85	*Daphoenodon superbus*	innominate (r)	7-8-85	5-90	small carnivore	ungual phalanx	6-13-90
71-85	*Merychyus*	proximal phalanx (p)	7-8-85	6-90	*Daphoenodon superbus*	rib, proximal (9th)	6-19-90
72-85	*Merychyus*	ungual phalanx	7-8-85		small mammal	2 vertebral centra (p)	
	Oxydactylus	distal phalanx (p), 14 bone fragments		7-90	*Menoceras arikarense*	proximal phalanx (side toe, l, juv)	6-18-90
73-85	NI	bone fragment	7-8-85	8-90	*Cormocyon*	tarsus (l, p) and proximal MT1-5	6-18-90
74-85	NI	4 bone fragments	7-8-85				
75-85	*Cormocyon*	calcaneum (r, juv)	7-9-85	8A-90	lizard	skull bone	6-18-90
76-85	NI	5 bone fragments	7-9-85	9-90	small mustelid	distal femur (p), vertebral fragments	6-18-90
77-85	NI	5 bone fragments	7-10-85				
78-85	*Promartes olcotti*	proximal ulna (l)	7-1-85	10-90	*Daphoenodon superbus*	distal femur (l, p, juv)	6-19-90
	Promartes olcotti	distal tibia (l, juv)			small mammal	proximal tibia (juv), 2 bone fragments	
	Merychyus	ungual phalanx			small carnivore	vertebral neural arch	
84-85	NI	9 bone fragments	6-29-85	11-90	*Cormocyon*	median and ungual phalanges, articulated	6-19-90
85-85	NI	proximal phalanx (juv)	6-29-85				
86-85	*Merychyus*	distal metapodial	6-29-85	12-90	*Promartes*	fragment (p, juv) with dp4 (l)	6-19-90
87-85	*Stenomylus*	distal femur (l, p, juv)	7-10-85	13-90	NI	diaphysis fragment	6-19-90
6700-89 to 6702-89	NI	25 bone fragments	7-7-89 to 7-12-89	14-90	small carnivore	posterior mandible (r), edentulous	6-19-90
6703-89	*Merychyus*	proximal phalanx (p)	7-12-89	15-90	*Stenomylus*	cervical vertebra (p)	6-19-90
	NI	petrosal (p), 13 bone fragments		16-90	*Cormocyon*	maxilla with M1-M2	6-22-90
6704-89	NI	bone fragment	7-13-89	17-90	*Daphoenodon superbus*	entocuneiform (l)	6-22-90
6705-89	*Daphoenodon superbus*	vertebral epiphysis (juv)	7-13-89	18-90	*Merychyus*	proximal phalanx	6-22-90
6706-89	NI	4 bone fragments	7-13-89	19-90	*Daphoenodon superbus*	proximal phalanx, forefoot, digit I (r)	6-22-90
6707-89	*Merychyus*	calcaneum (l, p, juv)	7-13-89				
6708-89	*Merychyus*	median phalanx (juv)	7-13-89	20-90	*Daphoenodon superbus*	proximal phalanx, forefoot, digit I (l)	6-22-90
6709-89	NI	2 bone fragments	7-13-89				
6710-89	NI	numerous small bone fragments	7-13-89	21-90	*Stenomylus*	ungual phalanx	6-29-90
6711-89	NI	17 bone fragments	7-13-89	22-90	*Merychyus*	proximal phalanx (juv)	6-29-90
6712-89	NI	25 bone fragments	7-14-89	23-90	*Daphoenodon superbus*	baculum (p, juv)	6-29-90
6713-89	*Daphoenodon superbus*	patella	7-14-89	24-90	*Daphoenodon superbus*	mesocuneiform	6-29-90
6715-89	*Daphoenodon superbus*	zygoma (r), alisphenoid (r)	7-15-89	25-90	*Megalictis simplicidens*	ungual phalanx, forefoot	6-29-90
6716-89	*Daphoenodon superbus*	P4 (l, p)	7-15-89	26-90	*Daphoenodon superbus*	proximal phalanx	6-30-90

Table 2. (Continued) Fossil Material Excavated in Carnegie Quarry 3, Beardog Hill, Agate Fossil Beds National Monument, Nebraska (1981–1990). *Abbreviations:* r, right; l, left; p, partial; juv, juvenile; NI, indeterminate

UNSM No.	Taxon	Description	Date Collected
27-90	*Promartes olcotti*	distal tibia (l)	6-30-90
28-90	*Cormocyon*	distal humerus (l, p)	6-30-90
29-90	NI	bone fragment	6-30-90
30-90	*Promartes olcotti*	distal radius (r, p)	6-30-90
31-90	NI	proximal phalanx (juv)	6-30-90
32-90	NI	bone fragment	6-30-90
33-90	*Merychyus*	proximal metapodial	6-30-90
34-90	*Daphoenodon superbus*	cuboid (r)	6-30-90
35-90	*Merychyus*	astragalus (r, p), 5 bone fragments	6-30-90
	Daphoenodon superbus	median phalanx (p)	
36-90	*Merychyus*	proximal phalanx (juv)	6-30-90
37-90	*Daphoenodon superbus*	terminal caudal vertebra	6-30-90
38-90	anguid lizard	vertebra	6-30-90
39-90	*Promartes olcotti*	proximal radius (l)	6-30-90
	Merychyus	podial (p)	
	turtle	carapace plate	
40-90	*Daphoenodon superbus*	i3 (r)	6-30-90
41-90	*Promartes olcotti*	MT4 (l), podial	7-7-90
	Merychyus	distal metapodial (juv)	
42-90	NI	metapodial (p)	7-7-90
43-90	*Promartes olcotti*	distal tibia (r)	7-7-90
44-90	*Oxydactylus*	thoracic vertebra (juv)	7-7-90
45-90	*Merychyus*	astragalus (r, p), median phalanx	7-7-90
46-90	*Cormocyon*	m1 (r)	7-7-90
46A-90	*Stenomylus*	i3 (r)	7-7-90
47-90	*Promartes olcotti*	distal fibula (l)	7-8-90
48-90	*Merychyus*	DP4 (l, juv)	7-8-90
49-90	*Merychyus*	proximal phalanx (juv)	7-8-90
50-90	turtle	carapace plate	7-8-90
51-90	*Daphoenodon superbus*	median phalanx[6]	7-9-90
52-90	NI	bone fragment	7-9-90
53-90	*Megalictis simplicidens*	upper canine (r)	7-11-90
54-90	*Cormocyon*	distal radius and ulna (l, p), articulated[7]	7-11-90
55-90	*Daphoenodon superbus*	distal rib	7-11-90
56-90	*Stenomylus*	median phalanx (neonate)	7-11-90
57-90	small rodent or insectivore	proximal humerus	7-11-90
	Merychyus	proximal phalanx (juv)	
58-90	*Merychyus*	proximal phalanx	7-11-90
59-90	regurgitated meal?	carpus (p), proximal MC1-5 and bone hash[7]	7-11-90
60-90	*Megalictis simplicidens*	thoracic vertebra T6	7-13-90
61-90	*Megalictis simplicidens*	thoracic vertebra T7	7-13-90
62-90	*Stenomylus*	distal humerus (r, juv)	7-13-90
63-90	*Merychyus*	proximal metapodial	7-13-90
64-90	*Daphoenodon superbus*	complete rib (~11th)	7-13-90
65-90	*Daphoenodon superbus*	distal tip of rib	7-13-90
66-90	*Daphoenodon superbus*	scapholunar (l)	7-13-90
67-90	small mammal	centrum (juv) and rib head	7-13-90
68-90	small artiodactyl	tooth fragment, 10 bone fragments, vertebral epiphysis (juv)	7-13-90
69-90	*Merychyus*	astragalus (l)	10-19-90

UNSM No.	Taxon	Description	Date Collected
70-90	*Daphoenodon superbus*	proximal MT4 (r)	10-19-90
71-90	*Stenomylus*	cuboid (r)	10-19-90
72-90	*Daphoenodon superbus*	calcaneum (l, p)	10-19-90
73-90	NI	10 bone fragments	10-19-90
74-90	*Promartes olcotti*	MT3 (l, p)	10-19-90
5004-006	*Merychyus*	astragalus (l)	7-21-006

———

The following material was numbered in the laboratory after field work in 1990. It represents bone from screening and excavation of Dens 5A, 5B, 5C and Den 6 and surrounding area collected from 6-11 to 7-13-90 from the north quarry metric grid.

UNSM No.	Taxon	Description
90-90	NI	petrosal (p), 20 bone fragments
91-90	*Megalictis simplicidens*	lower canine (l, p), 4 bone fragments
92-90	NI	3 bone fragments
93-90	*Menoceras arikarense*	mandibular fragment
94-90	*Merychyus*	median phalanx (juv)
95-90	amphicyonid	sesamoid
96-90	*Merychyus*	cuboid (l, juv)
97-90	NI	bone fragment
98-90	NI	bone fragment
99-90	*Promartes olcotti*	distal radius (r), 2 bone fragments
100-90	*Merychyus*	proximal phalanx, 3 bone fragments
101-90	NI	3 bone fragments
102-90	NI	bone fragment
103-90	mammal	femoral condyle, 5 bone fragments
104-90	NI	9 bone fragments
105-90	NI	3 bone fragments
106-90	*Merychyus*	median phalanx, proximal metapodial
		4 bone fragments
107-90	small mammal	femoral condyle, 3 bone fragments
108-90	small mammal	sesamoid, 5 bone fragments
111-90	small mammal	cervical vertebra, 8 bone fragments
112-90	*Promartes*	2 lumbar vertebrae (p)
	small artiodactyl	femoral condyle (p)
	small mammal	thoracic vertebral fragment
	NI	5 bone fragments
113-90	*Promartes*	femoral head (l)
	small artiodactyl	femoral condyle (p), sesamoid
		9 bone fragments
114-90	carnivore	cervical centrum, 2 bone fragments
115-90	*Merychyus*	median phalanx (juv), 15 bone fragments
116-90	*Merychyus*	proximal metapodial
117-90	*Merychyus*	centrum (juv)
	rodent or insectivore	trunk vertebra
	small mammal	centrum (p)

TABLE 2. FOSSIL MATERIAL EXCAVATED AT BEARDOG HILL 1981–1990   121

Table 2. (Continued) Fossil Material Excavated in Carnegie Quarry 3, Beardog Hill, Agate Fossil Beds National Monument, Nebraska (1981–1990). *Abbreviations:* r, right; l, left; p, partial; juv, juvenile; NI, indeterminate

UNSM No.	Taxon	Description	UNSM No.	Taxon	Description
118-90	*Menoceras arikarense*	tooth fragment, 7 bone fragments	157-90	NI	10 bone fragments
119-90	NI	2 bone fragments	158-90	*Merychyus*	astragalus (r, p), tooth fragment 3 bone fragments
120-90	anuran	sacrum and urostyle	159-90	NI	2 bone fragments
121-90	mammal	sesamoid, bone fragment	160-90	NI	skull fragment, ?metapodial (p)
122-90	*Merychyus*	proximal metapodial	161-90	NI	7 bone fragments
123-90	mammal	rib fragment	162-90	NI	3 bone fragments
124-90	NI	6 bone fragments	163-90	NI	bone fragment
125-90	*Merychyus*	tooth fragment, 14 bone fragments	164-90	NI	rib (p), 3 bone fragments
126-90	*Cormocyon*	proximal phalanx	165-90	*Merychyus*	vertebral centrum 12 bone fragments
127-90	NI	7 bone fragments	166-90	NI	vertebral neural arch
128-90	NI	13 bone fragments	167-90	NI	bone fragment
129-90	NI	8 bone fragments	168-90	turtle	carapace plate
130-90	rodent or insectivore	2 trunk vertebrae	169-90	NI	bone fragment
	mammal	proximal tibia (juv), 2 bone fragments	170-90	NI	bone fragment
			171-90	NI	bone fragment
131-90	NI	3 bone fragments	172-90	NI	7 bone fragments
132-90	NI	2 bone fragments	173-90	NI	10 bone fragments
133-90	*Merychyus*	distal metapodial (juv)	174-90	NI	8 bone fragments
134-90	rodent or insectivore	proximal ulna (l)	175-90	NI	5 bone fragments
135-90	NI	4 bone fragments	176-90	NI	7 bone fragments
136-90	*Merychyus*	proximal metapodial, vertebra (p) 7 bone fragments	177-90	mammal	vertebral centrum fragment (juv)
			178-90	NI	5 bone fragments
			179-90	NI	2 bone fragments
137-90	NI	13 bone fragments	180-90	small mammal	vertebral centrum fragment
138-90	small mammal	femoral condyle (p)	181-90	NI	2 bone fragments
139-90	small carnivore	proximal phalanx (p) 6 bone fragments	182-90	NI	bone fragment
			183-90	NI	7 bone fragments
140-90	*Daphoenodon* or *Megalictis*	canine (p)	184-90	NI	bone fragment
			185-90	NI	bone fragment
141-90	NI	6 bone fragments	186-90	NI	bone fragment
142-90	NI	5 bone fragments	187-90	*Merychyus*	podial (juv), bone fragment
143-90	NI	2 bone fragments	188-90	NI	4 bone fragments
144-90	*Merychyus*	proximal phalanx (juv) tooth fragment, 4 bone fragments	189-90	NI	2 bone fragments
			190-90	NI	10 bone fragments
			191-90	NI	2 bone fragments
145-90	turtle	carapace plate	192-90	NI	bone fragment
146-90	turtle	carapace plate	193-90	NI	2 tooth fragments
147-90	NI	bone fragment	194-90	lizard	trunk vertebra, 3 bone fragments
148-90	bird	diaphysis, 3 bone fragments	195-90	NI	bone fragment
149-90	*Merychyus*	proximal radius (r)	196-90	small carnivore	proximal phalanx (p)
	small carnivore	baculum	197-90	NI	2 bone fragments
	NI	11 bone fragments	198-90	NI	bone fragment
150-90	*Merychyus*	proximal phalanx (juv), 3 bone fragments	199-90	small mammal	sesamoid, 4 bone fragments
			200-90	*Daphoenodon superbus*	caudal vertebra (p)
151-90	fish	pectoral fin spine	201-90	*Daphoenodon superbus*	chevron bone
	amphicyonid	proximal phalanx (p) 4 bone fragments	202-90	small mammal	centrum, metapodial (p, juv) 3 bone fragments
152-90	*Daphoenodon superbus*	median phalanx, 4 bone fragments	203-90	NI	5 bone fragments
	Merychyus	proximal metapodial	204-90	NI	bone fragment
	turtle	carapace plate	205-90	NI	3 bone fragments
153-90	turtle	carapace plate	206-90	small mammal	proximal ulna
154-90	small mammal	vertebral neural arch		carnivore	canine fragment 6 bone fragments
155-90	NI	bone fragment	207-90	*Promartes*	vertebra (p), 4 bone fragments
156-90	*Cormocyon*	proximal phalanx 10 bone fragments	208-90	NI	9 bone fragments
			209-90	*Cormocyon*	astragalus (r)

Table 2. (Continued) Fossil Material Excavated in Carnegie Quarry 3, Beardog Hill, Agate Fossil Beds National Monument, Nebraska (1981–1990). *Abbreviations:* r, right; l, left; p, partial; juv, juvenile; NI, indeterminate

UNSM No.	Taxon	Description
210-90	*Cormocyon*	vertebra (1st lumbar, p, juv)
210A-90	small carnivore	tooth fragment
		edentulous jaw fragment
		3 bone fragments
211-90	*Megalictis simplicidens*	unciform (l)
212-90	NI	3 bone fragments
213-90	*Daphoenodon superbus*	proximal MC5 (l)

Much bone that cannot be identified to skeletal element (NI) is in the form of small broken angular pieces, frequently poorly preserved and some apparently scavenged. These pieces are described in the list as "bone fragments." This fragmented bone occurred within and outside burrows throughout the den complex in the northern half of Quarry 3 during our excavation.

Notes

1. MC5 (UNSM 9-81) was found near MC3-4 and the skull of *Delotrochanter* (UNSM 8-81) in Den 2 and at first was not recognized as part of the same forefoot.

2. This astragalus was found in surface talus between Carnegie and Beardog Hills but is not from the carnivore den area.

3. This very small calcaneum suggests that neonatal calves of *M. arikarense* were probably taken as prey by the larger carnivores found in the dens (*Daphoenodon*, *Delotrochanter*).

4. This calcaneum found near Dens 1 and 2 demonstrates the presence of a second adult of *Delotrochanter oryktes* at Quarry 3.

5. This distal metapodial fragment belongs to either a dromomerycine or large moschid cervoid. Its size and form compare with the earliest records of the dromomerycine *Barbouromeryx*.

6. This beardog phalanx (UNSM 51-90) was the carnivore bone found farthest to the east on Beardog Hill during the excavation of Quarry 3.

7. Articulated bones of the small canid *Cormocyon* occur near a comminuted mass of angular bone fragments (the "bone hash") in Den 5B in the SW1/4 of meter O2 and SE1/4 of meter P2.

UNSM No.	Taxon	Description	Date Collected

During our geologic mapping of the national monument, some bones of *Daphoenodon* had been found on Beardog Hill prior to 1981 before UNSM excavations had relocated the den complex.

UNSM No.	Taxon	Description	Date Collected
UNSM 26397	*Daphoenodon*	distal humerus (l, p)	7-16-71
UNSM 423-78	*Daphoenodon*	calcaneum (r, p)	7-14-78
		proximal MT5 (l)	
		proximal MC3 (r)	
		distal metapodial	
		distal humerus fragment (r)	

Table 3. Postcranial Bones of Carnivores, Quarry 3
Abbreviations: l, left; r, right; juv, juvenile.
Carnegie Museum numbers are preceded by CM; UNSM numbers are those without a prefix.
Measurements are in millimeters (mm).

CM or UNSM No.	Taxon[a]	Description	Length	Width
Scapula				
CM1589	Daphoenodon	glenoid (l)	34.2[b]	23.6
CM1589	Daphoenodon	glenoid (r)	33.8	23.7
CM1589B	Daphoenodon	glenoid (r)	36.4	22.6
CM1589A	Daphoenodon	glenoid (r, juv)	37.1	23.3
700-82	Daphoenodon	glenoid (r)	40.5	~26
Humerus				
CM1589	Daphoenodon	complete (l)	209	35.4[c]
CM1589	Daphoenodon	complete (r)	210	34.2[c]
CM1589B	Daphoenodon	distal (l)	—	38.5[c]
CM1589D	Daphoenodon	distal diaphysis (l)	—	36.4[c]
CM1589B	Daphoenodon	proximal (r)	64.0	—
CM1589	Daphoenodon	proximal (l)	53.6	41.3
CM1589	Daphoenodon	proximal (r)	52.2	42.0
CM2774	Daphoenodon	diaphysis (r)	—	18.1
16-84	Daphoenodon	distal (l)	—	40.3[c]
18-84	Cormocyon	distal (r)	—	10.5[c]
28-90	Cormocyon	distal (l)	—	~12[c]
Radius				
17-84	Daphoenodon	proximal (l)	—	25.2[d]
91-84	Daphoenodon	distal (r), diaphysis	—	33.3[e]
4-90	Daphoenodon	diaphysis (l)	—	—
CM1589	Daphoenodon	complete (l)	182	34.7[e]
CM1589	Daphoenodon	complete (r)	182	34.1[e]
700-82	Daphoenodon	complete (r)	210	34.8[e]
CM1589B	Daphoenodon	proximal (l)	21.3	29.0[d]
CM1589B	Daphoenodon	proximal (l)	17.2	26.1[d]
CM1589	Daphoenodon	proximal (r)	16.8	23.0[d]
700-82	Daphoenodon	proximal (r)	20.5	28.7[d]
CM1589B	Daphoenodon	distal (r)	26.7	37.3[e]
CM1589	Daphoenodon	distal (l)	23.5	34.7[e]
CM2774	Daphoenodon	proximal (r)	—	24.3[d]
25-85	Promartes	distal (r)	—	10.0[e]
30-90	Promartes	distal (r)	~50	10.9[e]
39-90	Promartes	proximal (l)	—	6.5[d]
99-90	Promartes	distal (r)	—	10.6[e]
54-90	Cormocyon	distal (l)	—	12.5[e]
Ulna				
12-81	Daphoenodon	fragment	—	—
700-82	Daphoenodon	complete	259	—
CM2774	Daphoenodon	lacks distal end (r)	—	27.0[g]
CM1589	Daphoenodon	complete (r)	222	26.3[g]
CM1589	Daphoenodon	complete (l)	223	26.6[g]
78-85	Promartes	proximal (l)	—	3.7
22-84	Megalictis	complete (r)	~160	22.0[f]
CM2774	Megalictis	distal (r)	—	17.4[f]
54-90	Cormocyon	distal (l)	—	3.9[f]
Size comparison of proximal ulnae				
CM1589B	Daphoenodon	proximal (l)	37.8	13.6[h]
CM1589B	Daphoenodon	proximal (r)	34.2	13.0
CM1589B	Daphoenodon	proximal (l)	33.7	12.5
CM1589	Daphoenodon	proximal (r)	32.8	11.7
CM1589	Daphoenodon	proximal (l)	33.3	11.9
CM2774	Daphoenodon	proximal (r)	32.1	10.9
Carpus, articulated (includes scapholunar, carpal cuneiform, pisiform, unciform, magnum, trapezoid, trapezium) and proximal MC1-5				
59-90	Cormocyon	complete	—	~15
Scapholunar				
66-90	Daphoenodon	complete (l)	18.5	30.0[i]
CM1589	Daphoenodon	complete (l)	15.9	24.9
CM1589	Daphoenodon	complete (r)	14.9	25.1
CM1589B	Daphoenodon	complete (l)	17.9	27.7
CM1589B	Daphoenodon	complete (r)	19.3	31.2
Carpal cuneiform				
CM2774	Daphoenodon	complete (r)	19.5	14.2[j]
CM1589	Daphoenodon	complete (l)	19.4	13.5
CM1589	Daphoenodon	complete (r)	20.4	15.1
CM1589D	Daphoenodon	complete (l)	20.9	15.1
Magnum				
18-85	Daphoenodon	complete (r)	22.8	17.3[k]
CM1589	Daphoenodon	complete (l)	20	16
8-81	Delotrochanter	complete (l)	19.4	14.7
Unciform				
24-85	Daphoenodon	complete (l, juv)	16.4	15.1[l]
CM1589	Daphoenodon	complete (l)	16	17
CM1589A	Daphoenodon	complete (l)	15.6	19.0
211-90	Megalictis	complete (l)	13.9	14.0
CM2389	Megalictis	complete (r)	13.0	15.0
Metapodials				
CM1589	Daphoenodon	MT1 (r)	42	11[m]
CM1589B	Daphoenodon	MT1 (l)	—	13.0
CM1589C	Daphoenodon	MT1 (l)	41.3	12.2
CM1589	Daphoenodon	MT2 (r)	59	10
CM1589B	Daphoenodon	MT2 (l)	—	10.0
733-82	Daphoenodon	MT2, (l, juv)[n]	48.7	8.5
CM1589A	Daphoenodon	MT2, (l, juv)[n]	52.3	9.4
CM1589A	Daphoenodon	MT2, (r, juv)[n]	60.8	9.7
CM1589B	Daphoenodon	MT2 (l)	—	9.7
CM1589C	Daphoenodon	MT2 (l)	62.6	9.2
CM1589	Daphoenodon	MT3 (r)	70	14
CM1589A	Daphoenodon	MT3, (r, juv)	71.6	15.5
CM1589B	Daphoenodon	MT3 (l)	—	14.7
CM1589B	Daphoenodon	MT3 (r)	73.8	16.3
CM1589C	Daphoenodon	MT3 (l)	73.3	16.4
CM1589	Daphoenodon	MT4 (r)	73	12
CM1589B	Daphoenodon	MT4 (r)	—	11.0
CM1589C	Daphoenodon	MT4 (l)	77.3	11.0
730-82	Daphoenodon	MT4 (l)	76.4	13.7
41-85	Daphoenodon	MT4 (l)	76.5	13.5
70-90	Daphoenodon	MT4, proximal (r)	—	10.9
CM1589	Daphoenodon	MT5 (r)	62	19
CM1589C	Daphoenodon	MT5 (l)	66.7	17.8
423-78	Daphoenodon	MT5 (l)	—	17.7
CM1589	Daphoenodon	MC1 (l)	32	11
26-84	Daphoenodon	MC1 (r)	—	10.4
CM1589B	Daphoenodon	MC1 (r)	—	11.9
CM1589B	Daphoenodon	MC1 (l)	—	13.2
CM1589B	Daphoenodon	MC1 (r, juv)	29.7	10.0

Table 3. (Continued) Postcranial Bones of Carnivores, Quarry 3

CM or UNSM No.	Taxon[a]	Description	Length	Width	CM or UNSM No.	Taxon[a]	Description	Length	Width
CM1589B	*Daphoenodon*	MC1 (l, juv)	29.6	9.8	CM1589B	*Daphoenodon*	proximal	27.6	12.0
CM1589	*Daphoenodon*	MC2 (l)	51	16	CM1589B	*Daphoenodon*	proximal	24.4	10.6
CM1589B	*Daphoenodon*	MC2 (l)	—	11.8	CM1589B	*Daphoenodon*	proximal	24.3	10.8
CM1589B	*Daphoenodon*	MC2 (l)	58.3	12.4	CM1589B	*Daphoenodon*	proximal	23.6	10.0
CM1589	*Daphoenodon*	MC3 (r)	62	11	CM1589B	*Daphoenodon*	proximal	20.6	10.1
CM1589B	*Daphoenodon*	MC3 (l)	68.5	12.5	CM1589D	*Daphoenodon*	proximal	27.7	12.7
CM1589B	*Daphoenodon*	MC3 (l)	—	12.5	CM1589D	*Daphoenodon*	proximal	29.3	13.7
CM1589B	*Daphoenodon*	MC3 (r)	—	13.3	CM1589D	*Daphoenodon*	proximal	24.9	11.4
423-78	*Daphoenodon*	MC3 (r)	—	12.8	8-81	*Delotrochanter*	proximal	33.0	15.2
CM2774	*Daphoenodon*	MC3 (r)	60.4	11.2	CM1589B	*Daphoenodon*	median	22.5	13.4
CM1589	*Daphoenodon*	MC4 (r)	60	12	CM1589B	*Daphoenodon*	median	21.0	11.6
CM1589B	*Daphoenodon*	MC4 (l)	—	12.7	CM1589B	*Daphoenodon*	median	19.9	13.5
CM1589B	*Daphoenodon*	MC4 (r)	—	13.7	CM1589B	*Daphoenodon*	median	19.6	11.3
CM1589D	*Daphoenodon*	MC4 (l)	—	13.6	CM1589B	*Daphoenodon*	median	18.9	11.4
CM1589	*Daphoenodon*	MC5 (l)	47	13	CM1589B	*Daphoenodon*	median	17.7	11.4
CM1589A	*Daphoenodon*	MC5 (r, juv)	50.6	12.3	CM1589B	*Daphoenodon*	median	15.8	10.3
213-90	*Daphoenodon*	MC5 (l)	—	12.7	CM1589B	*Daphoenodon*	median	15.8	—
8-81	*Delotrochanter*	MT2 (l)	74.1	7.9	43-84	*Daphoenodon*	median	21.6	11.4
8-81	*Delotrochanter*	MT3 (l)	90.9	12.6	35-90	*Daphoenodon*	median	18.3	~12
8-81	*Delotrochanter*	MT4 (l)	91.0	12.9	51-90	*Daphoenodon*	median	20.4	12.9
CM1589B	*Delotrochanter*	MT5 (r)	~74	11.8	152-90	*Daphoenodon*	median	18.5	10.2
8-81	*Delotrochanter*	MC3 (l)	82.6	11.4	35-85	*Daphoenodon*	ungual	21.7	7.9
8-81	*Delotrochanter*	MC4 (l)	83.9	12.5	CM1589B	*Daphoenodon*	ungual	17.0	6.5
9-81	*Delotrochanter*	MC5 (l)	65.0	12.7	CM1589B	*Daphoenodon*	ungual	17.5	7.3
7-81	*Megalictis*	MT2	50.3	10.8	CM1589B	*Daphoenodon*	ungual	17.6	6.8
CM1589B	*Megalictis*	MT3	—	11.7	CM1589B	*Daphoenodon*	ungual	21.2	8.1
CM2389	*Megalictis*	MC1 (r)	26.1	7.4	CM1589B	*Daphoenodon*	ungual	23.4	8.6
CM2389	*Megalictis*	MC2 (r)	36.9	~9	CM1589D	*Daphoenodon*	ungual	17.3	—
CM2389	*Megalictis*	MC2 (l)	37.0	9.3	25-90	*Megalictis*	ungual, forefoot	25.3	9.3
CM2389	*Megalictis*	MC3 (r)	40.8	10.3					
9-84	*Megalictis*	MC4 (r)	—	9.4	*Phalanges of CM 1589 and 1589A could not be measured.*				
58-84	*Promartes*[o]	MC3 (l, ?juv)	—	2.6					
47-85	*Promartes*[o]	MC4 (r, juv)	14.9	2.7	7-81A	*Cormocyon*	proximal	15.3	4.9
41-90	*Promartes*[o]	MT4 (l)	24.1	3.4	126-90	*Cormocyon*	proximal	12.9	4.7
74-90	*Promartes*[o]	MT3 (l)	—	3.6	156-90	*Cormocyon*	proximal	16.5	5.1
63-85	small carnivore	MT5 (l)	—	—	18-84	*Cormocyon*	proximal	16.4	6.9
					55-84	*Cormocyon*	median	7.9	3.8
Phalanges					21-85	*Cormocyon*	median	9.0	4.0
701-82	*Daphoenodon*	proximal	30.1	13.8[p]	11-90	*Cormocyon*	median	9.3	4.2
705-82	*Daphoenodon*	proximal, MT digit I	22.9	10.9	11-90	*Cormocyon*	ungual	9.7	3.6
719-82	*Daphoenodon*	proximal	31.1	14.4	5-90	small carnivore	ungual	8.1	3.0
17-84	*Daphoenodon*	proximal	27.8	12.2	196-90	small carnivore	proximal	—	—
33-84	*Daphoenodon*	proximal	27.6	12.0	6726-89	small carnivore	proximal	—	—
		proximal	28.1	—	139-90	small carnivore	proximal	—	—
51-84	*Daphoenodon*	proximal	25.9	11.5					
83-84	*Daphoenodon*	proximal	28.0	11.9	*Sesamoids*				
10-85	*Daphoenodon*	proximal	31.9	13.7	95-90	amphicyonid	complete	11.9	6.4
55-85	*Daphoenodon*	proximal	30.0	13.2	CM1589B	*Daphoenodon*	16	—	—
26-90	*Daphoenodon*	proximal	29.1	12.7	CM1589	*Daphoenodon*	7	Figured by	
19-90	*Daphoenodon*	proximal, MC digit I	26.1	10.3				Peterson	
20-90	*Daphoenodon*	proximal, MC digit I	25.9	10.2				(1910)	
CM1589B	*Daphoenodon*	proximal	31.6	13.7					
CM1589B	*Daphoenodon*	proximal	31.5	12.9	*Sacrum*				
CM1589B	*Daphoenodon*	proximal	31.0	13.4	3-90	*Megalictis*	complete	52.6	62.9[q]
CM1589B	*Daphoenodon*	proximal	30.8	13.1	CM1589	*Daphoenodon*	complete	75.9	59.1[q]
CM1589B	*Daphoenodon*	proximal	30.2	13.5					
CM1589B	*Daphoenodon*	proximal	30.0	14.1	*Innominate*				
CM1589B	*Daphoenodon*	proximal	30.0	13.4	48-84	*Daphoenodon*	acetabulum (r)	25.2	24.8
CM1589B	*Daphoenodon*	proximal	29.5	13.4	CM1589	*Daphoenodon*	acetabulum (r)	28.1	25.4
CM1589B	*Daphoenodon*	proximal	28.1	12.1	CM1589A	*Daphoenodon*	acetabulum (r, juv)	30.7	29.5
CM1589B	*Daphoenodon*	proximal	28.1	11.9	70-85	*Daphoenodon*	acetabulum (r)	29.9	31.7

Table 3. (Continued) Postcranial Bones of Carnivores, Quarry 3

CM or UNSM No.	Taxon[a]	Description	Length	Width
CM1589B	*Daphoenodon*	ischium	—	—
CM1589B	*Daphoenodon*	ischium	—	—
11-81	*Daphoenodon*	ischial fragment (l)	—	—
Baculum				
CM1589A	*Daphoenodon*	juvenile	90.4	8.2
23-90	*Daphoenodon*	juvenile	51.9	7.5[r]
149-90	small carnivore	adult	—	3.9
36-85	small canid	adult	~44	3.2
Femur				
10-90	*Daphoenodon*	distal epiphysis (l, juv)	—	~40
CM1589	*Daphoenodon*	complete (r)	229	43.1[s]
CM1589	*Daphoenodon*	complete (l)	230	44.8[s]
CM1589B	*Daphoenodon*	distal femur (l)	—	49.2[s]
CM1589B	*Daphoenodon*	diaphysis	—	—
CM2389	*Megalictis*	complete (r)	171	43.2[s]
CM1589	*Promartes*	distal (l)	—	13.8
113-90	*Promartes*	femoral head	7.6	7.1
9-90	small mustelid	distal	—	—
Comparison of the femoral head				
CM1589	*Daphoenodon*	femoral head (r)	27.0	25.4
CM1589	*Daphoenodon*	femoral head (l)	26.8	25.3
CM1589B	*Daphoenodon*	femoral head (r)	30.0	29.6
Patella				
15-85	*Daphoenodon*	complete	—	—
6713-89	*Daphoenodon*	complete	—	—
Tibia				
701-82	*Daphoenodon*	distal (r)	24.6	40.2[t]
CM1589	*Daphoenodon*	distal (r)	23.6	33.4[t]
CM1589	*Daphoenodon*	length, estimated	~200	—
CM1589B	*Daphoenodon*	head (r), large	—	—
CM1589B	*Daphoenodon*	head (r), small	—	—
CM1589B	*Daphoenodon*	diaphysis (r), large	—	—
CM1589B	*Daphoenodon*	diaphysis (r), small	—	—
CM1589B	*Daphoenodon*	diaphysis (l)	—	—
CM1589B	*Daphoenodon*	distal (r)	—	—
CM1589B	*Daphoenodon*	distal (l)	—	—
10-81	*Daphoenodon*	proximal (l, juv)	—	~35
12-85	*Megalictis*	distal (l)	—	34.2[t]
78-85	*Promartes*	distal (l, juv)	—	10.5[t]
27-90	*Promartes*	distal (l)	—	9.9[t]
43-90	*Promartes*	distal (r)	—	10.1[t]
Fibula				
CM1589	*Daphoenodon*	complete (l)	188	19.6[u]
CM1589	*Daphoenodon*	complete (r)	190	18.4[u]
701-82	*Daphoenodon*	distal (l)	21.3	11.7
CM1589	*Daphoenodon*	distal (l)	19.7	9.7
CM2389	*Megalictis*	complete (r)	131	17.8[u]
47-90	*Promartes*	distal (l)	7.5	4.4
Tarsus, articulated (includes cuboid, ecto-meso-entocuneiforms) and proximal MT1-5				
8-90	*Cormocyon*	nearly complete	—	16.3
Calcaneum				
423-78	*Daphoenodon*	partial (r)	~58	27.9[v]
72-90	*Daphoenodon*	partial (l)	~65	33.0

CM or UNSM No.	Taxon[a]	Description	Length	Width
CM1589	*Daphoenodon*	complete (l)	58.7	31.3
CM1589	*Daphoenodon*	complete (r)	59.1	31.4
CM1589B	*Daphoenodon*	complete (l)	67.5	31.9
CM1589B	*Daphoenodon*	complete (r)	63.8	30.6
CM1589B	*Daphoenodon*	partial (l)	—	—
CM1589C	*Daphoenodon*	complete (l)	64.3	30.3
3-84	*Delotrochanter*	distal (l)	—	27.3
8-81	*Delotrochanter*	complete (l)	71.1	26.0
49-84	*Promartes*	complete (r)	18.1	9.8
26-85	*Promartes*	complete (r)	16.7	8.5
75-85	*Cormocyon*	complete (r, juv)	16.9	7.3
Astragalus				
730-82	*Daphoenodon*	complete (l)	38.5	21.9[w]
47-84	*Daphoenodon*	complete (r)	39.1	20.6
CM1589	*Daphoenodon*	complete (l)	35.3	20.1
CM1589	*Daphoenodon*	complete (r)	35.2	20.9
CM1589B	*Daphoenodon*	complete (l)	41.0	22.3
CM1589B	*Daphoenodon*	partial (r)	—	20.9
CM1589B	*Daphoenodon*	partial (r)	—	~22
CM1589C	*Daphoenodon*	complete (l)	38.2	22.1
CM2389	*Megalictis*	complete (l)	33.0	16.0
26-85	*Promartes*	complete (r)	11.6	6.3
209-90	*Cormocyon*	complete (r)	15.0	7.8
Navicular				
50-84	*Daphoenodon*	complete (l, juv)	17.7	19.4
CM1589	*Daphoenodon*	complete (r)	24	21
CM1589	*Daphoenodon*	complete (l)	21.8	19.1
CM1589C	*Daphoenodon*	complete (l)	22.7	22.0
CM1589A	*Daphoenodon*	complete (r, juv)	22.9	21.8
Cuboid				
44-84	*Daphoenodon*	complete (r)	24.5[x]	18.2[x]
34-90	*Daphoenodon*	complete (r)	22.4	16.1
CM1589	*Daphoenodon*	complete (r)	20.7	17.8
CM1589	*Daphoenodon*	complete (l)	20.5	17.1
CM1589C	*Daphoenodon*	complete (l)	21.5	16.9
CM1589A	*Daphoenodon*	complete (r, juv)	22.2	17.3
Ectocuneiform				
CM1589	*Daphoenodon*	complete (l)	—	12.1
CM1589	*Daphoenodon*	complete (r)	21	12.3
CM1589B	*Daphoenodon*	complete (l)	22.5	13.8
CM1589B	*Daphoenodon*	complete (r)	23.0	15.0
CM1589C	*Daphoenodon*	complete (l)	24.8	14.7
CM1589A	*Daphoenodon*	complete (r, juv)	22.7	12.7
Mesocuneiform				
CM 1589	*Daphoenodon*	complete (l)	—	9.6
CM 1589	*Daphoenodon*	complete (r)	13	9.8
67-85	*Daphoenodon*	complete (l)	11.2	9.9
24-90	*Daphoenodon*	complete (l)	12.1	9.9
CM1589C	*Daphoenodon*	complete (l)	13.3	9.8
CM2389	*Megalictis*	complete (r)	11.0	6.0
Entocuneiform				
28-84	*Daphoenodon*	complete (r)	16.7	6.7
17-90	*Daphoenodon*	complete (l)	13.5	6.8
CM1589	*Daphoenodon*	complete (r)	13	7
CM1589	*Daphoenodon*	complete (l)	13.1	—
CM1589B	*Daphoenodon*	complete (l)	14.8	8.1
CM1589C	*Daphoenodon*	complete (l)	14.0	7.5

Table 3. (Continued) Postcranial Bones of Carnivores, Quarry 3

CM or UNSM No.	Taxon[a]	Description	Length	Width
Vertebrae				
37-90	*Daphoenodon*	terminal caudal	23.8	7.8
24-84	*Daphoenodon*	caudal	—	—
32-85	*Daphoenodon*	caudal (5th)	—	—
67-85	*Daphoenodon*	caudal chevron	—	—
200-90	*Daphoenodon*	caudal	—	—
201-90	*Daphoenodon*	caudal chevron	—	—
CM2774	*Daphoenodon*	caudal	38.8	14.9
CM1589A	*Daphoenodon*	caudal	43.9	15.8
CM1589A	*Daphoenodon*	caudal	39.1	13.2
CM1589B	*Daphoenodon*	caudal	50.0	19.0
CM1589B	*Daphoenodon*	caudal	27.9	10.5
CM1589B	*Daphoenodon*	caudal	37.1	18.8
CM1589B	*Daphoenodon*	cervical (C4)	34.0	25.5[y]
CM1589B	*Daphoenodon*	cervical (C5)	32.3	25.1[y]
CM1589B	*Daphoenodon*	cervical (C6)	31.0	24.4[y]
CM1589B	*Daphoenodon*	thoracic	29.0	33.6[y]
CM1589B	*Daphoenodon*	thoracic	31.9	30.6[y]
31-85	*Daphoenodon*	thoracic (juv)	—	—
CM1589B	*Daphoenodon*	atlas	—	53.3[z]
713-82	*Daphoenodon*	lumbars (2)	—	—
734-82	*Daphoenodon*	lumbar	—	—
10-84	*Daphoenodon*	lumbar	—	—
6705-89	*Daphoenodon*	vertebral epiphysis	—	—
47801	*Megalictis*	cervical	—	—
60-90	*Megalictis*	thoracic (T6)	19.6	26.4[y]
61-90	*Megalictis*	thoracic (T7)	20.1	27.2[y]
112-90	*Promartes*	lumbars (2)	—	10.8[y]
207-90	*Promartes*	vertebral centrum	13.9	8.7[y]
18A-84	*Promartes*	cervical vertebra	8.6	6.1[y]
114-90	carnivore	cervical centrum	—	18.4[y]
10-90	small carnivore	neural arch	—	—
210-90	*Cormocyon*	vertebra (lumbar, juv)	16.6	~10.5

Vertebral measurements of the holotype CM 1589 are given in Peterson (1910).

Ribs

64-90	*Daphoenodon*	complete (~11th)	16.0 (chord)	
8.5 (head)				
701-82	*Daphoenodon*	partial	—	8.4
702-82	*Daphoenodon*	partial (4)	—	—
715-82	*Daphoenodon*	partial	—	5.6
6-90	*Daphoenodon*	proximal (9th)	98.5 (p)	6.3
55-90	*Daphoenodon*	distal (8th or 9th)	67.3 (p)	6.3
65-90	*Daphoenodon*	distal (tip)	—	12.0

Ribs of the holotype CM1589 were not well preserved but some are figured in Peterson (1910). Ribs of the juvenile CM1589A are much more complete. Almost no ribs were found in the dens during the UNSM excavations.

Notes

a. Only the genera are listed in Table 3 for convenience. Assigned species are found in Table 2.

b. Length measured from the coracoid process to the base of the glenoid; width taken perpendicular to length.

c. Width of the articular surface of the trochlea and capitulum.

d. Greatest width and antero-posterior length of the radial head.

e. Greatest width and antero-posterior length of the distal radius.

f. Greatest width of the distal ulna.

g. Greatest width measured at base of the trochlear notch.

h. Anterior-posterior length measured from the anconeal process to the posterior border of the olecranon; width of olecranon measured posterior to the trochlear notch.

i. Antero-posterior length of the lateral face; greatest transverse width.

j. Measured as greatest length; greatest width perpendicular to length.

k. Measured as greatest antero-posterior length; width taken as height of magnum.

l. Measured as greatest antero-posterior length; width taken as height of unciform.

m. All metapodial widths measure the greatest width of the proximal head; a distal width was taken for UNSM 7-81, 41-85, and 730-82.

n. UNSM 733-82 is from a smaller juvenile of *D. superbus* than is CM 1589A, the latter a large juvenile male with baculum. These metatarsals establish that at least two juveniles of the species were present in the dens. UNSM 733-82 is little ossified and appears to be very young. Both 733-82 and the left CM 1589A lack their distal epiphyses hence their shorter length measurements. CM 1589A (right) is a complete juvenile MT2.

o. Metapodials of the *Promartes olcotti* holotype (Loomis, 1942) approximate the size of metapodials of the small mustelid from the dens under numbers UNSM 58-84, 47-85, 41-90, and 74-90.

p. All phalangeal widths measure the greatest width of the proximal head.

q. Length measured from anterior face of 1st sacral vertebral centrum to posterior face of terminal sacral vertebral centrum; width measured across ilial articular surfaces.

r. Distal portion of the baculum lost but proximal part identical in size to CM1589A.

s. Greatest width of the distal femur.

t. Greatest width of the distal tibia.

u. Width measured as the long dimension of the fibular head.

v. Greatest calcaneal width measured transversely at the level of the sustentaculum.

w. Width of the astragalus measured across the trochlea.

x. Length measured as greatest height of cuboid, anterior face; width measured as the greatest width of the proximal calcaneal facet.

y. Length and greatest width of the centrum.

z. Width measured across the anterior condyles.

TABLE 4. POSTCRANIA AND TEETH OF UNGULATES   127

Table 4. Postcrania and Teeth of Ungulates, Quarry 3
Abbreviations: l, left; r, right; juv, juvenile.
Carnegie numbers are preceded by CM; UNSM numbers are those without a prefix.
Measurements are in millimeters (mm).

CM or UNSM No.	Taxon	Description	Length	Width
18-81	*Merychyus*	astragalus (r)	20.1	12.1[a]
704-82	*Merychyus*	astragalus (r)	19.7	11.8[a]
25-84	*Merychyus*	astragalus (l)	~19.9	12.8[a]
35-90	*Merychyus*	astragalus (r)	—	~13
45-90	*Merychyus*	astragalus (r)	—	—
69-90	*Merychyus*	astragalus (l)	20.9	12.4[a]
158-90	*Merychyus*	astragalus (r)	—	—
5004-006	*Merychyus*	astragalus (l)	20.5	11.9[a]
CM1589A	*Merychyus*	astragalus (l)	22.4	12.2[a]
CM1589A	*Merychyus*	astragalus (r)	20.8	12.9[a]
6707-89	*Merychyus*	calcaneum (l, juv)	—	8.0[b]
96-90	*Merychyus*	cuboid (l, juv)	12.6	7.6[c]
38-84	*Merychyus*	proximal phalanx (juv)	15.2	~5.6
71-85	*Merychyus*	proximal phalanx	—	~4.6
29-85	*Merychyus*	proximal phalanx (juv)	14.2	4.9[d]
22-90	*Merychyus*	proximal phalanx (juv)	11.9	5.2[d]
36-90	*Merychyus*	proximal phalanx (juv)	13.4	4.4[d]
49-90	*Merychyus*	proximal phalanx (juv)	12.1	5.9[d]
CM1589D	*Merychyus*	proximal phalanx (juv)	18.5	7.4[d]
57-84	*Merychyus*	proximal phalanx	18.2	8.0[d]
24-85	*Merychyus*	proximal phalanx	18.2	5.6[d]
25-85	*Merychyus*	proximal phalanx	15.4	—
39-85	*Merychyus*	proximal phalanx	18.5	5.1[d]
18-90	*Merychyus*	proximal phalanx	19.0	7.7[d]
57-90	*Merychyus*	proximal phalanx (juv)	14.4	5.7[d]
58-90	*Merychyus*	proximal phalanx	18.5	6.6[d]
100-90	*Merychyus*	proximal phalanx	17.5	6.0[d]
144-90	*Merychyus*	proximal phalanx (juv)	—	5.5[d]
150-90	*Merychyus*	proximal phalanx (juv)	13.1	5.8[d]
CM1589D	*Merychyus*	proximal phalanx (juv)	13.5	5.6[d]
6703-89	*Merychyus*	proximal phalanx	—	~4.4
6708-89	*Merychyus*	median phalanx (juv)	5.3	3.9[d]
45-90	*Merychyus*	median phalanx	10.7	6.3[d]
94-90	*Merychyus*	median phalanx (juv)	6.3	4.8[d]
106-90	*Merychyus*	median phalanx	8.2	4.2[d]
115-90	*Merychyus*	median phalanx (juv)	7.0	5.0[d]
CM2774	*Merychyus*	median phalanx	10.6	6.1[d]
72-85	*Merychyus*	ungual phalanx	9.4	5.1[d]
78-85	*Merychyus*	ungual phalanx	7.9	3.6[d]
31-84	*Merychyus*	distal humerus (l)	—	19.9
CM1589A	*Merychyus*	glenoid of scapula (l)	—	13.4
42-84	*Merychyus*	distal humerus (r)	—	20.2
60-84	*Merychyus*	distal humerus (l)	—	19.0
CM1589A	*Merychyus*	distal humerus (l)	—	21.9
CM1589D	*Merychyus*	distal humerus	—	18.2
20-84	*Merychyus*	humerus, epiphysis (juv)	—	21.7
41-84	*Merychyus*	proximal radius	—	12.8
149-90	*Merychyus*	proximal radius (r)	—	16.7
56-85	*Merychyus*	tibial epiphysis (juv)	—	23.2
53-84	*Merychyus*	lunate (r, juv)	~10.5	5.4
86-85	*Merychyus*	distal metapodial	—	7.0
41-90	*Merychyus*	distal metapodial (juv)	—	5.7
133-90	*Merychyus*	distal metapodial (juv)	—	7.2
32-84A	*Merychyus*	proximal metapodial (juv)	—	—
33-90	*Merychyus*	proximal metapodial	—	5.9
63-90	*Merychyus*	proximal metapodial	—	9.0
106-90	*Merychyus*	proximal metapodial	—	4.4

CM or UNSM No.	Taxon	Description	Length	Width
116-90	*Merychyus*	proximal metapodial	—	6.1
122-90	*Merychyus*	proximal metapodial	—	7.0
136-90	*Merychyus*	proximal metapodial	—	8.7
152-90	*Merychyus*	proximal metapodial	—	8.1
45-85	*Merychyus*	patella	16.6	14.0
68-85	*Merychyus*	patella (juv)	11.9	10.9
46-85	*Merychyus*	carpal cuneiform	8.3	4.7
50-85	*Merychyus*	ecto-mesocuneiform (l)	7.6	5.2
39-90	*Merychyus*	podial	11.8	—
187-90	*Merychyus*	podial (juv)	9.7	5.7
48-90	*Merychyus*	DP4 (juv)	~10.5	—
19-84	*Merychyus*	dp3-dp4 (juv)	12.3 (dp4)	6.4 (dp4)
11-84	*Merychyus*	tooth fragment	—	—
125-90	*Merychyus*	tooth fragment	—	—
144-90	*Merychyus*	tooth fragment	—	—
158-90	*Merychyus*	tooth fragment	—	—
117-90	*Merychyus*	vertebral centrum (juv)	16.2	9.7
136-90	*Merychyus*	vertebral fragment	—	—
165-90	*Merychyus*	vertebral centrum	14.9	—
729-82	*Oxydactylus*	proximal phalanx	62.0	19.0[d]
CM1589D	*Oxydactylus*	proximal phalanx	—	10.7[d]
72-85	*Oxydactylus*	distal phalanx	—	—
49-84	*Oxydactylus*	distal metapodial	—	14.4
2-90	*Oxydactylus*	distal metapodial (juv)	—	13.3
709-82	*Oxydactylus*	distal metapodial (juv)	—	15.0
CM1589A	*Oxydactylus*	unciform (r)	—	12.2
13-81	*Oxydactylus*	unciform (l)	—	13.3
731-82	*Oxydactylus*	astragalus (l)	—	17.7[a]
CM1589A	*Oxydactylus*	navicular (l)	24.6	12.8
CM1589A	*Oxydactylus*	magnum (l)	19.2	16.4
CM1589A	*Oxydactylus*	ectocuneiform (l)	13.3	10.4
CM1589D	*Oxydactylus*	cuneiform (l)	20.1	—
CM1589D	*Oxydactylus*	cuboid fragment	—	—
15-85	*Oxydactylus*	distal calcaneum	—	—
6725-89	*Oxydactylus*	patella	33.3	19.0
44-90	*Oxydactylus*	thoracic vertebra (juv)	16.9[e]	20.7[e]
CM1589B	*Oxydactylus*	distal humerus	—	25.8
62-90	*Stenomylus*	distal humerus (r, juv)	—	~19
87-85	*Stenomylus*	distal femur (l, juv)	—	—
710-82	*Stenomylus*	distal metapodial (juv)	—	12.1
8-84	*Stenomylus*	rib head	—	—
12-84	*Stenomylus*	distal phalanx (juv)	—	8.2
15-90	*Stenomylus*	cervical vertebra	—	16.5[e]
CM2774	*Stenomylus*	lumbar vertebra	20.7	22.0[e]
21-90	*Stenomylus*	ungual phalanx	16.1	8.0[d]
56-90	*Stenomylus*	median phalanx (juv)	9.3	5.8[d]
71-90	*Stenomylus*	cuboid (r)	25.9	11.3[c]
717-82	*Stenomylus*	carpal cuneiform (juv)	11.1	6.1
46A-90	*Stenomylus*	i3 (r)	9.0	2.5
32-84	moschid	astragalus (r)	18.6	11.8[a]
37-84	dromomerycine	distal metapodial (juv)	14.4	—
55-84	moschid	phalanx (juv)	—	5.0[d]
CM1589B	cervoid	proximal phalanx[f]	—	9.2
2-84	*Menoceras*	calcaneum (l) neonate	46.2	31.1[b]
7-90	*Menoceras*	proximal phalanx (juv)	21.9	20.4

Table 4. (Continued) Postcrania and Teeth of Ungulates, Quarry 3

CM or UNSM No.	Taxon	Description	Length	Width
CM1589A	*Menoceras*	proximal phalanx (juv)	20.2	20.4
93-90	*Menoceras*	mandibular fragment	—	19.9
118-90	*Menoceras*	tooth fragment	—	—
712-82	small artiodactyl	astragalus	—	—
68-90	small artiodactyl	vertebra epiphysis (juv)	—	—
112-90	small artiodactyl	femoral condyle	—	—
113-90	small artiodactyl	femoral condyle	—	—

Notes

a. Measured as greatest medio-lateral width of the proximal astragalus.

b. Width measured transversely at the level of the sustentaculum.

c. Proximal width measured across cubo-navicular facets.

d. Greatest proximal width.

e. Length and greatest width of the centrum.

f. This partial phalanx is without doubt a cervoid; CM1589B does not appear on the bone, but it was found in a box with only CM1589B material.

———

CM or UNSM No.	Taxon	Description
	Postcrania and teeth of small mammals, Quarry 3	
14-84	small mammal	femoral epiphysis (juv)
67-90	small mammal	centrum (juv)
111-90	small mammal	cervical vertebra
177-90	small mammal	centrum (juv)
180-90	small mammal	centrum
206-90	small mammal	proximal ulna
45-84	rodent	proximal radius (juv)
57-90	rodent or insectivore	proximal humerus
134-90	rodent or insectivore	proximal ulna
117-90	rodent or insectivore	trunk vertebra
130-90	rodent or insectivore	2 trunk vertebrae
53-85	lagomorph	lower molar

———

CM or UNSM No.	Taxon	Description	Length	Width
	Skeletal elements of lower vertebrates, Quarry 3			
14-81	anguid lizard	osteoderms, vertebra	—	—
38-90	anguid lizard	vertebra	5.9	5.1
8A-90	lizard	pterygoid	—	—
194-90	lizard	vertebra	5.9	5.5
CM1589F	snake	vertebra	—	—
15-81	anuran	distal humerus	—	3.4
120-90	anuran	sacrum and urostyle	10.3	—
23-84	anuran	pterygoid	9.7	—
57-84	anuran	sacral vertebra	5.9	5.2
49-85	tortoise	dentary fragment	30.2	—
1-90	turtle	carapace plate	10.2	9.2
39-90	turtle	carapace plate	9.6	6.9
50-90	turtle	carapace plate	13.7	18.6
145-90	turtle	carapace plate	14.0	8.9
146-90	turtle	carapace plate	22.7	10.1
152-90	turtle	carapace plate	10.9	10.4
153-90	turtle	carapace plate	13.7	9.2
168-90	turtle	carapace plate	20.9	13.1
148-90	bird	diaphysis	—	8.5
1-84	bird	phalanx (talon)	13.8	3.7
726-82	bird	coracoid	—	8-10
CM 1589F	bird	coracoid	—	—
151-90	fish	pectoral fin spine	11.4	1.4

All noncarnivoran material from the den site (Quarry 3) collected from 1905 to the present by UNSM and by the Carnegie Museum is included in Table 4.

Table 5. Dental Measurements (length × width in mm) of Lower Teeth of *Daphoenodon superbus*

Mus no.	p2	p3	p4	m1	m2	c-m2	p1-4
CM1589	10.3 × 5.2	12.8 × 5.8	16.2 × 7.9	24.2 × 11.6	13.9 × 9.8	92.0	47.7
CM1589A	12.7[a] × —	12.7[a] × —	18.6 × 8.8	26.2 × 11.4	15.7[a] × —	87.5[a]	
CM1589B	12.8[a] × —						
CM1589B		14.8 × 6.8					
CM1589B					17.4 × 11.5		
CM1589B					14.6 × 10.4		
CM1589D				25.9 × 11.6			
CM2774	11.3 × 5.5	13.6 × 6.1	17.2 × 8.6	24.2 × 11.1	14.2 × 9.8	92.5	51.0
UNSM 723-82					14.8 × 10.6		
UNSM 92-84	12.2[a] × —	14.1[a] × —	18.5[a] × —	~27.8 × —	14.5[a] × —		~49[a]
UNSM 700-82	12.6 × 5.6	13.6 × 6.4	19.3 × 8.9	26.4 × 11.6	15.2 × 10.1	104.9	56.0
UNSM 40-90						i3 [7.3 × 5.2]	

a. Alveolar measurement

Table 6. Dental Measurements (length × width in mm) of Upper Teeth of *Daphoenodon superbus*

Mus no.	P2	P3	P4	M1	M2	C-M2	P1-4
CM1589	11.5 × 5.3	13.1 × 7.1	22.3 × 13.7	18.6 × 23.5	12.6 × 19.1	84.6	55.1
CM1589A	12.3 × 5.7	14.1 × 7.2	25.1 × 15.0	18.7 × 24.3	13.6 × 19.4	83.1	56.8
CM1589B		16.3 × 8.7[a]	23.8 × 14.6[a]		12.8 × 19.6[a]		
CM1589B					13.6 × 21.0		
CM2774	11.1 × 5.2	12.2 × 6.4	22.8 × 13.9	17.8 × 23.8	12.3 × 19.0	80.6	52.4
UNSM 703-82				19.0 × 23.8			
UNSM 5-84				~18.3 × —			

a. These three teeth are not necessarily from a single individual.

Table 7. Dental Measurements (length × width in mm) of Upper Teeth of *Delotrochanter oryktes*, *Megalictis simplicidens*, *Promartes olcotti*, *Phlaocyon annectens*, and *Cormocyon* sp.

Mus no.	P2	P3	P4	M1	M2	C-M2	P1-4
Delotrochanter							
UNSM 47800	15.9 × 8.0	18.2 × 9.8	22.8 × 17.9	17.5 × 23.9	8.9 × 15.3	83.5	64.2
Megalictis							
UNSM 732-82			18.0 × 12.9				
UNSM 12-85	8.9 × 6.5	12.5 × —	19.1 × —	6.7 × 16.2			
Promartes							
UNSM 38-85		5.3 × 3.4	8.7 × 5.8	5.5 × 9.3			
UNSM 34-85			7.3 × 5.5				
Phlaocyon							
CM1602	4.2 × 2.3	4.9 × 2.5	8.6 × 5.7	6.0 × 8.4	3.6 × 6.0	28.3	21.0
Cormocyon							
UNSM 16-90				7.4 × 10.1	5.9 × 8.5		

Table 8. Dental Measurements (length × width in mm) of Lower Teeth of *Megalictis simplicidens*, *Promartes olcotti*, *Phlaocyon annectens*, and *Cormocyon* sp.

Mus no.	p2	p3	p4	m1	m2	c-m2	p1-4
Megalictis							
UNSM 54-85	8.6 × 5.6[a]	10.5 × 7.3	13.3 × 7.9	18.9 × 8.5	3.6 × 2.9[a]	58.1	34.4
UNSM 27-85	8.9 × —						
CM1553[b]	8.7 × 5.7	10.1 × 7.0	11.7 × 7.0	16.3 × 7.6	5.8 × 4.9	55.3	33.4
CM2389		10.3 × 7.6		17.9 × 8.3	4.2 × 3.1[a]		
Promartes							
UNSM 13-85					4.0 × 2.6[a]		
UNSM 16-85					4.0 × 3.2		
UNSM 58-85				9.0 × 4.4			
UNSM 12-90			5.6 × 2.9 (dp4)	7.8 × 3.1[a]			
Phlaocyon							
CM1602	4.2 × 2.1	4.8 × 2.3	5.7 × 2.9	9.9 × 4.5	4.9 × 3.4	30.7	17.2
CM1589B				— × 4.9			
Cormocyon							
UNSM 46-90				11.5 × 5.0			
UNSM 64-85				— × 4.1			

a. Alveolar measurement.
b. CM1553, the holotype of the species, is from the Harrison Formation and not from Quarry 3.

Table 9. Measurements of Canines (length × width in mm) of *Daphoenodon superbus*, *Megalictis simplicidens*, and a Small Carnivore

Mus no.	C	c
Megalictis		
UNSM 53-90	12.2 × 9.1 (r)	
UNSM 91-90		~21.6 × ~9 (l)
Daphoenodon		
CM1589	12.5 × 10.1 (l)	12.2 × 9.4 (r)
CM1589	13.3 × 10.1 (r)	12.0 × 8.8 (l)
CM1589B		15.2 × 10.4 (l)
CM2774	14.0 × 10.3 (r)	13.8 × 10.2 (r)
UNSM 701-82	17.4 × 12.5 (–)	
Small carnivore		
UNSM 7-84	4.36 × 3.1 (–)	
Megalictis or *Daphoenodon*		
UNSM 140-90	— × 13.0	

Abbreviations: l, left; r, right

All dental measurements of Carnegie Museum carnivores (CM1589, 1589A, 1589B, 1589D, 2774, 1602, 2389) from Quarry 3 are included in Tables 5 to 9.

Table 10. Cranial and Mandibular Measurements of Carnivorans from the Dens

UNSM 12-85	*Megalictis simplicidens*	Length of skull, ~172 mm (condyle of skull to I3)
		Length of lower jaw, 121 mm (articular condyle to i3)
		Depth of jaw below m1, 27 mm
CM1589	*Dapoenodon superbus*	Length of skull, 226 mm
		Length of lower jaw, 178 mm
CM1589A		Length of skull, ~184 mm
		Length of lower jaw, ~154 mm
CM2774		Length of skull, 228 mm
		Length of lower jaw, 175 mm
UNSM 700-82		Length of lower jaw, 218 mm
UNSM 47800	*Delotrochanter oryktes*	Length of skull, 256 mm

Three chalicotheres (Moropus) at the waterhole during the drought with others approaching — mural by Mark Marcuson (Visitors Center, Agate Fossil Beds National Monument).

Appendix A

Carnegie Hill Quarries— A Brief History of Excavations of the Bonebed

Exploration of the Miocene waterhole bonebed on Carnegie and University Hills experienced its zenith during the first quarter of the twentieth century (1904 to 1923). Recognition of its importance in 1904 by Carnegie paleontologist Olaf Peterson motivated the Carnegie Museum to initiate major excavations on Carnegie Hill in 1905, 1906, and 1908. During those same years, and prompted by Peterson's discovery, the University of Nebraska not to be outdone opened its only quarry on nearby University Hill under the direction of Erwin Barbour. Both Peterson and Barbour during those years were encouraged in this effort by James Cook, the cattleman who controlled access to the bone deposit near his Agate 04 ranch in the valley of the Niobrara River and who had previously noticed bones there.

Despite the immense accumulation of bones at the waterhole, the skeletons of only three species of mammals made up nearly the entire bonebed: a small rhinoceros (*Menoceras arikarense*), a large chalicothere (*Moropus elatus*), and a formidable scavenger, the entelodont (*Dinohyus hollandi*). It was evident to Peterson that complete skeletons of these animals, all extinct and unknown to science, could be reconstructed from the quality of the fossil material in the bonebed. He understandably looked forward to unimpeded access to Carnegie Hill because of his discovery. However, as Peterson's excavations from 1905 to 1908 began to reveal the enormous potential

133

Olaf Peterson 1865–1933

James Cook 1857–1942

W. J. Holland 1848–1932

H. F. Osborn 1857–1935

of the bone deposit, James Cook came to regard the great number of bones as "surplus," particularly due to the abundance of the small rhinoceros. To Peterson's chagrin, Cook not only encouraged Erwin Barbour's excavation at University Hill but openly welcomed the interest of other institutions in sampling the bonebed.

Working in the region at this time were paleontologists from the American Museum of Natural History (New York) who likewise recognized the potential of the Carnegie Hill bonebed for research and for acquiring fine skeletons for public exhibition.

Prompted by word of Peterson's discoveries and a developing friendship with James Cook and his son, Harold, the American Museum men opened a small test excavation on the north side of Carnegie Hill during the absence of Peterson and Barbour at Agate in 1907. Unfortunately, by this time disagreements had developed between James Cook and the Carnegie Museum's difficult director, W. J. Holland, who had quietly attempted to lease Carnegie Hill in order to control access to the bonebed. Aware of Holland's intent, James Cook had no intention of permitting such a lease, believing he owned the quarry

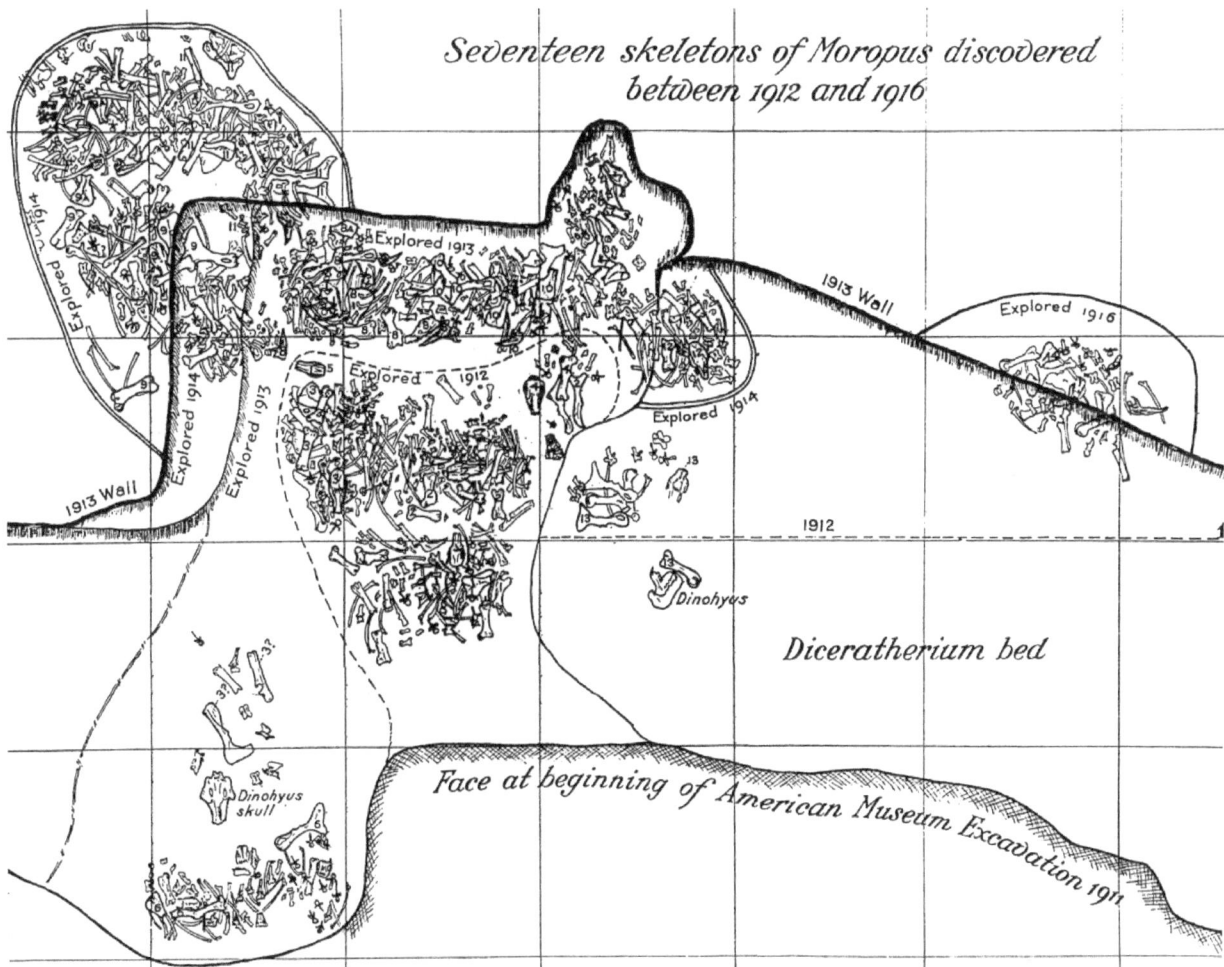

Albert (Bill) Thomson's map of the 17 chalicotheres discovered in the deepest part of the waterhole in the Southwest Excavation at Carnegie Hill — the map recorded the apparent synchronous mass death of young, subadult, and mature individuals of Moropus elatus [On the map the name 'Diceratherium' used by Thomson for the common bonebed rhinoceros has been replaced by the genus Menoceras]

hills. Cook immediately undertook a land survey, realized the bonebed was not on his ranch, and filed on the quarry land himself in 1908. By now Peterson also had found it difficult to work for Holland. As a result, the 1908 field season was Peterson's last at Carnegie Hill. His mapping and analysis of the bonebed had been exemplary and are still in use today.

By this time, the evident interest of the New York men in the bonebed was supported by James and Harold Cook, working in cooperation with the American Museum's director, H. F. Osborn, and paleontologist W. D. Matthew. In 1911 the American Museum reopened Peterson's Carnegie Quarry 1, which would prove to be the most productive of the Carnegie Hill quarries. From 1911 to 1916 the American Museum vigorously pressed the excavation and extended this prolific quarry further into the hill—among numerous fossils of the small rhinoceros *Menoceras*, the common mammal of the bonebed, they recovered an unprecedented mass burial of the large chalicothere *Moropus*. Over a number of years, Albert (Bill) Thomson, the American Museum's principal field paleontologist at Agate, excavated 17 to 20 of these chalicotheres found together in the waterhole. They appear to have been a family group and the only known occurrence in the fossil record of a small band of these mammals that perished together and were buried essentially intact.

From 1917 to 1919, the American Museum opened the north side of Carnegie Hill with an excavation 200 feet (60 m) in length that yielded rhinoceros and some chalicothere—here Bill Thomson identified a lower bonebed and, about a meter above, an upper layer of bone confirmed in 1986 by the University of Nebraska. Bones here were water-worn and not as concentrated as in the large American Museum excavation that had developed from Carnegie Quarry 1. Curiously, there is no indication that Peterson during his exploration ever entered the north side of Carnegie Hill.

The American Museum concluded its excavations at Carnegie Hill in 1920 with removal of an exceptional two-ton block of rhinoceros bones from their work in Quarry 1, now exhibited in the American Museum Hall of Mammals in New York. It is currently the best prepared and most remarkable intact example of the bone accumulation at the waterhole.

An unsuccessful opening in 1923 of a small site on the south margin of Carnegie Hill ended work by the American Museum at Agate. From that time until the establishment of the national monument in 1965 no significant excavations or investigative research took place either at Carnegie or University Hill—a few institutions cut out small slabs of the remaining bonebed at Quarry 1 on Carnegie Hill for exhibition but did not continue in-depth research in the quarries. Such slabs had been removed as early as 1917 by the Denver Museum, later in 1920 by the University of Chicago, in 1922 by the University of Kansas and University of Michigan, and in 1929 by Harvard.

Albert "Bill" Thomson 1874–1948
American Museum of Natural History (1923)

Appendix B

Reopening of the Carnegie Hill Quarries by the University of Nebraska in 1986

The quarries on Carnegie Hill were reopened by the University of Nebraska in 1986 following a preliminary investigation in 1984–85 using test pits to explore the sediments enclosing the bonebed and the distribution of bones. The plan for exploration of the quarries in 1986 was developed from the field records, maps, photographs, and publications available in the archives of the Carnegie Museum (Pittsburgh), the American Museum of Natural History (New York), and the University of Nebraska, all of which had previously excavated at Carnegie Hill in the early twentieth century.

The location and extent of each of the quarries on Carnegie Hill was established by survey with alidade and plane table. An aluminum bolt (Datum No. 1) was embedded in concrete at the northwest corner of Carnegie Hill as a *principal reference datum*. Placement of three additional aluminum bolts (Nos. 2, 3, 4) allowed any point in the quarries on the north, west, or south sides of the hill to be mapped in relationship to the principal reference datum and were intended to serve as a permanent reference system for future exploration.

In 1986 additional test pits (each 1 m²) were placed at intervals around the perimeter of Carnegie Hill in the surveyed quarries to more accurately locate and sample the bonebed. These test excavations were worked with hand tools from the ground surface downward to the base of the bone bed. Bones were identified to skeletal element and taxon, and their condition and orientation in the bonebed were recorded. As bones were discovered, they were removed from six of these meters, and in eight others left in place as exhibits for future study. Sediments were examined for composition, bedding, facies relations, and sedimentary structures. Diagenetic features (the chemical, physical, and biologic changes undergone by sediment after its initial deposition) were studied, including development of *paleosols*. In order to construct measured stratigraphic sections that described in detail the sedimentary rock layers, the face of each quarry was exposed using shovels, brushes, and other hand tools, and where necessary, when a large volume of fallen rock and debris had accumulated, a backhoe cleared colluvium that obscured the quarry face. The profiles of the quarries revealed by this method demonstrated the spatial relations and character of the different types of sediment (*lithofacies*) which proved essential to understanding the origin and history of the waterhole. In this way, measured sections from the North Excavation (American Museum Quarry of 1917–19) were combined to create a sedimentation profile 50 m in length used to reconstruct the environment of the waterhole and its history of sedimentation at the time the bonebed formed.

Appendix C

Sediments at Quarry 3

The waterhole and the den community centrally located in the broad, shallow valley of the Agate paleoriver developed at a time of aridity and drought. Waterholes appeared in abandoned channels and topographic lows along this sandbed river. Until an active streamflow returned, water ponding in these waterholes accumulated calcareous mud and fine wind-blown sand and ash. Occasionally a brief rainfall event introduced a thin bed of stream-deposited sand.

Although these sediments that tell the story of the river and its waterhole are best seen on Carnegie Hill, the same stream and pond sediments are also present on Beardog Hill at Quarry 3. There in the northern portion of the quarry, white ponded mudstone is interbedded with laminated gray river sand just as at Carnegie Hill, demonstrating intervals of ponding alternating with periods of stream inflow. The bedload of the stream was a volcaniclastic sand with a high percentage of volcanic ash and minimal detrital sediment from mountains to the west.

As the stream dried and the waterhole came into existence, the volcaniclastic sand began to grade into and intertongue with the ponded calcareous mud and wind-blown ash that accumulated in and dominated the southern portion of the waterhole. During this time, the waterhole hosted a biota of small crustaceans (ostracods), molluscs (pulmonate snails), frogs, and a singular fish that confirmed the existence of the ponded environment. The fine-grained calcareous mud (micrite) was likely precipitated from carbonate-rich (Ca-Mg) water evaporating in the mildly alkaline waterhole.

This ponded sediment over time became a consolidated calcareous mudstone: its composition is key to understanding the placement of the carnivore dens. The mudstone is made up of microcrystalline calcite (micrite) and clay, the latter montmorillonite and rare zeolite from diagenesis of the volcanic ash. Montmorillonite and zeolites are recognized common byproducts from the dissolution of volcanic glass (Fisher & Schmincke, 1984); the pronounced surface area of the volcanic glass shards promotes their rapid hydration followed by destruction of the glass matrix and development in the resulting pore space of authigenic montmorillonitic clay and opaline silica cement. Silica-rich waters from devitrification of the ash infiltrated the porous carbonate mud contributing to the rapid growth of opaline cement and clay that created the consolidated mudstone fabric. Periodic drying of the waterhole added to the diagenesis of the volcanic glass and unstable mineral grains.

The transformation of the pond mud to a mudstone must have happened over a geologically brief interval since broken fragments of consolidated mudstone floating in burrow fill indicate the Miocene pond mud underwent a rapid diagenetic conversion to the consolidated mudstone fabric evident today at Quarry 3. Precipitation of secondary (authigenic) minerals in silica-rich pore waters and the dissolution of volcanic glass shards and their replacement by new minerals filling that pore space are some of the most rapid low-temperature lithification processes known (Fisher and Schmincke, 1984). At the time the carnivores excavated the burrows, the conversion of the primary porous mud to a secondary consolidated mudstone must have already begun—the hardened mud prevented the caving-in of the burrows, allowing the carnivores to construct their tunnel network in the consolidated pond sediment.

Significantly, only thick ponded carbonate mud was present in the southern half of Quarry 3 where we found Dens 1 and 2 burrowed into the white consolidated mudstone, the burrows later filling with gray wind- and stream-deposited sediment. It was the contrast in color between the gray sand and white mudstone that allowed us to recognize and define the walls and floor of the dens. However, in the northern half of the quarry, burrow margins were less evident where carnivores were forced to bur-

row through pond mudstone interbedded with gray stream-deposited sand. Because the gray sand that filled burrows in the northern quarry was identical in color and lithology to the gray stream-deposited sand, burrow walls in the northern den area were sometimes difficult to recognize.

The composition of sediment filling the burrows was uniform throughout Quarry 3. A thin section that sampled the burrow fill 2 cm from the *Delotrochanter* skull in Den 2 showed it to be a very fine silty sand, light gray (10YR-7/1: Munsell Soil Color Charts, Baltimore, Maryland), friable, tuffaceous, notably rich in volcanic glass shards, with angular to subangular grains, well-sorted, having thin (<1 mm) linear fissures that appeared to be root traces filled by very fine silt.

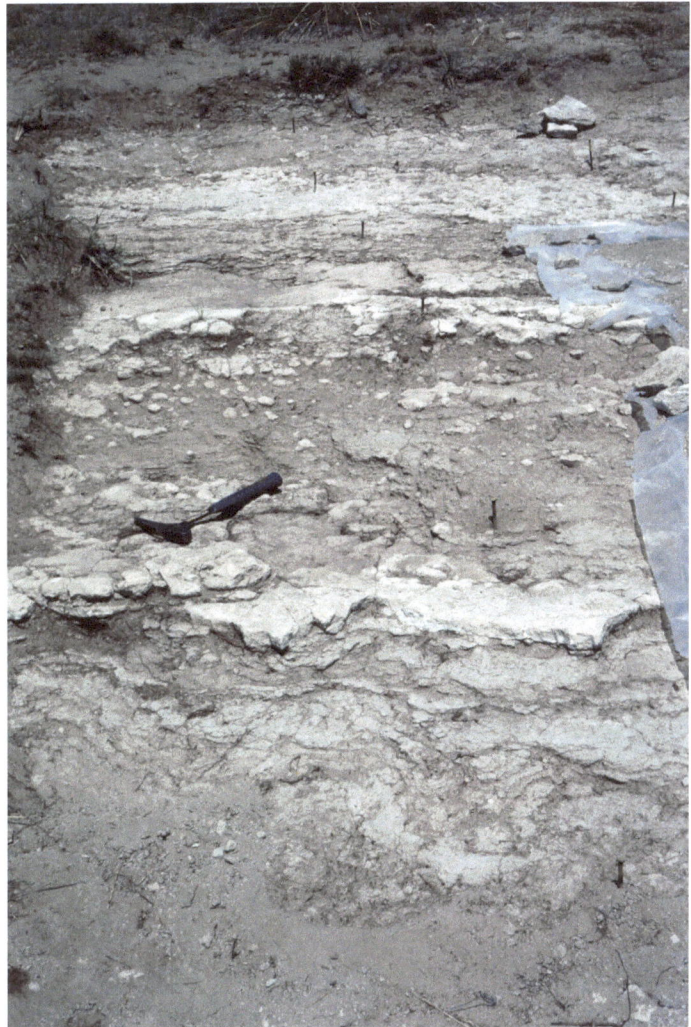

At the north end of Quarry 3, alternating beds of white calcareous mud and gray stream-transported sand do not show evidence of burrowing. Here at the margin of the waterhole, a ponded environment was periodically interrupted by the inflow of low-energy stream currents depositing the sand.

Appendix D

Analysis of Bone at Quarry 3

Condition of Fossil Bone

The partial skeletons and isolated bones in the quarry show that condition ranged from intact and undamaged to fragmented and degraded. Bone from Quarry 3, white in color in the living mammal, is only slightly discolored during residence in the burrows. Color determination using the Munsell Soil Color Chart (1954 edition) showed that almost all bone could be termed light gray (10YR-7/1,7/2) to white (10YR-8/2).

Bone found within a den in the layered sediment of unbreached burrows often appears as if taken from a living animal. Yet as burrows were breached by erosion and exposed to the elements, breakdown of bone took place as it worked into soil where plant roots completed disintegration. Much fragmented bone from the northern half of the quarry represents the residue from such disturbed burrows. However, hundreds of small angular bone fragments from our excavations lack evidence of either chemical dissolution or physical abrasion and compare to fragmented bone seen in the dens of living canids such as the gray wolf (*Canis lupus*) and Asiatic wild dog (*Cuon alpinus*) (Fox, 1985: Figs. 5.3, 5.4).

In the south quarry at Den 1, the two beardogs buried in their sand-filled burrow show what the condition of some carnivore skeletons must have been before destruction of the burrows. We learn that some individuals died and were scavenged in the den when it was occupied and in active use. In this case the scavenged skeleton of the youthful male *Daphoenodon* (CM1589A) with its gnawed limb bones

lacking their epiphyses in the company of the adult female (CM1589) is a prime example. At Den 3 the foreleg of the aged male *Daphoenodon* at burial was still held together by ligament and tough connective tissues as were foot bones of the beardog *Delotrochanter* in Den 2. These fossils found in the better-preserved burrows at Quarry 3 demonstrate that the condition of skeletons found in undisturbed burrows can be exceptional and suggests that renewed excavation at Beardog Hill could discover additional skeletons where such burrows may still be preserved.

Diagenesis of Bone

X-ray diffraction analysis of bone from the dens and waterhole shows it to be a recrystallized carbonate fluorapatite ($Ca_5[PO_4, CO_3]_3F$). The fluorapatite of fossil bone is influenced only by physicochemical processes such as dissolution, reprecipitation, and incorporation of foreign ions whereas the carbonate hydroxylapatite of living bone is continually being remodeled and redeposited by cellular activity (Boskey, 2007). For living bone to recrystallize to a carbonate fluorapatite, its organic tissue (primarily collagen) must decay. The loss of collagen (which makes up ~30% of the bone by volume) and other organics opens pore space for crystal growth and consequent addition of fluorine and other elements to the crystal lattice, leading to an increase in crystallinity (Lebon et al., 2010). Once bone is buried and in contact with pore-waters, the apatite crystals over time can dissolve, recrystallize, and progressively fill collagen-free pore space with crystallites of increasing size. Recrystallization of bone appears to be essential for its preservation as fossil bone in geologic time (Trueman et al., 2008). At Quarry 3, recrystallization of apatite, addition of trace elements, and permineralization has occluded bone porosity, resulting in an increase in the mass, density, and hardness of the bone. In some skeletons silica from dissolved volcanic ash has substituted for bone mineral.

Recent analyses (Koenig et al., 2009; Lebon et al., 2011; Trueman et al., 2004; Trueman, 2013) have shown that bone diagenesis can be complex: recrystallization does not necessarily proceed evenly through fossil bone but can be quite "patchy." Recently, identification of highly resolved gradients

of trace elements (REE) in fossil bone recognized at submicrometer (μm) scales has demonstrated such patterns of recrystallization.

Diffusion profiles of trace elements in bone have been employed to estimate rates of recrystallization, which are thought to range widely over thousands to millions of years (Trueman et al., 2008; Koenig et al., 2009). Mammal bone from a Javan cave dated at ~60 ka lacked evidence of collagen and included partially recrystallized fluorapatite (Lebon et al., 2010, 2011). The degree of crystallinity varied through the mapped area of the bone and was not uniform (histological sections examined by microspectroscopy at a resolution of < 10 μm demonstrated differential spatial crystallinity).

Acknowledgments

Excavation of Quarry 3 was carried out by the Division of Vertebrate Paleontology of the University of Nebraska State Museum of Natural History in Lincoln. The project could not have been undertaken without the support and cooperation of the Midwest Region of the National Park Service and staff of Agate Fossil Beds National Monument over several decades. Superintendents Jerry Banta and Larry Reed (Scotts Bluff National Monument) and James Hill (Agate Fossil Beds National Monument) provided continual logistical support and encouragement. Tom Richter, Chief of Interpretation, Midwest Region, assisted us throughout the duration of the project. During the earlier years, Rangers John Rapier, Bob Todd, Bill Taylor, and Reid Miller aided our initial excavation with useful advice and collaboration. Later, park rangers (Lil Mansfield, Mark Hertig, Betty Mack, Anne Wilson, A. J. LeGault, Alvis Mar, and Fred Macvaugh) provided essential interpretation for the visiting public. We relied on the capable park maintenance staff (Bill Matthews, Don Mack, Bud Buckley, and Jeff Jones) for their support at Quarry 3 during out fieldwork; we thank them for their current management and protection of the den site on Beardog Hill. In planning of wayside exhibits and those at the Visitor Center, we benefited from the collaboration of NPS Media Specialist Roberta Wendel. Artist Mark Marcuson brought to life in his exceptional murals the life of the waterhole; scientific illustrator Angie Fox contributed her expertise in digital editing of our field photographs. For more than a decade, Mary Dawson and Elizabeth Hill provided indispensable access to Peterson's fossils and archival records at the Carnegie Museum.

UNSM personnel: Bob Hunt (paleontologist), Rob Skolnick (field crew chief and paleontologist), Joshua Kaufman (paleontologist), and Ellen Stepleton (editor).

UNSM Field Crew: John Morgenson, Cindy Loope, Xiang-xu Xue, Mary Rebone, Hannon LaGarry, Richard Ehrman, Susan Hueftle, James Phipps, King Richey, Natalie Marovelli, and Paola Villa.

Office of Scholarly Communications, University of Nebraska–Lincoln: Paul Royster, Coordinator, and Linnea Fredrickson, Production Specialist.

It is not possible to adequately thank the many individuals whose interest and unselfish cooperation allowed us to complete a project of this length and complexity—we hope the publication of the results of the UNSM excavations will encourage others to continue research at the national monument to add to our understanding of the geological history of the region and the evolving history of life revealed there.

References

Banfield, A. W. F. 1974. The Mammals of Canada. University of Toronto Press, Toronto. 438p.

Bekoff, M. 1975. Social Behavior and Ecology of the African Canidae: A Review. *In* M. W. Fox (editor), The Wild Canids: Their Systematics, Behavioral Ecology, and Evolution: 120–142. Van Nostrand Reinhold, New York.

———. 1982. The Coyote (*Canis latrans*). *In* J. A. Chapman and G. A. Feldhamer (editors), Wild Animals of North America: 447–459. Johns Hopkins University Press, Baltimore, MD.

Boskey, A. L. 2007. Mineralization of Bones and Teeth. Elements 3: 387–393.

Boydston, E. E., K. M. Kapheim, and K. E. Holekamp. 2006. Patterns of den occupation by the spotted hyena (*Crocuta crocuta*). African Journal of Ecology 44: 77–86.

Bradley, R. M. 1971. Warthog (*Phacochoerus aethiopicus*) burrows in Nairobi National Park. East African Wildlife Journal 9: 149–152.

Brown, L. E., and E. S. Brown. 2014. A new genus of fossil frogs (Amphibia: Anura: Hylidae) from the Miocene of the northern Great Plains (USA), with a commentary on vertebrate diversity. Life: The Excitement of Biology 2(3): 136–145.

Bueler, L. E. 1973. Wild Dogs of the World. Stein and Day, Briarcliff Manor, New York. 274p.

Corbett, L. K. 1995. The Dingo in Australia and Asia. Cornell University Press, Ithaca, NY. 200p.

Darton, N. H. 1899. Preliminary report on the geology and water resources of Nebraska west of the 103rd meridian. U.S. Geological Survey 19th Annual Report 1897–1898, Part 4—Hydrography: 719–785. U.S. Geological Survey, Washington, DC.

Elbroch, M. 2003. Tracks and Sign: A Guide to North American Species. Stackpole Books, PA. 778p. (p. 447, dens of wolves)

Fisher, R. V., and H.-U. Schmincke. 1984. Pyroclastic Rocks. Springer Verlag, New York. 472p.

Fox, M. W. 1985. The Whistling Hunters: Field Studies of the Asiatic Wild Dog (*Cuon alpinus*). State University of New York Press, Albany. 150p.

Gier, H. T. 1975. Ecology and social behavior of the coyote. *In* M. W. Fox (editor), The Wild Canids: Their Systematics, Behavioral Ecology, and Evolution: 247–262. Van Nostrand Reinhold, New York.

Grinnell, J., J. S. Dixon, and J. M. Linsdale. 1937. Fur-Bearing Mammals of California, Vol. 2: 377–763. University of California Press, Berkeley.

Hill, A. 1989. Bone modification by modern spotted hyenas. *In* R. Bonnichsen and M. H. Sorg (editors), Bone Modification: 169–178. Center for the Study of the First Americans, University of Maine, Orono.

Hunt, R. M., Jr. 1990. Taphonomy and sedimentology of Arikaree (Lower Miocene) fluvial, eolian, and lacustrine paleoenvironments, Nebraska and Wyoming: a paleobiota entombed in fine-grained volcaniclastic rocks. Geological Society of America Special Paper 244: 69–111.

———. 1995. The Miocene carnivore dens of Agate Fossil Beds National Monument, Nebraska: Oldest known denning behavior of large mammalian carnivores. *In* National Park Service Paleontological Research, Technical Report NPS/NRPO/NRTR-95/16, V. L. Santucci and L. McClelland (editors), pp. 3–7.

———. 2011. Evolution of large carnivores during the mid-Cenozoic of North America: the temnocyonine radiation (Mammalia, Amphicyonidae). Bulletin of the American Museum of Natural History 358: 1–153.

Hunt, R. M., Jr., and R. Skolnick. 1996. The giant mustelid *Megalictis* from the Early Miocene carnivore dens at Agate Fossil Beds National Monument, Nebraska: earliest evidence of dimorphism in the New World Mustelidae (Carnivora, Mammalia). Contributions to Geology, University of Wyoming 31(1): 35–48.

Hunt, R. M., Jr., X-X. Xue, and J. Kaufman. 1983. Miocene burrows of extinct bear dogs: Indication of early denning behavior of large mammalian carnivores. Science 221: 364–366.

Kerbis-Peterhans, J. C., and L. K. Horwitz. 1992. A bone assemblage from a striped hyena (Hyaena hyaena) den in the Negev Desert, Israel. Israel Journal of Zoology 37(4): 225–245.

Kinlaw, A. 1999. A review of burrowing by semi-fossorial vertebrates in arid environments. Journal of Arid Environments 41: 127–145.

Koenig, A. E., R. R. Rogers, and C. N. Trueman. 2009. Visualizing fossilization using laser ablation-inductively coupled plasma-mass spectrometry maps of trace elements in Late Cretaceous bones. Geology 37(6): 511–514.

Kruuk, H. 1972. The Spotted Hyena: A Study of Predation and Social Behavior. University of Chicago Press, Chicago. 335p.

Lacruz, R., and G. Maude. 2005. Bone accumulation at brown hyena (Parahyaena brunnea) den sites in the Makgadikgadi Pans, northern Botswana: taphonomic, behavioral, and paleoecological implications. Journal of Taphonomy 3: 43–53.

Lansing, S. W., S. M. Cooper, E. E. Boydston, and K. E. Holekamp. 2009. Taphonomic and zooarchaeological implications of spotted hyena (Crocuta crocuta) bone accumulations in Kenya: A modern behavioral ecological approach. Paleobiology 35(2): 289–309.

Larson, E. E., and E. Evanoff. 1998. Tephrostratigraphy and source of tuffs of the White River sequence. Geological Society of America Special Paper 325: 1–14.

Lebon, M., I. Reiche, J.-J. Bahain, C. Chadefaux, A.-M. Moigne, F. Frohlich, F. Semah, H. P. Schwarcz, and C. Falgueres. 2010. New parameters for the characterization of diagenetic alterations and heat-induced changes of fossil bone mineral using Fourier transform infrared spectrometry. Journal of Archaeological Science 37: 2265–2276.

Lebon, M., K. Muller, J.-J. Bahain, F. Frohlich, C. Falgueres, L. Bertrand, C. Sandt, and I. Reiche. 2011. Imaging fossil bone alterations at the microscale by SR-FTIR microspectroscopy. Journal of Analytical Atomic Spectrometry 26: 922–929.

Lopez, B. H. 1978. Of Wolves and Men. Charles Scribner's Sons, New York. 309p.

Mech, L. D. 1970. The Wolf: The Ecology and Behavior of an Endangered Species. The Natural History Press, Garden City, NY. 384p.

Mills, G., and H. Hofer. 1998. Hyaenas: status survey and conservation action plan. IUCN/SSC Hyena Specialist Group.

Moskowitz, D. 2013. Wolves in the Land of Salmon. Timber Press, Portland, OR. 334p.

Nowak, R. M. 1991. Mammals of the World (5th ed.), Vol. II. The John Hopkins University Press, Baltimore. 1629p.

Owens, D. D., and M. J. Owens. 1979. Communal denning and clan associations in brown hyenas (Hyaena brunnea, Thunberg) of the Central Kalahari Desert. African Journal of Ecology 17: 35–44.

Owens, M. J., and D. D. Owens. 1978. Feeding ecology and its influence on social organization in brown hyenas (Hyaena brunnea, Thunberg) of the Central Kalahari Desert. East African Wildlife Journal 16: 113–135.

———. 1984. Cry of the Kalahari. Houghton Mifflin, Boston. 341p.

Packard, J. M. 2003. Wolf behavior: Reproductive, social, and intelligent. In L. D. Mech and L. Boitani (editors), Wolves: Behavior, Ecology, and Conservation: 33–65. University of Chicago Press, Chicago.

Peterson, O. A. 1907. The Miocene beds of western Nebraska and eastern Wyoming and their vertebrate faunae. Annals of the Carnegie Museum 4(1): 21–72.

———. 1909. A new genus of carnivores from the Miocene of western Nebraska. Science 29(746): 620–621.

———. 1910. Description of new carnivores from the Miocene of western Nebraska. Memoir of the Carnegie Museum 4(5): 205–278.

Peterson, R. O. 1977. Wolf Ecology and Prey Relationships on Isle Royale. National Park Service Scientific Monograph Series 11: 1–210.

Peterson, R. O., and P. Ciucii. 2003. The wolf as a carnivore. In L. D. Mech and L. Boitani (editors), Wolves: Behavior, Ecology, and Conservation: 104–130. University of Chicago Press, Chicago.

Pokines, J. T., and J. C. Kerbis-Peterhans. 2007. Spotted hyena (Crocuta crocuta) den use and taphonomy in the Masai Mara National Reserve, Kenya. Journal of Archaeological Science 34: 1914–1931.

Rausch, R. A. 1967. Some aspects of the population ecology of wolves, Alaska. American Zoologist 7: 253–265.

Riggs, E. S. 1942. Preliminary description of two Lower Miocene carnivores. Geological Series, Field Museum of Natural History 8(10): 59–62.

———. 1945. Some Early Miocene carnivores. Geological Series, Field Museum of Natural History 9(3): 69–114.

Riley, G. A., and R. T. McBride. 1975. A survey of the Red Wolf (*Canis rufus*). *In* M. W. Fox (editor), The Wild Canids: Their Systematics, Behavioral Ecology, and Evolution: 263–277. Van Nostrand Reinhold, New York.

Ross, K. 1987. Jewel of the Kalahari: Okavango. Macmillan, New York. 256p.

Schaller, G. B. 1972. The Serengeti Lion. University of Chicago Press, Chicago. 480p.

———. 1973. Golden Shadows, Flying Hooves. University of Chicago Press, Chicago. 293p.

Senzota, R. B. M. 1984. The habitat, abundance, and burrowing habits of the gerbil, *Tatera robusta*, in the Serengeti National Park, Tanzania. Mammalia 48: 185–195.

Skinner, J. D., J. R. Henschel, and A. S. van Jaarsveld. 1986. Bone-collecting habits of spotted hyenas (*Crocuta crocuta*) in the Kruger National Park. South African Journal of Zoology 21: 303–308.

Stanley, K. O., and Benson, L. V. 1979. Early diagenesis of High Plains Tertiary vitric and arkosic sandstone, Wyoming and Nebraska. Society of Economic Paleontologists and Mineralogists Special Publication 26: 401–423.

Swinehart, J., V. Souders, H. Degraw, and R. Diffendal. 1985. Cenozoic paleogeography of western Nebraska. *In* R. Flores and S. Kaplan (editors), Paleogeography of the west-central United States. Rocky Mountain Section, Society of Economic Paleontologists and Mineralogists: 209–229.

Trueman, C. N. 2013. Chemical taphonomy of biomineralized tissues. Palaeontology 56(3): 475–486.

Trueman, C. N., A. K. Behrensmeyer, N. Tuross, and S. Weiner. 2004. Mineralogical and compositional changes in bones exposed on soil surfaces in Amboseli National Park, Kenya: Diagenetic mechanisms and the role of sediment pore fluids. Journal of Archaeological Science 31(6): 721–739.

Trueman, C. N., M. R. Palmer, J. Field, K. Privat, N. Ludgate, V. Chavagnac, D. A. Eberth, R. Cifelli, and R. R. Rogers. 2008. Comparing rates of recrystallisation and the potential for preservation of biomolecules from the distribution of trace elements in fossil bones. Comptes Rendus Palevol 7: 145–158.

Valenciano, A., J. A. Baskin, J. Abella, A. Perez-Ramos, M. A. Alvarez-Sierra, J. Morales, and A. Harstone-Rose. 2016. *Megalictis*, the bone-crushing giant mustelid (Carnivora, Mustelidae, Oligobuninae) from the early Miocene of North America. PLOS ONE 11(4): 1–26.

Wang, X. 1994. Phylogenetic Systematics of the Hesperocyoninae (Carnivora, Canidae). Bulletin of the American Museum of Natural History 221: 1–207.

Wang, X., R.H. Tedford, and B.E. Taylor. 1999. Phylogenetic Systematics of the Borophaginae (Carnivora: Canidae). Bulletin of the American Museum of Natural History 243: 1–391.

Watson, R. M. 1965. Observations on the behaviour of young spotted hyena (*Crocuta crocuta*) in the burrow. East African Wildlife Journal 3: 122–123.

White, C. R. 2005. The allometry of burrow geometry. Journal of the Zoological Society, London 265: 395–403.

Young, S. P., and E. A. Goldman. 1944. The Wolves of North America. Dover Publications, NY. 385p.

www.ingramcontent.com/pod-product-compliance
Lightning Source LLC
Chambersburg PA
CBHW061135030426

42334CB00003B/52